A Lesson Learned
By Jeevan Brown

ISBN-13: 978-1523818877

ISBN-10: 1523818875

www.jeevanbrown.com

Written By: Jeevan Brown

Cover By: Julian Dangerfield

Edited By: Janis Carmichael and Maurice Garland

Connect

www.jeevanbrown.com

 Facebook - JeevanABrown

 Instagram - JeevanABrown

 Twitter - JeevanBrown

 Snapchat - KingJeevan

 YouTube - Jeevan Brown

Dedication

Dedicated to my late best friend Jeffrey Donnell Cox, my Grandmother Audrey Brown, and Grandfather James Thomas with love, respect, joy and gratitude.

Table of Contents

Introduction

Chapter 1: Live By Faith Not By Sight   1

Chapter 2: Let It Burn   23

Chapter 3: Achieving While Grieving   39

Chapter 4: HIGHway Patrol   59

Chapter 5: Cold Summer   71

Chapter 6: 19 & Pregnant   89

Chapter 7: Big Man on Campus   107

Chapter 8: iRacist   123

Chapter 9: Passion for Fashion   141

Chapter 10: Draft Day   159

Chapter 11: Co-Sign   171

Chapter 12: Quarterbook Sneak   189

Chapter 13: A Different World   205

Chapter 14: Under The Influence   217

Chapter 15: Panhellenic Commitment   233

Chapter 16: Two Heartbeats   251

Acknowledgements   287

Notes   289

Bibliography   291

Connect   293

Introduction

My senior year in college was one of the most difficult times in school and maybe even life. I was thrown into a roller coaster of emotions that I couldn't guide or fix. My plate was full, and just when I thought it was over, more problems were coming in for seconds and thirds. There was nobody I could talk to who could fully give me the answers for which I was looking. Sure, there were some who gave encouraging advice, but none of it really stuck. Somehow I still pulled through and graduated. I wish I had somebody who related to my ongoing trials. Somebody wiser, who'd been there and done that; but the older adults, teachers, parents, and mentors couldn't fully relate. As Millennials, we sometimes reject the attitudes of the Baby Boomers and take a smidge of advice from Generation X. We do things our way and on our terms. We saw the past mistakes of our elders and decided to take our own route instead of following the status quo.

I decided to write this book to help the Millennials and generations to come that might go through similar experiences. This book is from a Millennial's perspective with the guidance Baby Boomers and Generation X couldn't give us because technology wasn't that advanced while they were growing up. Social media wasn't a thought, and college debt wasn't surpassing $1 trillion. Violence also didn't hit so close to home while you were trying to succeed and obtain a career that was financially stable, creative, and meaningful.

I didn't have a blueprint to guide me through those years, but I did have my friends and peers who were going through similar situations. With my Bachelor's Degree in Communication and background in journalism I thought to myself why not interview them? Not only will I tell their stories, but detail what they learned while giving advice to the reader. During this process I discovered things about them I never knew, and these were some of my closest friends. I knew what was on the surface; but didn't know the pain, agony, and suffering they endured. I had heard their stories before, and were part of a few, but I didn't realize how deeply rooted their stories were to the people they've become. Through their tribulations came some of their darkest and deepest moments, birthing their divine purpose and destiny. Not all of their stories have happy endings, but one thing we all have in common is that we learned a lesson from each experience.

A Lesson Learned is not just for college students, but also for adolescents and young adults. Almost every story is relatable. This book may also give a feeling of nostalgia and cause others to reminisce on the past, good or bad. These short stories aren't your average everyday problems; they're raw, uncut, and honest. Not only will this book help, it will bring a sense of conscience to the readers' souls while also taking them through a range of emotions leaving them happy, sad and even laughing. This book is the guidance I didn't have that will change the outcome of millions that are dealing with or may go through the same dynamic. There are no losses in life, just lessons learned

Author's Note

Excluding chapters 1, 3, and 10 which contain the real names and places, the remaining chapters' names and identifying details have been changed to protect the innocence and privacy of individuals.

Chapter 1: Live By Faith Not By Sight

"Yes!" I said quietly walking into my room noticing my roommate was gone. I could take my nap in peace without any interruptions of snoring, heavy breathing, or sounds from the TV. My roommate was notorious for all three. I lay on my twin bed trying to get comfortable, but it was almost impossible with my 6-foot long frame. Looking out the window I could see my friends mingling on the yard, kicking up the autumn leaves. I wanted to join them, but after last night's party I needed some rest. Slowly I drifted into dreamland, but before I could sleep there was a knock at the door. *Why can't people just leave me alone?* I prayed they would go away, but then I heard another knock. Geesh he's persistent!

"Who is it!" I yelled.

"Shawn it's me, Terrell, open the door. I have to show you something," he said anxiously.

"Man, I'm trying to get some sleep. Go away and come back another day," I replied in a humorous voice.

"Go away and come back another day? Man, this ain't no children's rhyme book. I hear you laughing. You can sleep later; it's the middle of the day. Open up!"

I opened the door and immediately got back in my bed. I didn't care what he had to show me, I was going to get some sleep one way or another.

"Man, what do you want?" I said sarcastically.

"Look I still got it," he said.

As he pulled his .22 black handheld gun from his pants, his face beamed with pride. I didn't understand why he was so happy. But standing at 5'4, I guess it fitted him well - small guns for small people.

"What is up with you and this gun? You've been playing with it for months," I said.

Terrell has been obsessed with this gun ever since he found it in the woods at the beginning of the school year. It was almost October and he still couldn't resist. He brought it to parties and sometimes he even brought it to class. A few guys carried guns on campus, but I didn't get it. We were in Orangeburg, South Carolina attending South Carolina State University. None of us needed guns. I guess showing off their gun gave them some sort of satisfaction, like a badge of honor.

"Would you put that thing away, you should only have it out when it's time to use it,"

"Man, I know what I'm doing, calm down, this isn't my first gun. Look at her. Isn't she a beauty? She's so clean."

"Yeah, she's clean, I guess," I laid back down hoping he would see I wasn't interested, but he continued to play with the gun. I could hear the clicks of the trigger and clip as he took it in and out. He was such a big kid.

Pop! A single shot rang out echoing throughout the building. It was so loud. I felt a sharp pain on the left side of my head and abruptly everything became dark. I felt something dripping down the left side of my face, but I couldn't make out what it was. Suddenly Terrell gasped.

"Oh my God," he murmured as I heard the gun drop to the floor.

"What?"

"I'm so sorry Shawn, I'm so sorry!" he said while holding my body up in his arms while I laid in bed. Quickly he reached for the room phone.

"Hello, 911! Please come quick. I just shot my friend. Please hurry. Please! I'm at South Carolina State University."

Within minutes I could hear the ambulance sirens outside of my window.

2

"Shawn, man, I'm so sorry. Stay with me; fight through it. The paramedics just arrived. Oh my God!" he yelled as I could hear other students arriving at my door.

"Terrell what did you do?" one of them said.

I couldn't respond. I could only feel the blood rolling down the side of my face. Suddenly the paramedics barged into the room.

"Let's make a hole through here guys! We're going to have to carry him through this hallway and right now timing is everything!" a female paramedic yelled out.

"What's your name, honey?" the paramedic asked.

"Shawn Callaway."

"How old are you?"

"19 ma'am. I can't breathe, I can't breathe," I said slowly.

"I think we're losing him. Let me get some oxygen, now!" she screamed.

Placing the oxygen mask over my face, she grabbed her two-way radio: "19 year old, black male, shot on the left side of his head. We're going to need a helicopter to Palmetto Hospital, now! Let's move it people!" Dazing in and out of consciousness, I could hear the helicopter hovering over the dorm as they carried me down the steps, but as the paramedics pushed me through the front doors, my mind faded to black.

As I arose from my sleep the following morning, my head was pounding. The headache was excruciating. *Where is the aspirin?* Touching my cheek I could feel bandages wrapped around my head and face. I could feel the IV pumping fluids into my arm and I could feel the finger pulse oximetry on my finger. Attempting to sit up, I heard a familiar soft voice in the background.

"Baby, don't move too much."

"Mom? Mom is that you?" I asked glancing to the right.

3

"Yes, baby, your father and I flew down yesterday as soon as we heard about what happen," she replied.

My parents had flown down from Riverdale, Maryland in the middle of the night. I didn't even know what time it was, but before I could ask I heard a knock at the door.

"Mr. Callaway, I see you're awake. How are you feeling?" I heard from a foreign voice, the accent sounded Indian.

"Who are you?" I asked.

"I'm sorry, forgive me. I'm Dr. Gupta, one of the doctors who performed surgery on you yesterday."

I knew he was Indian, I had science and math professors with the same last name and they both were Indian.

"Are you feeling better today?"

"Not really, my head is killing me."

"The pain shouldn't last much longer. I must say Mr. Callaway, you are blessed, I mean really blessed. It's simply a miracle you're still alive."

"How long will I have this bandage on my face?" I asked.

"For a few days, and you'll be able to leave the hospital in about a week."

"Can you at least take the bandage off my eyes so I can see while I'm in here?

Silence filled the room. The only things I could hear were soft talking and footsteps from outside of my door.

"Hello, did you hear me? I just want this off my eyes," I said pointing to the bandage on my face.

"I'm sorry to tell you this Shawn, but the bullet hit your temple, rupturing your optic nerve. You're…" he paused before finishing his sentence.

"I'm sorry, but you won't be able to see," Dr. Gupta said.

"For how long?" I replied.

He took a deep breath before answering.

"Mr. Callaway, you're permanently blind. Again, I'm sorry."

"Wait, what do you mean I'm blind? Mom, Dad, is this true?"

I sat in disbelief. *Was this some sort of horrible nightmare? I was only 19 years old. How was I going to finish school?*

"Are you sure there's nothing else the doctors can do?" my father asked.

"Again, Shawn's optic nerve was ruptured and there is currently no procedure to restore it. You all are welcome to get a second opinion if you like."

I could feel my mom grabbing my hand as she sat next to me on the hospital bed.

"Don't worry baby. We're going to get a second opinion, ok?" she said. Tears welled in my eyes, but the bandages on my face prevented them from rolling down.

Each day I woke up in the hospital bed hoping, praying, and wishing for a miracle. I had no track of time; I didn't know if it was day or night. My dreams were better than my reality. Every chance I got I went to sleep and when I wasn't sleeping I was daydreaming. Sitting on my bed, my mother read a plethora of cards and letters that were sent from my classmates and professors. While she was reading, I heard a knock at the door followed by a cautious, timid voice.

"Shawn, Mr. and Mrs. McCree hi," he said.

"You must be one of Shawn friends. Come on in. Please have a seat. What's your name?" my mom asked.

"Thank you ma'am. I'm Terrell."

Instantly my anger grew as memories from that day replayed in my head. I couldn't believe he had the nerve to show his face; he was the last person I wanted to hear from.

"Oh, you're Terrell!" my mother's tone quickly went from sweet to livid, leaving Terrell speechless.

"Yes, ma'am," he uttered.

"I just wanted to say sorry. I shouldn't have been so reckless. If I could change places with you I would," he pleaded.

"It's a little too late for that," my father replied.

"I know sir, I feel so bad, and I should've listened. My friends told me numerous times to stop playing with the gun. I hope you can find it in your heart to forgive me."

"Did you hear that I was blind?" I said.

"Yes, President Oden held a meeting in the auditorium and told everybody what happened. I felt so bad watching everybody cry and ask the president multiple questions about you. Everybody's worried sick."

"Yeah," was the only thing I could say, I didn't have any words for Terrell. I turned my head away from him, lying back on my pillow. I could only imagine him standing there looking pitiful with that usual dumb look on his face.

"Mr. and Mrs. McCree I know it's really nothing I can do, but I'm truly sorry," he said.

"We're very disappointed in you young man. I hope this is a lesson to you and all of your friends; a gun is nothing to play with. My son can't see. He won't be able to see me, his father, his sister, brother, his family, friends, or anything else! Look what you did. Look!" my mom said in a stern voice.

"I know ma'am, I'm so sorry. If you ever need anything from me, please don't hesitate to call me, Shawn. I'm so sorry."

Need him? Terrell was from North Augusta, SC I didn't want to be around him or even think about him. I wish I never knew him.

Two weeks later I was back at home. I missed college already. Luckily my parents worked nights, so they were able to help me during the day. I didn't need that much help. I'd been living in this house for most of my life, so I knew how to navigate it without a problem. A lot of things had changed, but one thing remained the same - my love for football. "Come on! I can't believe this game! This is a joke; two fumbles and one turnover! I could play this damn game!" my dad yelled in the living room as he watched the Washington Redskins take on the Buffalo Bills for the 1992 Super Bowl. Ironically, I was standing and yelling right with him, but there was a difference. I wasn't watching; I was listening. My screams were delayed as I waited for the commentator to report the recent play. I still loved sports just as much as I did before I went blind.

"Mmm, that food smells delicious, baby!" my dad said to my mom, who was in the kitchen cooking.

"What food?" I asked my dad.

"You don't smell that, boy? You don't smell your mother cooking fried chicken. "What's wrong with you?"

"Nah, I don't smell anything."

Mom must be losing her touch, back in high school I could smell her cooking from a mile away. As I continued to yell at the TV, I became light headed. The game was so serious I was getting dizzy from it. As I sat on the couch, my breaths became intense and shorter. I didn't understand what was going on; I was only watching the game, not playing in it. Suddenly, I felt a sharp pain zip through my head, leaving me discombobulated. The pain came straight from the gunshot wound. Placing my hand on the wound, I felt sweat pouring. Standing up, I attempted to walk to the kitchen but became light headed, losing my balance and abruptly collapsing to the floor. "Shawn? Shawn!" My dad yelled out. "Baby, call 911. Shawn's convulsing, his eyes are going into the back of his

7

head. Hurry up baby! Hurry!" my dad yelled to my mom as she ran to my side with the phone to her ear.

Waking up the next morning I was confused.

"How are you feeling?" I heard my mom say as she softly touched my head.

"What happened? Where am I?" I replied.

"You're at the Washington Hospital Center. Yesterday during the game you had a seizure and your wound was leaking fluid."

"That was fluid? I thought it was sweat," I replied.

"You were sweating too; to be honest you were drenched. But I do have some good news. You have a new doctor who specializes in eye and vision care. Her name is Dr. Reed." In the middle of her talking, I could hear the door opening and footsteps walking into the room.

"Did I hear my name? Sounds like I'm right on time," she said with a smile in her voice.

"Hello, Shawn, I'm Dr. Reed. I'm going to be your Ophthalmologist for the time being," she said, grabbing my hand so I could shake hers. Gosh! Her hands are so soft, she has to be pretty.

"Hi Dr. Reed," I replied in a somber tone.

"Aww come on Shawn. I know it's rough, but you have to make the best of the situation and be positive," she replied, noticing the anguish in my voice.

"I'm trying ma'am, but I have a question."

"I'm listening."

"Yesterday, before I had the seizure, I noticed I couldn't smell my mother's cooking. Now that I think about it, I haven't smelled her cooking since I've been back. Is something wrong with my sense of smell?"

"Funny you asked that question. I was reading your medical records; the nerves that ruptured were a part of that sense."

"So, it's confirmed. I can't smell?" I asked.

"Yes, Shawn, you can't smell. I'm sorry," she said compassionately.

"Ok, I have one last question."

"I'm listening."

"Well, when I was in South Carolina the doctor said I would never see again. Is that true? My parents and I wanted a second opinion."

"We actually discussed that while you were resting. I showed them a picture of a human brain, so I want you to imagine one too. The optic nerve is located in the back of the eye. The responsibilities of the optic nerve are to transfer visual information from the retina to the vision centers. Trauma to the optic nerve makes it hard for fibers to grow the full length of the visual pathway. If the bullet would have traveled any further, it would have reached your brain. I think you know what would have happened after that," she explained.

As she continued to talk, I started zoning out; I didn't want to hear anything else. If I was a musical genius like Stevie Wonder or Ray Charles, or like the deaf and blind author Helen Keller, this would be different; but I'm not. I'm just a blind kid from Maryland. "I know this is hard Shawn, believe me I do. I deal with blind patients all the time. I know it's especially hard for you because you weren't born blind. But I really want you to think about rehabilitation. There are centers where you can get accustomed to being blind," said Dr. Reed.

I shook my head in disbelief. *Was there really no cure? Was I really going to live my life without ever seeing or smelling again?*

9

As time went by, family and friends stopped by every day to visit and lend a helping hand. They poured in by the numbers. Their reactions when first seeing me were always somber. I could hear the sympathy in their voices; I could hear them sniffling and crying every time they walked out the door. Just like me, they were praying for a miracle. One day my best friend, Shawnda came to visit me. We've been friends since high school and she got wind of my accident while away at North Carolina Central University. Her mother happened to be getting married one weekend and while she was home she came to see me.

"So you came over to see me huh?" I asked sarcastically.

"You know I had to come see my boy. I'm worried about you," she said.

"Oh please, I'll be alright. Don't you worry about me."

"I can't lie, I've been so nervous about this," she said.

"Nervous about what? I'm still the same Shawn; nothing has changed, but my sight."

"I know, but I just can't imagine."

"I can. I imagine all the time," I said as she laughed. I knew that would break the ice and it did.

"I see you still got your sense of humor," she replied.

"Yeah I don't think I can lose that sense too."

A slight moment of silence filled the air. I knew this feeling all too well. I knew she had questions; everybody did.

"Ok, get it out. I know you have questions, go ahead and ask. I'm used to it."

"Well since you insist," she said laughing.

"So there's nothing the doctors can do? I mean, nothing at all?"

"Nope. The bullet shattered my optic nerve, which is one of the only nerves that can't be restored."

"You can't sue the school for that?"

"I mean, I'm not sure. The school didn't shoot me, Terrell did. We probably could because there's no procedure in place for an accident of that magnitude. Terrell didn't receive punishment for what he did, but I think he should've been expelled. I know it was an accident, but still." I replied.

"Right, he needs to have something happen to him!" Before Shawnda left she explained that her mother wanted to talk to me, so she dialed her number.

"Hey, Ms. Thomas."

"Hey, Shawn how are you holding up?"

"I'm good, Ms. Thomas, I can't complain."

"I want you to know that I'm praying for you. Shawnda has been taking it real tough since she found out, but don't tell her I told you," she said whispering as if Shawnda could hear her.

"Oh, it's too late for that. She already walked in here crying."

We both started laughing, but what Ms. Thomas said next would have a great effect on me and stick with me for the rest of my life.

"You know the bible says we have to live by faith and not by sight. Now you're the perfect example of that, not only physically, but mentally. Don't you think for one second that you can't accomplish everything you set out to do. God will lead you to your path of success."

When she said that it made so much sense to me. I've heard that phrase before, but now it seemed to connect.

As Shawnda was leaving I could hear my little brother and sister coming up the driveway returning from their day at school. They were full of energy, but before I could go to my room I felt a small hand touch me.

"Fern is that you?" I said to my little sister who was only 6 years old.

"Yes it's me." She said in her little voice.

"Well, what's up little one?"

"I wanted to help you to your room. Aren't you about to go to your room?"

"Aww. You don't have to help me; I can do it. I'm a big boy," I said.

"I want to; mom said that's what family is for. Helping right?"

"You're just full of surprises today huh? Thank you."

"You're welcome. I love you." She said as she giggled running down the steps.

Numerous thoughts started to clutter my mind as I sat alone in my room. *I have to do something with my life.* Having my little sister help me to my room and hearing Ms. Thomas say, "Live by faith and not by sight" sparked something within my soul. I can't continue to just sit around collecting my social security disability check from the government. I had to set an example for my little siblings. Dr. Reed suggested that I attend the Maryland Rehabilitation Center located in Baltimore, Maryland. As I pondered, I made a choice that I wasn't going to let my circumstance inhibit me from moving forward.

I tried to take a brief nap after making my decision, but couldn't. My eyes were itching uncontrollably. It was spring, but my allergies never affected me this badly. I just couldn't stop scratching my eyes. As I dug deeper and deeper into the crevices of my left eye, I started to feel something. It was solid and felt like a rock. My eye started throbbing and within a second severe pain ricocheted through my eye. I heard something fall to the ground. Nervous about what had just come out, I searched the floor feeling for the piece, hoping it wasn't some organ. I located the object and picked it up off the floor, examining it with my hands. It was small, made of metal, and felt just like a bullet. I couldn't believe it. It was the bullet! I remember Dr. Gupta saying they couldn't remove the bullet because it would cause more damage, but I never thought the bullet would come out of my eye socket.

The following month was my first day at the rehabilitation center. I was nervous and didn't know what to expect, but I was here.

"Welcome to the Maryland Rehabilitation Center," said Mr. McBride, the director of the center. "Today begins the first day of the rest of your life. During your stay here you will become a new person - changed from within. You will learn daily tasks that others take for granted. For example, learning how to boil water to make a cup of tea. You'll also learn how to color-code your closet, and small things such as choosing the right flavors to make a peanut butter and jelly sandwich. You may be blind, but there is still a path in front of you. You just have to take it," he lectured.

As the weeks went by I realized that counseling for blind mobility and independent living skills was beneficial. I might have lost my sight and sense of smell, but learning how to walk and navigate with my white cane gave me a sense of independence. I also learned how to count and separate money, which was a lifesaver. One dollar bills stayed unfolded, $5 bills folded crosswise, $10 bills folded lengthwise, and larger bills are a combination of the two. I thought I would become a master of reading braille, but to my surprise braille wasn't encouraged. One standard textbook converted to braille equals 30 braille books. The majority of my books were on tape because listening to an audio book was much easier.

Group discussions became therapeutic for me. I met Ryan, who was from Washington D.C., which was a relief. The Baltimore natives were quite different from the Prince Georges County and D.C. residents. Ryan understood me and my lingo; we were like kindred spirits.

"I have a question?" Ryan said

"What's your question, Ryan" the director said.

"I think certain aspects about being blind are pure BS." I laughed at his statement even though I had no idea what he was talking about. I could imagine him sitting there with his shades on holding his white cane blurting out that statement. He was blunt.

"What do you mean?"

"For example, they say your senses are heightened when you lose your sight; but I don't smell, touch, or hear any better." he said, causing the entire group to burst into laughter.

"Well, Ryan, you're right, that is a myth. Your other senses don't become heightened; you just become more aware of them."

"Thank you! I knew I wasn't tripping. It's like every day I'm waiting to hear a penny drop from a mile away and nothing ever happens."

"I can't smell, so I never thought about that." I murmured.

"What did you say Shawn?" Ryan asked.

"Well, when I got shot I lost my sight and sense of smell."

"For real?" Ryan said.

That day was the first time I told my story to the group and it was a great experience. Not only did everybody understand, but they could somewhat relate, making it easy for me to let go of the anxiety.

I completed the rehabilitation course within six months and celebrated with my close family and friends.

"I'm so proud of you, baby," my mom said.

"Thanks mom," I replied smiling.

"So what's next, son?" my dad asked.

"Well, Mr. McBride said this is only half of the battle and I have to be twice as good to make it in the real world, so I think I want to enroll in college."

"Really? Is that possible?" my mom replied as I laughed at her response.

"Of course mom. I've actually researched it. Mr. McBride said I can stay at the rehabilitation center while I attend Essex Community College, which is down the street from the center. Then when I graduate from Essex, I can transfer to the University of Maryland, College Park (UMD)."

There was a slight pause before my mother answered. I could sense something was wrong.

"That sounds great and all, baby, but UMD is a huge campus. I'm worried that it won't be accessible for you," she said.

"I already looked into that too. UMD is one of the top schools in the country for people with disabilities. I'll be fine, mom, don't worry. I'm a big boy," I said, giving her a kiss on the cheek.

"Seems like you got it all figured out," she said.

"I think our son is transforming into a man right in front of our eyes, baby." My dad said.

Today was the day. After two years of hard work and studying, I was about to walk across the stage and receive my Associates Degree in Psychology. I could feel the tassel hanging from my graduation cap sliding across my face as the warmth of the sun beamed down on me. With my black shades on, grinning from ear to ear, I proudly walked across the stage with my white cane. I could hear my family yelling from the stands. "Go Shawn! I Love You, baby!" When I sat down I started to reminisce. I was so grateful for the rehabilitation center. If my little sister never would have walked me to my room that day, I would still be sitting on the couch feeling like a complete loser collecting my check.

After moving all of my belongings back home from Baltimore, my mother and father took turns reading the UMD college pamphlet to me.

"Shawn, somebody's on the phone for you," My father yelled interrupting my mother while she was reading.

"Who is it, pops?" I asked.

"I don't know. Sounds like some white kid."

"White kid? I don't have any white friends." I replied.

"Hello, this is Shawn. How may I help you?" I said in a professional voice, just in case it was a job calling.

"Shawn this is Neil, your roommate. I was just calling to touch bases with you."

"My roommate from the University of Maryland?" I asked.

"Yup."

"Man, I didn't know who this was." I replied laughing. I had no idea my roommate would be calling. As the conversation went on I figured this would be the perfect time to tell him that I was blind. That would be the best way to avoid the awkwardness when we finally meet.

"Hey, Neil I think I should tell you a little secret about me before we move in." I said stopping him mid-sentence.

"Secret? Secrets already?" he said laughing.

"Well, a few years ago, I was involved in an accident where I became permanently blind."

"Oh, that's no secret, bro. I knew that. The university told me that in the profile they sent me about you."

"Really?"

"Yeah man, it's not a big deal. I'm here to help you whenever you need me."

"Aww man, you don't know how much relief that gave me. I'm really looking forward to meeting you now."

"Same here."

Hanging up the phone I now understood why the University of Maryland was rated one of the top colleges for disabled students.

Two months later I was all moved in. I lay in my dorm bed and took it all in. *I was a student at one of the best and biggest colleges in Maryland and I lived on campus.* I could hear keys jingling from outside of the door. The knob turned and I felt a brief gust of wind hit my legs.

"Shawn! I wasn't expecting to see you here. Welcome!" It was Neil. I could tell from his voice, and I'm pretty sure he was the only other person with a key to my room.

"Neil is that you?" I asked, just to be sure.

"Yeah, it's me. How was everything moving in?"

"It was cool; my parents helped me. They actually just left not too long ago; you just missed them."

"I wish I could've met them."

Then there was a silence. The awkward silence people feel when they don't know what to make of the situation or what to say next.

"My friends and I are about to get a bite to eat. Do you want to come?" Neil said.

"Nah, I'm fine"

"Aww come on, you can't stay in here forever. I'll introduce you to my friends."

I felt reluctant to go, not only because I was blind, but I also didn't know these people. I sat quietly for a moment, but then I thought about everything I learned at the rehabilitation center. *"You may be blind, but there is still a path in front of you. You just have to take it."*

Walking on campus with Neil and his friends I realized that I was in good hands. Neil helped me across the street and told me to watch my step repeatedly. I was surprised by how well he was taking to my disability and his friends were no different. They weren't treating me like some disabled kid.

"Did you guys see the Wizards play the Lakers? That game was bananas," Neil said.

I could hear Neil whispering under his breath as if he had just made a mistake.

"Shawn, I'm so sorry. I didn't mean to say "see". I totally forgot."

"It's cool, I'm used to it. It doesn't bother me at all. You can actually keep saying see."

"Really? Would that be right?" Neil asked.

"No, but it wouldn't be right if you replaced see with hear because you did see it. When I was in the rehabilitation center we were encouraged to tell people to use the right words because we can see with our white canes or other senses. Believe me it's ok."

"Wow, that's different." Neil responded.

"What happened, if you don't mind me asking?"
I knew he would ask me about my accident, but telling my story was a form of therapy - letting it all out and living my truth.

My first weeks of class were slightly difficult. I was late a few times, but eventually got the hang of it. I was appointed an assistant who recorded my notes for me and helped me get from class to class. While other students had to read their books, I was listening. My memory was becoming stronger and stronger. At times I could hear a tape and remember everything I needed to know. My grades were good, but social life was a struggle. Neil and I hung out, but not often. It was a major difference from South Carolina State University. Going from an all-black school to a public state school where most of the students were white was a culture shock.

I graduated within two years from the University of Maryland majoring in Psychology, but I didn't stop there. I always knew I had to be twice as smart as the next person, so I enrolled in Catholic University in Washington D.C. where I became a member of the Alpha Phi Alpha Fraternity Incorporated and received my masters in Social Work.

Lesson Learned: I was shot in the head, became permanently blind, had multiple seizures, was rehabilitated, and still graduated from college. What a journey! Receiving my masters was one of the most gratifying days of my life. To walk across that stage knowing nine years before I was lying in the hospital bed receiving the worst news of my life felt great. I didn't know how I was going to make it, but I had to let go of the fear. The rehabilitation center helped me tremendously. A lot of people shun away counseling, not knowing it'll help heal their emotional wounds. When you ask for help you'll sometimes develop a relationship with people who'll take you to the next level. Some may even become a staple leading you into a new dimension of God's intention.

My family and friends were very supportive, but I lost a few friends when I became blind. They thought I was a burden. There's a joke in the blind community, "if you want to know who your real friends are, then lose your sight." In reality they weren't really my friends. This happens to all of us. As you grow and mature you'll lose people who weren't really your friends and you have to let them go. Everybody can't go with you. Bringing them along will only cause misguided energy and you should only want synergy.

All grudges must come to an end, and I was blessed to find my closure. 20 years after becoming permanently blind I visited South Carolina State University as the keynote speaker for White Cane Day, a national observance celebrating the achievements of people who are blind or visually impaired. After I spoke with the students I was able to visit my old dorm room. Once I sat in the room I started thanking God for all of my success. It's a blessing to have come this far. It was a struggle finding a job after I graduated, but when I did I knew it was only God. When I started working for the Federal Government I didn't know who I could trust or who would assist me, but I had faith that everything would work out. Coincidentally, Ms. Thomas worked in my building and I was able to hire my best friend as my assistant. You may not understand the turmoil going on in your life, but if your heart and intentions are pure everything will work together for good. You have to find your treasure in your tragedy.

I am now the president of The National Federation of The Blind for the District of Columbia. I never thought I would be in a leadership role, but it's one of the best things I could have ever done. When I first went to college I took school and life for granted, but after the accident I appreciated life and took everything serious. Gun violence has become prevalent on college campuses, especially since the 2015 deadly massacre at Umpqua Community College in Roseburg, Oregon which caused a somewhat debate on if guns should be allowed on college campuses. America is divided on the issue. A survey of students at 15 Midwestern colleges found 4 in 5 would prefer to keep guns off college grounds.[1] During a press conference regarding the Oregon shooting, former President Barack Obama was visibly angered not only by the Oregon shooting, but from the 15 mass shootings that have happened during his tenure as President. "The United States of America is the one advanced nation on earth in which we do not have sufficient common sense gun safety laws, even in the face of repeated mass killings. There is a gun roughly for every man, woman, and child in America,"[2] said Obama.

Time will only tell if gun regulations will come to pass, but if there was some kind of regulation when I was in school Terrell might've thought twice about having a gun on campus and I would be able to see today. Through all of this I've found that my life is no different from anybody else's. I am now married with a daughter; and yes, I may have obstacles, but I know I'll get through it because I live by faith and not by sight. If I can find success in my circumstance, then you can too. You have to be patient and trust the timing - God works in mysterious ways.

"The only thing worse than being blind is having sight, but no vision." - Helen Keller

Chapter 2: Let It Burn

"Happy Birthday, Chase!" My friends yelled as the clock struck midnight on my golden birthday. I was 19 on April 19th. Relaxing on my mom's indoor, screened back porch we struggled to keep the laughter from disturbing the neighbors. My mother worked late, so her house was the perfect place to escape the woes of Virginia Commonwealth University (VCU). The back porch was filled with empty cups and containers from the local carry out; it was a mess. If my mom saw this, she would have my head on a platter.

"So Chase, what are you doing this weekend," my friend Nick sarcastically asked, elbowing my friend Kenneth because he knew my answer.

"No real plans, but Allison and I are going to The Cheesecake Factory."

"Y'all go out every weekend and you've known her for two years. Did you make her your girl yet?" he asked jokingly.

"We haven't made it official, but she did purchase me an outfit from Urban Outfitters," I replied with a smirk.

I've been dating Allison since winter, but I've known her since high school. We were associates back then, only saying "hi" and "bye" in passing, until one day her sister Melissa requested me on Facebook. Looking through Melissa's Facebook page, I came across a picture of Allison and immediately sent her a message. She had blossomed since high school, which piqued my interest. That same day we exchanged information. The rest was history.

Walking to the cooler to grab a drink, my bladder stopped me in my tracks, causing me to rush to the bathroom. I couldn't believe what I saw in the bathroom mirror. Sweat was dripping from my forehead and my eyes were bloodshot. *What did*

Kenneth put in these drinks? Smiling at myself in the mirror, I realized I was on cloud nine. I attempted to urinate, but couldn't. I waited and waited, still nothing. I didn't understand; I had just ran to the bathroom because I had to go, but now I was clogged. After waiting for what seemed like a century, I exhaled and released. After Nick and Kenneth left, I decided to stay at my mom's house since I didn't have classes on Thursdays, not to mention I didn't feel like having my slumber disturbed by my roommate. He usually came into the room at the wee hours of the morning.

While brushing my teeth the following morning, I looked at myself in the mirror and laughed when I remembered the night before. But it wasn't funny when I lifted the toilet seat and had the same problem when I tried to urinate again. *Was this déjà vu?* A sharp pain ripped through my urethra as I urinated, causing me to flinch and aim for the seat. I didn't understand what was happening. As I wiped off the seat, I started to wonder: *Did I drink too much liquor last night? Should I quit smoking? Is this the true meaning of a golden birthday?* Flushing the toilet I could smell the aroma of bacon in the air. Mom was home and cooking up a storm.

"There's my birthday boy! What do you have planned for today?" my mom said as I walked into the kitchen.

"I'm going out with Allison tomorrow, but I'm going over grandmother's house later."

"I figured that. You have to collect your birthday money from grandma huh?" she said with a smile.

"Yeah, I know she'll have something for me."

"Tell your father to give you some money too, even though I know he probably will. How is he anyway?"

"He's good, still the same cool guy," I said as she rolled her eyes.

My parents divorced when I was in the 8th grade, but they still had to co-parent. Unlike some college students, I attended school in my hometown. Sometimes I wished I could've left Richmond, but staying on campus would have to suffice. I decided to attend VCU because it was cheaper than out of state colleges. My parents couldn't afford out of state tuition, so I played the hand I was dealt.

I wanted to make sure I was back to normal before leaving out, so I went back into the bathroom. I unzipped my pants and instantly went into shock. *What the hell is this?* My penis was oozing with milky white and yellowish pus that was half crusted over. My stomach rumbled, tossed, and turned like waves crashing against a ship. I felt seasick, but I was truly sick from what I was seeing. After wiping the pus off, I tried to pee again and another sharp pain burned me as the urine drained into the toilet. "Ugh!" I murmured to myself so my mother wouldn't hear me. She always said not drinking enough water would catch up with me. Leaving the bathroom, I became distressed knowing that my golden birthday was turning into rusted trash.

Lying across my bed, I pondered telling my mom; but, knowing her, she would ask a million questions, making me uncomfortable. I wasn't a little boy anymore, so any questions about my private parts would just be weird. I couldn't stop thinking about what was going on; then it hit me! A year ago Nick caught gonorrhea from his ex-girlfriend, and the symptoms were similar to mine. Allison is the only girl I've been with in the past four months; I believe she would've told me if she had a Sexually Transmitted Disease (STD). If she had gonorrhea, how could she live with the fact that every time she peed it burned, especially if it's curable? I haven't been sleeping with multiple people; hell, I'm not half as promiscuous as some of my friends. I can count on one hand how many sexual partners I've had. I remember going to Freshmen Orientation and the counselor told us that 1 in 4 students would catch an STD before graduating. Now I was a statistic. Shaking my head as I left the bathroom, I didn't understand. *God why me? Why is this happening?*

I ended up leaving my grandmother's house early because I was so discombobulated. I had to figure out what was going on. I went home and took a nap but was irritated by the tingling irritation in the opening of my urethra. Finally, I got up and went into the bathroom. Standing at the toilet, I saw the same fluids from this morning except this time it was completely crusted over and dried out. "Ugh!" I murmured as I urinated. The pain was getting more and more extreme as time went by. I had to get this taken care of now. Hopefully the health center at school could do something. I looked around as I pulled into the Student Health Center parking lot and suddenly became paranoid. Multiple thoughts ran through my head as I walked towards the entrance. *What if somebody sees me? What if somebody asks why I'm here?* Sticking my hand out to open the door, I quickly changed my mind. I couldn't risk somebody knowing I had an STD. I don't want to be known as the guy on campus who has an STD.

Returning to my mother's house, I grabbed the Yellow Pages phone book from the top of the refrigerator. As I searched for the nearest clinic, I realized they were all in proximity of the campus. Then I saw a listing for the Hanover Health Department, which was 20 minutes away from campus. Perfect!

"Hanover Health Department; how may I help you?" said the secretary who answered the phone. I became frozen with a loss for words. I didn't want her to know what was going on.

Do I say I want to get tested? Do I tell her I might have an STD?

"Hello is anybody there?" she asked in her southern accent.

"Yes, umm"

"Hello!" she irritably replied.

"I'm sorry. Is it possible I can get tested today?" I asked.

"I'm sorry we're all booked for today, but we have openings for tomorrow. What tests did you want?"
Oh God, what do I say?

"Umm, I guess everything?"

"Ok we have an opening at 8:30 a.m. tomorrow morning. There will be a fee of $35.00. Do you have insurance?"

"Yes, I'm under my mom's insurance with Aetna."

"Ok, and your name?"

A million thoughts scattered through my mind. *Why does she need to know my name? What if she finds out what school I attend and tells somebody?*

"My name? Why do you need to know that?" I asked.

"It's protocol sir? Don't worry, all of your information is protected," she said as if she knew what I was thinking.

"My name is Chase Alexander, ma'am."

"Ok, Mr. Alexander please be here promptly at 8:30 a.m.; you're allowed a 15 minute grace period."

I hung up the phone and plopped my head down between the yellow pages, banging my fist against the kitchen table. It was my 19th birthday and I was about to get tested for every STD in the book, and one might be positive. My phone started to vibrate; it was Allison. *What the hell does she want?* I wanted to curse her out and call her every name in the book, but I had to wait for the test results.

"Hey, baby! Happy Birthday!" she yelled into the phone.

"Hey," I replied in a somber tone.

"What's wrong with you? It's your birthday."

"Nothing, just a little tired. I had a long night of partying."

"You getting old; one night of chilling with your friends and you still tired at 2:00 p.m.," she said.

Already irritated, I pulled the phone away from my ear to avoid cursing her out. I was a ticking time bomb waiting to explode.

"Yeah, I'm just tired."

"Well, get some sleep. We're still on for tomorrow right?"

"We sure are," I sarcastically replied.

Friday night was perfect because I would have my results and could let her know the cold-hearted truth.

The next morning my stomach churned and my head pounded with a headache from thinking about my appointment. *Was this the day the Lord made or the devil made?* I was on fire; burning physically and emotionally. Usually I would be listening to the latest rap songs in the car, but not today. Right now I needed God. Kirk Franklin and The Family's *Whatcha Lookin 4* album played through the speakers as I drove to the clinic. My mother and father used to play this album when I was younger and it's stuck with me ever since. Pulling into the parking lot, I stared at the clinic and shook my head. I couldn't believe this was about to happen. Turning down the music, I prayed before leaving the car. "Father God, please let my tests come back negative. Please let it be a bladder problem and not an STD problem. Please heal me. In Jesus name, I pray, Amen." Grabbing my iPod, I put my headphones on and walked in. I needed this anointed music to play throughout my visit.

I was shocked when I walked into the clinic and saw that it was filled to capacity. I expected a few people, but not like this! Young mothers skimmed through magazines as their children played with games and young teens like me sat in fear. "We'll be with you in a moment Mr. Alexander, please have a seat," the female secretary said. Her voice didn't sound like the lady from yesterday, so half of my nervousness went away. Suddenly, the front door opened. A young girl with dark shades, a hat, and a magazine covering her mouth, chin and nose walked in talking softly on her cell phone. I tried to contain my giggles as she attempted to look inconspicuous; but the guy beside me couldn't contain his. Immediately he burst out laughing as other patients quietly laughed with him. "You're only attracting more attention to yourself walking in here trying to look all incognito. We're all in here for a reason, so it's nothing to be ashamed of," he said out loud. Covering my face, I started laughing even more. Quickly removing the magazine from her face, she sat staring at the guy with a look of disgust. The stress and tension that had been building up from yesterday seemed to have faded after laughing so hard. The guy was right; there's nothing to be ashamed of, especially if we're all in here. "Mr. Alexander?" the nurse yelled from the door waiving for me to come back.

Walking into the room, I became anxious as I stared at the STD pamphlets on the wall. There was one for HIV/AIDS, Gonorrhea, Chlamydia, Herpes, Pubic Lice, Syphilis, and Human Papillomavirus (HPV). "Dr. Thompson will be in soon," the nurse said as she exited the room. Standing up, I grabbed the Chlamydia pamphlet off the wall and instantly cringed as I looked at the pictures. These pictures didn't reflect my symptoms; I started to wonder if I had an STD at all. Neither my genitals nor mouth were covered in white and red bumps. The only picture I could relate to was the one of discharge oozing out of the male genital. Abruptly, I put the pamphlet down. Looking at those pictures was torture.

Startled by a knock at the door, I put the pamphlet back and turned towards the front. "Good Morning, Mr. Alexander. I'm Dr. Thompson; I will be your doctor for the day," she said. Dr. Thompson reminded me of my grandmother, she was short, wore glasses, and her long, salt and pepper hair flowed down her medicine jacket.

"How are you doing today, Mr. Alexander?" she asked.

"Umm, I'm ok; a little nervous."

"A little nervous? I'm sure I can take care of it. Now tell me why you're here."

"I was hanging with my friends for my birthday, and when I went to the bathroom I couldn't pee for a few seconds. The same thing happened the following morning, but this time I saw white and yellowish pus."

"And all of this happened on your birthday?"

"Yes ma'am, it was yesterday."

"Geesh what a birthday!"

"It sounds like you have an STD, but let me ask you a few questions. Are you sexually active?"

"Yes."

"The last time you had sex, did you use protection?"

"No," I replied letting out a deep sigh. *Why would I do that? I always use a condom and the one time I don't this happens.*

"Do you participate in group sex?"

"No."

"Are you gay or bi-sexual?"

"No."

"Do you engage in anal sex?"

"No!" I replied raising my voice. Didn't she just hear me say I'm not gay or bi-sexual?

"No need to get upset Mr. Alexander. Heterosexuals engage in anal sex too. You know, like with females," she said giggling.

"Oh," I replied feeling dumb. Apparently I was on edge and needed to calm down.

Putting on her latex gloves, she stood up from the desk, grabbed a large Q-tip, and turned towards me.

"Mr. Alexander please drop your pants and undergarments."

"What are you about do?" I asked nervously.

"I have to stick this Q-tip in the opening of your penis to swab the discharge. This will determine what STD you have."

"What!" I yelled. My stomach turned as I thought about the pain.

"It won't hurt Mr. Alexander. It's just a little sting."

"Yeah right, I'm not stupid," I murmured.
I started quivering as I stood up to undo my belt buckle and pull down my pants. This is about to be the most painful thing ever; nothing is supposed to go in there. Jesus why me! Dr. Thompson came towards me while sitting on the stool. I felt her grab my genital.

"Oh wow, this is a significant amount of discharge," she said. Looking away I clenched my teeth and braced myself for the pain. In an instant, a sharp pain twisted and savagely ripped through my urethra. The pain caused me to flinch making the Q-tip go further into me.

"Ahhhhhh!" I yelled. *Just kill me now, please!*

"Hush up with all that screaming. You shouldn't be having unprotected sex," she said as I looked down at her. She acted like my grandmother too, feisty with a no holds barred attitude.

I could still feel the pain in my urethra as I pulled up my pants. "Now I'm going to draw some blood. This won't hurt," she said with a devious smile. As she took the plastic off of the needle, I took a deep breath, thanking God this was almost over.

"I'll be back with the discharge results in 10 minutes, but your blood work will take a few days." My right leg shook nervously as I bowed my head and prayed one last time.

"Ok Mr. Alexander the results are in. You have Chlamydia," she said.

"So what does that mean? How did I get it?"

"You got it from having unprotected sex or oral sex, but there have been accounts where patients did use condoms and they still caught the disease. Remember condoms aren't 100% effective, so if you want to avoid coming back here, don't have sex. Or make sure your partner has been tested and you're in a monogamous relationship."

"Is it possible that she knew because she's not dating anybody else but me? She's the only one I've been with," I asked.

"Sometime females have no symptoms or they ignore the signs, so maybe she didn't. When you're sexually active and don't use protection this is bound to happen, especially with young adults. Just tell her the truth and see what she says, either way you'll be cured in a week."

"A week?"

"Yes a week. The antibiotics I'm prescribing for you will clear it up by then. You also shouldn't have sex, drink alcohol, or smoke within the next week. The secretary at the front will have all of your information."

Taking the walk of shame through the hallway, I prayed none of the other patients heard my cries. I jumped in shock from hearing a familiar loud scream from a patient in the next room. That person has to be going through the same thing as me. There was no charge for my visit, thanks to my insurance. It would have been stupid if I paid, especially since VCU covers these types of expenses. With my medicine in hand, I opened the bottle and popped a pill as I exited the clinic. Getting in the car, I looked at my cell phone; I had seven missed calls from Allison. *What did she want?* She never called me this much. *Was this some sort of women's intuition? Did she know something was wrong?* I dialed her number; she picked up on the first ring.

"Mmmhmm," she said answering the phone.

"Hello, Allison?"

"I said mmmhmm, Chase," she said with an attitude.

"What's wrong with you?" I asked.

"Why were you ignoring my calls?"

"I wasn't ignoring your calls I was at the doctor."

"Stop lying, you weren't at the doctor. You never told me you had an appointment."

"Well, I went to the damn doctor, ok!" I yelled. She had some nerve having an attitude after the hell I just went through. I wasn't going to curse her out like I planned since Dr. Thompson explained that she might not have known.

"Are you home?" I asked

"Yeah I'm here."

"I'm about to come over. I have to talk to you about something."

"About what? I don't want to argue Chase."

"We're not about to argue. I'll see you in 30 minutes."

Opening the door to her apartment she embraced me with a hug as she played with her half curled and half straighten hair. "Hey birthday boy, I missed you." Grabbing my hand she dragged me to the bathroom so she could finish curling her hair. Sitting on the edge of the bathtub I pondered how I would tell her. She could see the nervousness in my face as she looked in the mirror at my reflection. "Ok what's wrong,

Chase?" she asked. With my hand slightly shaking I had to tell her.

"Yesterday when all of my friends were over my house I went to the bathroom and I couldn't pee. Then that same morning I saw a white, yellowish discharge coming out the opening."

"What!' She yelled.

"So today I went to the doctor and she diagnosed me with Chlamydia and you're the only one I've been with and had unprotected sex with." The curling iron dropped to the ground as she slowly sat next to me. Pausing before speaking she took a deep breath and wiped her eyes.

"Babe, I'm so sorry," she said.

"You didn't know did you?" I asked.

"Of course not; if I did I would've got checked. I wouldn't want to walk around in pain," she said.

"I believe you. Dr. Thompson said most females don't have any symptoms or they're not that severe."

"Yes, I swear I didn't know. I'm going to make an appointment and go in the morning. I promise."

Later that afternoon, as I walked into my mother's house, I could see her bedroom light on. Still feeling ashamed of what happened, I attempted to avoid her by going straight to my room, but before I could she stopped me. "Chase come here, I need to talk to you." Walking in her room she had her scarf on while lying in the bed watching The Price is Right.

"Yes, Mom."

"Can you hand me that remote off the dresser, baby?" Looking at her like she was crazy I grabbed the remote and headed to my room.

"Wait a minute, I'm not done. Do you have something to tell me?" she asked, as I looked around confused. *Is this woman's intuition day?*

"No, what do you mean?"

"Well when I walked in the house the Yellow Pages phonebook was left opened to a list of clinics. I know you haven't gone and gotten one of these girls pregnant, Chase!" She yelled. Trying to convey my best poker face and laugh it off I couldn't believe I was so stupid to leave the phonebook open on the kitchen table. "No, Mom, I was looking for a friend," I said. She looked at me with a smirk as if she didn't believe me. I didn't like lying to my mom, and I usually tell her everything, but this time I just couldn't. "Ok, Chase. I don't have time for no babies and you better be wrapping it up! There are all kind of sexually transmitted diseases out here. Sex isn't worth risking your life over a feeling that will only last a few minutes or longer. As a matter of fact, you shouldn't be having sex anyway; you're not married." Opening my room door, I quickly laid on my bed feeling drained and stressed.

Awakening from my nap, the first thing I did was go to the bathroom to see if there were any improvements. Lifting the toilet seat I examined my genitals. Surprisingly, there was no discharge; and when I urinated the sting was less painful. Thank God things were getting back to normal. I decided to go on campus since I hadn't seen my friends.

"Chase where the heck you been?" Nick and Kenneth said as I walked in Nick's room.

"You know he probably been laid up with Allison," Kenneth jokingly said.

"Man, y'all won't believe this," I said as I sat in the wooden chair.

"Remember the other day on my mother's back porch?"

"Yeah," they both said in sequence.

"When I went to the bathroom that night I couldn't pee, and when I did it burned like hell."

"Man, don't tell me you got burnt," Nick said.

"Yeah man, I went to the clinic. The doctor put the Q-tip in my penis and swiped all around the opening."

"Ugh!" they both yelled, cringing while briefly closing their legs and clenching their teeth."

"Wait a minute, it wasn't Allison was it?" Nick asked.

"I don't know. She's going to get tested tomorrow. It had to be her though; she's the only one I've been with."

"Dang, so it happened to you too?" Kenneth said.

"What do you mean you too? You had Chlamydia?" I asked.

"Yup. Rosa from Regency Mall gave it to me, but mine was worse. Remember that time I couldn't walk and my knees kept collapsing?"

"Yeah I remember that. We all thought you were just getting old," I replied as me and Nick laughed.

"Well, that's why. I had the symptoms, but after two weeks it went away. Then a few months later my knees started sporadically going out and I could barely walk. I didn't know what was going on. When I went to urgent care they diagnosed me with Reactive Arthritis, which was caused by Chlamydia. Right then and there I knew the symptoms I had before must have been the disease."

I couldn't believe what I was hearing. Kenneth almost couldn't walk because of Chlamydia! This is worse than I thought; not only are the symptoms painful, but Chlamydia can leave you handicapped.

As I lay in bed Saturday afternoon, my phone started ringing; it was Allison. I took a deep breath before answering the phone; I knew she had received her results.

"Chase," she said nervously.

"Good Afternoon, Allison. Don't sound so scared," I said with a smile to try and lighten the mood.

"Well, I got my results back and I do have it."

"I only have one question, Allison. Who did you get it from, because you're the only one I've been with," I said in a stern voice. She became silent, seemingly lost for words.

"Hello, you still there?" I asked sarcastically.

"Yes, I'm here. I saw my ex-boyfriend about two weeks ago. I contracted it from him. I'm so sorry, please forgive me."

"I'm not even that mad, you're not my girlfriend, but I thought we were being monogamous with each other. Well, I know I was."

"I was too, I just slipped up. He came over my house saying how much he missed me and that he was sorry for what he did and I gave in."

"But you gave in and didn't use a condom? Why would you do that?"

"I know, I know. All I can say is I'm sorry, I didn't mean to hurt you."

"I'm going to talk to you later. I'm going out with Nick and Kenneth. Just call me tomorrow or something," I said nonchalantly.

It wasn't ok, but I had too much pride to show her my true feelings. Not only did she risk our lives, but she also went behind my back with her ex. Granted, we weren't a couple; I couldn't be too mad, that's part of the reason why I acted as if nothing was wrong. The trust was gone; she burned me, so I had to let the relationship burn. We remained cordial and occasionally saw each other through mutual friends, but whatever relationship I thought we had was dead.

Lesson Learned: "Sex isn't worth risking your life over a feeling that will only last a few minutes or longer," was the advice from my Mom and she was right. Is sex worth catching a disease or even worse, a disease that's incurable? Absolutely not. I was naive to not use a condom; I put my trust in someone I really didn't know. We were only dating for four months and that's not enough time to fully know someone. I should've asked about her STD status. At times it can be awkward to ask somebody about their sexual status, but it's better to be safe than sorry. If you're sexually active, use protection no matter what, even if you think you're in a monogamous relationship. I thought I was and unfortunately I wasn't so lucky. Having multiple sex partners is like rolling dice; you might eventually crap out.

Find someone you can be in a relationship and truly monogamous with. Listen to your friends or associates; if they've been through similar experiences, learn from them. Nick told me a year prior that he had an STD and that was a clear warning. If your friend can catch it, then you can too. If you think you may have caught a disease, research it online and go to your local health provider. Do not throw it to the way side or the symptoms may worsen. People in the age range of 15-24 represent 25% of the active sexual population, but they account for more than half of the new STD diagnoses each year.[3] During freshmen orientation, the counselor explained that 1 in 4 college students would contract an STD before graduating. Thank God I walked across that stage STD free. I thought this would never happen to me, but it did. Nobody is invincible.

Chapter 3: Achieving While Grieving

I wish these last 30 minutes of class would hurry up; it's 11:30 a.m. and I'm ready to go. That's what I told myself as I sat in class watching the clock go around and around. "Jeevan, the time isn't going to move any faster if you keep looking at the clock," said Professor Wynn. Slowly lifting my head off the desk, removing my dreadlocks from my face, I could hear my classmates snickering at me. I was caught. I've been in Reporting 101 for an hour and can't remember anything she said. Opening my textbook, I smirked as I tried to catch up with the rest of the class. "What page are we on again?" I murmured to my classmate. It was only the third week of class. I usually wouldn't be visiting Maryland this early, but I wouldn't dare miss this weekend. Julian and I were headed home to celebrate his girlfriend, Kacey's, 21st birthday. This wasn't a normal celebration; she was going all out with her own party bus. As the clock reached 12 p.m., I hurdled out the classroom before Professor Wynn could finish her sentence. "Excuse me, Mr. Brown! Mr. Brown!" She said yelling, but it was too late. I was headed home and nothing could stop me.

It was Friday, the sun was shining, and there wasn't a cloud in the sky; a perfect beginning for the weekend. As I walked past the café, I could feel my phone vibrating in my pocket. It was my friend Jeff.

"Oh, so you, John, and Julian coming home this weekend and wasn't going to tell me?" he said laughing.

"Man, I told you last week I was coming for Kacey's birthday party. You need to try and come. Your old boo, Britney, is going to be there," I said.

"Oh yeah?"

"Yup! Are you going to come with us?"

"Nah, I'm going chill. You know I got a girl and I'm not trying to hear her mouth while I'm there." We both started laughing; I could see him now arguing on the phone with her while we partied.

Jeff and I have been friends since elementary school. We were so close our high school voted us "Best Friends" along with our other friends John and Laurence. When you saw one, you saw the other; if the other wasn't around, you could be rest assured he was close. Jeff attended World Technical College in Pittsburgh, Pennsylvania, but before that he went to North Carolina A&T State University in Greensboro, North Carolina, only an hour from my school, Johnson C. Smith University in Charlotte, North Carolina. There was no separating us; we were like brothers. Little did I know this would be my last time talking to him.

Parked outside of my cousin's Herb apartment, Julian and I waited for him to come outside as he took his precious time.

"Man, would you hurry up. You know we have to take this long trip home. I'm trying to hop on Highway 85 now!" I said to him as he walked towards my 1998 green Toyota Camry.

"For what? We're not going to get there any faster. It's a six hour ride from Charlotte to Maryland," he said with a grin.

"Why are you in such a rush?" Herb asked.

"I'm supposed to be hooking up with Jeff and everybody else when I get home. I'm going to be so busy I might not get to see everybody."

"Jeff, that's the dark skin guy with the low hair cut that went to North Carolina A&T right?" Herb asked.

"Yup."

I wanted to enjoy as much time as I could, but each second waiting on Herb was a second lost from my visit. Once we hit the highway, it only took us 5 hours to get home; my foot was heavy on the pedal. After arriving home, it seemed like the weekend went past in a blink of an eye. Herb decided to stay in Maryland, but Julian and I were exhausted as we struggled to make it back down Highway 85. With such a busy schedule, I wasn't able to hook up with Jeff or anybody else. The following Tuesday, while walking out the library, my phone rang; it was Charisma, Jeff's girlfriend. *Oh Lord!* Jeff must have pissed her off or something. She never calls me. I was always the scapegoat for my friends. I braced myself for the questions before answering.

"Hey, Jeevan. Have you talked to Jeff?" she asked.

"I talked to him last Friday. Why what's up? When's the last time you talked to him?" I asked.

"On Sunday and now its Tuesday. This isn't like him."

"He's probably busy; there's no need to worry. I'll call him, and if I talk to him I'll call you back." I said.

Hanging up the phone, I scrolled through my Blackberry contacts and stopped at "Birdman," Jeff's nickname. Jeff was fly, charismatic, and often listened to the rapper Birdman, so his nickname matched him perfectly.

"Hey, Jeff where you at? Hit me back. You got your girl calling me all worried. I'm sick of y'all girls calling me when they looking for y'all," I said laughing on his voicemail. I figured they must have gotten into an argument and he was avoiding her. Or maybe, just maybe, he was busy with school. He was serious about school this year; he had finally found his passion in automotive repair.

The following day I still hadn't heard from Jeff. I called his phone numerous times and still nothing. Sitting in my car before walking into the library, I called my friend Wesley; maybe he knew where Jeff was.

"You talk to Jeff lately?" I asked.

"Nah, but I've called his phone at least five times. Charisma called me yesterday and said she hadn't talked to him, but I figured they were just beefing." he said with a snicker.

"I know right. I thought the same thing, but he still hasn't called me back."

"Well, I did talk to his grandparents and they haven't heard from him either. They said if he doesn't call them by tomorrow they're going to his school," Wesley said.

"For real? Why the hell isn't he answering the phone? I'm getting kind of worried now."

"I talked to Laurence and he said he was coming home on Friday from Hampton University in Virginia. We were going to his school too, but since I talked to his grandparents we're not."

Hanging up the phone, I immediately called Charisma.

"Hey Charisma, you still haven't heard from Jeff?"

"No and I'm really starting to get worried, Jeevan," she said in a somber voice.

"What was he doing the last time you talked to him?"

"Well, he went to the hospital because he had a cold and a headache, but they sent him home. Later that day he was sitting in the car with the heat on because he was so cold; his apartment wasn't keeping him warm either."

"Hold up, hold up! You mean to tell me, it's the middle of September and he was sitting in his car with the heat on? What's wrong with him?"

"I don't know. He was supposed to call me yesterday to wake me up for school, but he never did. That's so unlike him; he calls me every morning."

"Damn. What is really going on? Well let me know if you hear anything, and I'll let you know if I do too."

It was Friday evening and I was set to interview one of Charlotte's local rap artists, Sosa, for my internship at Play Magazine. I usually would be excited about doing an interview, but the vibe was different this time. The energy wasn't there. After leaving the interview, I sat in the backseat of Play's managers blue Chrysler 300 exhausted. I drifted off to sleep on the brown leather interior and Jeff appeared in my dreams. I waited for an interaction, but he just stood there and stared, never taking his eyes off me. Just before I was able to speak I was awakened. "Jeevan, hey Jeevan! Get up, we're at your house," my manager said before putting the car in park. I didn't know if I had one too many snacks or if Jeff was just on my mind, but I took heed to my dream and called Wesley. If Jeff's grandparents hadn't heard from him then surely they drove to Pennsylvania, but Wesley hadn't talked to them. My mind was at ease. If they left today and Jeff's school was only two hours away, Wesley would have heard from them. Jeff was ok.

Awakening Saturday morning from the loud vibrations of my phone ringing on the dresser. I stretched my arms, yawning before answering it. It was Wesley. Doesn't he know its 7:30 in the morning; why is he calling me so early? Better yet, why is he up?

"Hello," I said while yawning into the phone.

"Dog," Wesley said in a dull voice.

"Yeah, what's up? What's wrong with you?" I asked.

"He's gone. Jeff is gone. They found him in his apartment lying under the covers."

Stunned I couldn't believe what I was hearing. Did I really just hear what I thought I heard, can't be.

"What do you mean he's gone? How? What happened?" I asked in a panic.

I could barely understand what he was saying; he was dazed and confused just like me.

"I'm going to call you back. I don't know what happened, man," he said, as his voice started to crack."

Before I could close my phone, it started to ring again. It was John, and he was in the same predicament; nobody knew what happened.

Lying in my bed, I was in denial, in disbelief. My best friend wasn't really gone, couldn't be. We're only 21, we're too young. I prayed to God it was all a big misunderstanding. I sat by the phone waiting for somebody to call and say it was a lie, an error, a mistake. *Who could I talk to? Who would give me answers?* I tried talking to God, but he wasn't answering yet, and my two roommates Ronald and Julian weren't home. I was alone. There was only one other person I could lean on for understanding, my mom. If anybody can make sense of this she could. She always had the answer. My body was buzzing with unbearable pain, like a hive of bees stinging and poisoning my soul. I started thinking of what to say. Jeff was like her son too. Plenty of times she's let us ravage the kitchen pantry and give us rides to the skating rink and Six Flags. She's seen him grow from an adolescent to a young man. Before I could think of anything else, she answered.

"Well good morning to you! To what do I owe this early morning call?" she said in a joyous voice.

"Hey, mom," I somberly said.

"Boy, what's wrong with you?"

Before answering I sat quietly, and as I started to talk my voice cracked.

"Jeevan what is going on? Are you crying?"

"Jeff...."

"Huh?"

"Mom, I got a call from Wes this morning, and he said Jeff's grandparents found him in his apartment."

"What do you mean found him? You're talking about your friend Jeff?"

"Yes mom. They found him dead under the covers in his apartment."

"What! You can't be serious right now, Jeevan," She screamed out.

"What happened?" she asked.

Wiping my tears, I explained the events leading up to this moment as she sat silently shocked by the news.

"I can't believe this," she murmured. "It's going to be ok. I really don't know what to say, baby. I just don't see how this could have happened. He's only 21, she said before pausing. "It'll be ok, baby, it will all make sense one day. Lord what is going on! I'm going to be calling you throughout the day, so answer your phone," she said.

It felt like the walls were closing in. Any other Saturday our house was filled to capacity; it was a haven for our friends who wanted to get away from campus. On any given day you could find them on the couch, floor, hallway and anywhere else they could fit, but today it was quiet. Julian and Ronald were back from Maryland, but there wasn't a sound; everybody was lost, nobody understood the imposing question "Why?" Jeff was a good guy and was loved by many, so none of us understood. It was Sunday and I should have been in church, but my mind was far from that. I was hurt. God had taken my best friend. There are worse people on earth who deserve a hearse. That was wrong to think, but that's how I felt. Lord knows I didn't need the stress; I had papers upon papers due and I couldn't afford to miss class.

Sitting at my iMac computer the following morning, I logged into Facebook and was surprised to see my wall filled with hundreds of people giving their condolences. The word about Jeff had spread like the speed of light thanks to social media. My phone started to ring; it was Wesley.

"I talked to Jeff's Grandparents earlier today.

"What they say?" I asked.

"They told me when they arrived at Jeff's apartment they had to get the rental property agent to open his room because it was locked," he explained.

"Where was his roommate?"

"That's what I don't understand because his roommate was there. When they found his body it was starting to decay and hemorrhage. He had been laying there for a few days."

"So you mean to tell me out of all those few days his roommate didn't check on him? He didn't think to knock on his door when he noticed he hadn't heard or seen Jeff?" I asked.

"That's what's confusing me. I was on Jeff's MySpace page, and I saw some of his classmates leaving some crazy post," Wesley said.

"Hold on, I'm sitting at my computer right now. I'm about to login," I replied.

Looking on Jeff's MySpace page, I scrolled down and saw the comments.

"You alright in there? Haven't heard from you lol," I said out loud reading the comment.

"I sure hope it wasn't any type of foul play," Wesley said.

"I know, right. I don't like the fact that he put "lol." What's so funny and why haven't y'all gone to check on him," I said.

Wesley and I didn't know his new college friends, but seeing those comments made us suspicious.

46

It seemed like things just kept getting worse. In the midst of this, my granddad was diagnosed with cancer and my grandmother had congestive heart failure, diabetes and kidney failure. I was also working at Circuit City with three internships. One at Play Magazine, another at Jungle Records Music Label, and another at Kanye West's G.O.O.D Music Label as a campus rep. Not to mention I had a full schedule of 19 credits. I was swamped. I prayed this was just some ephemeral stroke of bad luck, but it wasn't. It was reality. *How was I going to make it? How do I stay focused when the ones who love and support me are fading away?* I started mentally preparing myself for the funeral. It wasn't my first funeral, but it was going to be one of the most hurtful. Lying in bed staring at the obituaries of my past relatives and friends on the wall I became distressed, knowing I would be adding one more - my best friend's.

Tossing and turning in my bed, I gave up trying to rest. I was sleepless. Glancing around my room, it looked just how I felt - a mess. Sitting up to turn on my computer, I placed my iTunes on shuffle as I cleaned up. Scarface's 1997 song "Smile" featuring Tupac played through the speakers. Listening to the words seemed to help with my grieving. You would have thought Scarface, Tupac, and I were all suffering from the same thing. I've heard the song before, but that night it spoke to me, inspiring me to write a poem for Jeff. The following day I read the poem to John, his mother Ms. Monique, Laurence, and my mother.

"You should read your poem at the funeral, Jeevan," Ms. Monique said over the phone.

"Ummm I don't know, I'm going to be in front of a lot of people," I said shyly.

"When did you become shy," my mother chimed in as Ms. Monique laughed.

"That's just…"

"That's just what, boy." My mom said interrupting me.

"Stop acting scared. The poem described his personality and character flawlessly," she said.

"Ok, ok I'll do it." I said with a smile in my voice.

"I'm going to email the poem to Jeff's grandparents and see what they say," said Ms. Monique.

The next evening while sitting in the living room I decided to call Jeff's grandmother to check on her.

"Hey, Mrs. Cox, it's me Jeevan. How are you doing?"

"I'm good, baby just holding on. John's mother sent me the poem and I loved it. I can't wait for you to read it." She said with a smile in her voice. To hear her so excited brought me joy.

"I'm glad you liked it."

"I thought you might want to know we got the coroner's report back."

"Really? What did it say?" I asked.'

"Jeff died from meningitis."

"I'm sorry Mrs. Cox, meni- what?"

"Meningitis, it's a bacterial infection of the membranes that cover the brain and spinal cord."

"How in the world did he get that?" I asked in disbelief. With the suspicion of Jeff's roommate and classmates still on my brain, I started thinking the worst. *Did they put something in his drink? Was it a set up?*

"Baby, it could have come from a number of things. It could have come from eating off a utensil that wasn't thoroughly clean or it could have come from him being in contact with somebody who had it. The authorities are still investigating the case; I'll keep you and the guys updated."

After talking with Mrs. Cox, I quickly hopped on my computer and Googled the symptoms of meningitis. *Severe pains with aches in your back and joints, sleepiness or confusion, a dislike for bright lights, very cold hands and feet, shivering, rapid breathing, and red or purple spots that do not fade under pressure.* Some of the symptoms were an exact correlation to why he was blasting the heat in the middle of September. I pondered and grew somber thinking about the pain he might have gone through. Charisma said he was cold, but he could have been uncontrollably shivering and in pain at the same time. He didn't deserve this; it was unfair.

While preparing to go down the stairs Thursday morning to load my bags in Ronald's car, I went into panic mode when I noticed a pile of dishes in the sink. Remembering the causes of meningitis, I washed each utensil over and over, examining each one carefully making sure they were spotless. Riding through Greensboro, North Carolina, I noticed the exit for North Carolina A&T State University and instantly started reminiscing about the fun times we had there. From the homecoming Go-Go's to Aggie Fest, I usually would be excited passing A&T, but this time I was heavyhearted.

Later that night, arriving into Maryland, I went straight to John's house as we waited for everybody to arrive so we could follow each other to Jeff's grandparent's house. We were four cars deep as we hit the wooded back roads to their house. His grandparents lived in the new development around the corner from my neighborhood. The houses were beautiful, with long driveways and high ceilings, a complete difference from my neighborhood. Sorrow filled the air as we gathered together walking to the front. As we waited, a bright smile beamed through the glass door as Jeff's grandfather greeted us. With his glasses covering his brown skin and holding his oxygen tank in his left hand, Mr. Cox embraced me as I stepped through the doorway. Walking into the kitchen there stood Mrs. Cox, Jeff's aunt, and his father who resembled the rapper DMX. Smells of cake, baked chicken, macaroni with cheese, and pies filled the kitchen as balloons and a plethora of cards were placed throughout the dining room. While everybody stood around, I knew exactly what to do: grab a plate. Nothing helps grief like some food on your stomach.

"Go head, Jeevan, help yourself," Mrs. Cox said laughing as she looked down at me through her glasses.

"You haven't changed one bit, still eating everything," Jeff's father said with a smile.

"Well you know...," I said giggling.

"Is everything ready for tomorrow?" I asked.

"Yeah, as much as it's going to be. Since y'all are here, I might as well tell you the medical examiner's report came back. They found that Jeff most likely contracted meningitis from a dirty utensil in his school cafeteria," he explained.

I couldn't believe it. How could an established university not thoroughly clean their utensils? They needed me in the kitchen; my dishes were like brand new after I washed them yesterday.

"I also want to warn y'all. When they found Jeff's body he'd been there for a while, so the morticians did the best they could," Jeff's father said looking us in the eyes.

"Tomorrow, when you see Jeff, I want you to remember him how he looked the last time you saw him. Be prepared," he said with a look of anguish. Looking at Jeff's father, I admired how well he was taking the loss. He seemed so strong, but on the inside I knew there was pain; Jeff was his first-born.

A loud cry took over the silence as Jasmine; Jeff's ex-girlfriend, who went to North Carolina A&T with Jeff, ran into the bathroom with Wesley following behind her. Jeff's grandfather got all of our attention as he explained the pallbearer procedure.

"Make sure you're dressed nicely tomorrow. Follow the verbal directions of the funeral director. When you guys are carrying the casket, gage the tempo of each other to make sure you're on one accord," he explained. After gathering our belongings, we stood in a circle holding hands as his grandmother prayed for us. It was her grandson who passed, but she was consoling us. As I listened to her pray, it hit me that even though she was hurt, she was at peace. Only a person at peace can be this strong and soothe others when they should be the ones getting comforted.

The sun beamed down on my face the following morning while I was lying in bed, it was time. Taking my scarf off my dreadlocks, I ironed my black slacks, grey shirt, and tie to match. My house was the meeting place before the funeral, so my phone had been ringing all morning. Looking out the window, one by one, cars were pulling up in front of my house. Noticing my friend, Jonathan's 1996 dark blue Impala, I squinted as I tried to read the lettering on his tinted back window. When I finally realized what it said, I smiled. *R.I.P Jeff 7/3/86 - 9/22/07* were strategically placed on the window in white, bold lettering in honor of Jeff. Looking in the rearview mirror as we left my house there were 10 cars in all as Jonathan lead the fleet of vehicles.

Pulling into the church parking lot, I saw a large crowd outside of the church; it seemed like they were stalling, avoiding the pain of seeing their friend one last time. Arriving to the front of the church I saw my mom with her bob haircut and sepia-brown skin standing with Ms. Monique, who was the same complexion, but with long silver and black hair. Looking beautiful in their church attire, they embraced us with their motherly warmth. As I walked down the aisle, reality struck; I was about to say my final goodbye. With my mom by my side, there he was in his all black casket with golden trim and handles. It matched his style perfectly; he loved the color black. From the moment my eyes saw his face, I thought about what Jeff's father said. He was right, Jeff did look different. Sitting on the first row, I watched as old classmates and associates I hadn't seen in years came to show their respect. I also watched as a plethora of females fell out and passed out. Turning my head to the left, I watched as John, who was the bodybuilder of the crew, carried two girls out at once.

Multiple shades of lipstick covered my cheek as I received kisses from my past significant others who walked over to see me. "Why ain't nobody kissing me? That's messed up; I can't get no love," Ronald said jokingly, sitting there wrapped in white bandages from a motorcycle accident. His legs and arms were completely covered, resembling an Egyptian mummy. As I received more kisses, my friend Rasaan and I laughed at Ronald's facial expressions. Watching the choir sing, I took a closer look and realized it was our high school choir along with the Director, Mr. Mitchell, me and Jeff's high school piano teacher. Smiling when I saw him, I reminisced on the numerous times Jeff and I got kicked out for disrupting his class.

Browsing through the program, I realized it was time to read the poem, but I didn't want to go up alone. I wasn't just saying this for me, but from all of us. Looking around, I asked my friends to come up with me. As Ms. Monique introduced me, the butterflies in my stomach were so strong I could have flown to the stage. With my 10 friends standing behind me, I adjusted the microphone to my height and began to read:

Whoever thought this day would come
From racing bikes, to racing cars, to staying fly, to now saying
our last goodbye
My man Jeff, the calm one, the real one, the smooth one
Always staying calm no matter the situation
Always keeping it real no matter the altercation
And always being smooth no matter which girl you were
dating.
These past weeks I've done nothing but cry and laugh.
I laughed at all the funny moments we've shared.
I cried knowing having a friend like you is rare.
From elementary school, middle school, high school, and
college
Thinking about those days, man, the memories just keep on
piling.
I stayed up A&T, man you was the reason.
Not to mention the parties, and oh yeah homecoming season.
Speed racer Jeff that's what I called you.
I just knew NASCAR had a car waiting on you.
If you wasn't with your crew
We knew you was somewhere buning with your boo.
Jet skiing and skiing were the yearly trips we took.
I got all the pictures they right in my photo book.
Some say you don't know what you got until it's gone.
But not me the love I had for my brother could only be
weighed in tons.
Jeff, life is going to be hard here without you.
So whisper in my ear so that I make the right decisions
And give me a sign when you know that I'm on the wrong
mission.
And as you journey into outer space
May the angels help you lead the way

And may the prayers that we have made
Shine up on your soul and keep you safe.
And since D'Angelo and Deron has passed away
May they be there to greet you as you pass the gates
And as you head into the tunnel lights
I hope it leads you to eternal life.

Laughter and "aww's" filled the church as I read the poem. Looking up, I could see his whole family laughing at the NASCAR joke. Jeff had a heavy foot and a need for speed. Receiving a tumultuous applause from the crowd, I let out a deep sigh as I walked back to my seat. So many people were looking at me, but I kind of liked it. As the preacher finished his sermon, I kept looking at the casket. *How much does this thing weigh? I hope we can carry it?*

Arriving at the cemetery I measured the distance from the hearse to the grave. It was about 30 feet. I think we can make it, I said to myself. Grabbing the handle and stepping in the grass, we walked synchronized to the burial. Suddenly, my friend Sidney lost his balance when his dreadlocks swung across his pale skin, almost throwing us off balance. Quickly we held on tight, catching our steps and avoiding the fall.

"What the hell are you doing?" I murmured so nobody would hear me except my friends.

"Man, I slipped on that rock," Sidney said.

"You're in the gym all day, but can't carry a casket?" I said jokingly, causing the somber silence to instantly fade as we erupted in laughter. The funeral director instantly gave us a stern look.

"You're not supposed to talk when carrying the body to the grave," the funeral director said. I looked at him confused. *Why can't we talk? This is our friend* I said to myself. With the sun shining on the casket, I could see my reflection. *This is it,* I said while looking at myself. As the preacher said his last prayers, I grabbed a flower off the casket touching it one last time. Walking away, I wondered what life was going to be like without Jeff.

The following day, I visited my maternal grandfather in the hospital and my paternal grandmother who had recently gotten out the hospital. They both were battling for one of the most important things - life. Talking with them, they were more concerned about me, consoling, encouraging and telling me everything was going to be ok. They were just like Jeff's grandparents, showing sympathy when they were in pain. As they got older, it hurt knowing when I came back they would usually be sicker than before. They fought through the pain, always telling me to finish school and make them proud; I vowed to do so. Not only would I make them proud, but Jeff too.

Lesson Learned: Life is peculiar. My grandfather and grandmother weren't able to attend my graduation. The day after I graduated, I went home to visit my grandfather and he was unable to speak. I was aware of his sickness, but not to this extent. Within minutes of me being there, the ambulance arrived and he passed right before my eyes. There's no doubt in my mind he was waiting for me. I also believe God waited for me to graduate before taking him. God will never give you anything you can't handle. If he would have passed during my last months of school, there's no telling how I would have handled his death.

But sometimes your loved ones pass during a significant time in your life, just like Jeff did with me. What do you do? How do you handle it? Philippians 4:6-7 says "Do not be anxious about anything, but in every situation pray with thanksgiving and present your requests to God. And the peace of God, which transcends all understanding, will guard your hearts and your minds." When you're in emotional distress, there are two things hurting - your heart and your mind. Worrying will only leave your heart in emotional pain and your mind in mental anguish. Both cause nothing but stress, and stress leads to sickness. But through prayer, God will guard your heart and mind. Pray with thanksgiving and throw some gratitude next to your grief. Appreciate the times you shared with your loved one. Everyone isn't blessed with a family or friend like them - you're fortunate.

When you pray, ask for what you really want and leave all of your cares to God. In my poem I wrote, "Jeff, life is going to be hard here without you, so whisper in my ear so that I make the right decisions and give me a sign when you know that I'm on the wrong mission." I also prayed for this. It's funny; eight years later I wasn't making the best decisions and was headed down a path of destruction. One night, as I lay in bed, Jeff came to me in a dream. Unlike before, this time we interacted. He shook my hand and it felt just like his hand. I never imagined in a million years I would remember how his hand felt, but I did. Astounded by our interaction, I was almost frightened; it was surreal. Because I was timid and a little afraid, he smirked at me like he always did. Swiftly he said, "get your mind right," then vanished. It was so real that I got back on track immediately. Jeff was speaking from his grave and I was listening. This is my experience. I'm not saying it will happen to you, but I do believe that we speak things into existence. You may not have a dream, but you might have an intuitive nudge from within telling you to make the right choice. Your loved one may come across your mind and it might help with your current situation; but, it will only serve you if you listen and are aware of the signs.

Embrace your pain. Sure Jeff's grandmother and father were strong in front of us, but behind closed doors I'm positive they wept. They were at peace because God guarded their hearts and minds. Thinking you're strong or that you're simply ok is not an indicator of strength. Let your hurt out, cry in private if you feel you need to; but always know that your loved ones want nothing but the best for you. Keep them in the back of your minds while you go on with your life. Live with the peace of knowing you're making the right choices and making them proud. Death doesn't have to devastate you - it can motivate you.

A Lesson Learned

Chapter 4: HIGHway Patrol

"Hey James, make sure you check your oil and tires before you get on the road!" my Dad said yelling into the basement. In a rush, I continued to pack my bags, completely ignoring him. Walking to my bedroom door, I closed it softly making sure my dad wasn't coming down the steps. Grabbing a small plastic bag of marijuana from my desk, I opened it, inhaling the potent smell with a smile. It smelled so good! I quickly broke down the sticky nuggets and rolled them in a sweet, aromatic Backwood leaf. It was an 8-hour drive from Dover, Delaware to Salisbury, North Carolina and I wanted to be comfortable on the road. I was also stopping past my friend Tatum's house in Durham, North Carolina, and wanted everything rolled before I got there. I wasn't a heavy smoker. I only did it socially and on the weekends. I wasn't the type to study and smoke; I separated the two. There were enough distractions in college; I didn't need another one.

"Boy did you hear me!" my dad yelled again.

"Yeah, Dad I'm going to check it."

"Is that boy deaf or something? I know he heard me," he said grumpily while walking away from the spilt foyer. Summer was over and my junior year at Livingstone College was finally here. I was ready to get out of Delaware!

This was my first summer I didn't spend in Delaware; I visited two times this summer just to see my family and friends. Salisbury was my newfound love. I had my first internship as an entertainment journalist at www.charlottevibe.com. I interviewed American Idol winner Ruben Studdard and Kymani Marley, the youngest brother of the late reggae legend Bob Marley. I was VIP at every important event and the correspondent for the Charlotte

Bobcats NBA team. This summer was for the record books and I didn't plan on moving back to Delaware anytime soon. The freedom of doing what I wanted to do, being more responsible, and having my own place was remarkable. I felt like the man, and the way things were beginning to look, I was on my way to becoming - the man.

I rushed up the steps and out the house to check my oil and tire pressure, but only one thing was on my mind. *Where the hell am I going to stay this year?* I had recently moved out of the four-bedroom townhouse that I shared with my friend Nick, so I had nowhere to go - I was homeless. My friend Dontae and I were looking for a home to rent, but nothing had come through yet. My cousin, Elijah, had an apartment on the south side of Salisbury; I knew I could stay there for a while. Plus, he smoked like he was raised in the Marley household himself. My green 2001 Mazda 626 was packed to capacity with all of my clothes, shoes, big speakers, books, and computers looking just like a college student. Only thing missing was a bumper sticker sporting the name of my university.

"Dad, I'm gone," I hollered from the front door. I could see his bald head as he stood up in his room and walked out baring the smile of a proud father. Suddenly his smile turned to a frown.

"Why do you have that black bandanna on your head?" he asked.

"I just got my dreadlocks re-twisted. I can't mess them up."

He looked down, shook his head letting out a slight grunt.

"What, Dad? It's just a bandana!"

"I know what it is, James, but the cops and a handful of other people don't look at it like that. They're going to think you're some type of thug out to start trouble."

"Nobody is thinking that dad. I'm in college. It's not the 1960s anymore."

"They don't know that! All they see is a tall, black, big guy with tattoo's and dreadlocks."

"Dad, I have to go. I will see you soon, love you," I replied rushing him to finish his conversation.

"You're going to learn the hard way, boy."

"Bye Dad! I'll call you when I get to Salisbury."

Ever since I can remember, he's always had something to say about how I looked. When I got cornrows he didn't like that. I tried to wear one pants leg up like LL Cool J, he didn't like that. I still can't forget the look on his face when I got my first tattoo. He looked at me as if I was filth. But he couldn't stop me now. I wasn't under his roof anymore.

I stopped at the Wawa gas station before hopping on the highway, gassed up my car, purchased a big bag of Salt-N-Vinegar UTZ potato chips, and hopped on 95 South. Crossing into Virginia over the Woodrow Wilson Bridge, I grabbed my black iPod Classic and scrolled to Jay-Z's first album *Reasonable Doubt*. Jay-Z rapped about taking trips to Virginia, so I blasted every song because it was slightly relatable. I felt like I was on the road to riches just like him, but in two totally different ways. As I drove through Richmond and merged onto Highway 85, my phone rung; it was my mom. I was sure she was calling because I forgot to call her before leaving.

"I got some good news, baby?" she said with a smile in her voice.

"What happened?"

"You and Dontae got the 3 bedroom house on Braveheart Lane!"

"What? That's the one we wanted too!" I yelled.

61

"Yup, the leasing officer is going to call you tomorrow to let you know when you can move in. You've worked hard over the summer; you deserve it."
Just thinking about all the crazy times that were on the horizon made me want to celebrate. It was only going to be Dontae and me in that big house and he's one of the craziest friends I have. This school year was starting off good already.

The sun was shining and I was beaming all the way down 85 South thrilled with excitement. I was ready to celebrate now! Reaching in the backseat I grabbed my duffle bag to get the Backwood I had rolled just before leaving. I could smell the aroma as soon as I pulled it out my bag. I was saving it for Tatum, but I was so happy about getting the house I decided to smoke on the road. I'll see her another time. I patted my pockets searching for a lighter, but I couldn't find one. I looked in the glove compartment and still nothing. People loved stealing lighters and I guess I was the latest victim. I looked down at the console and immediately pushed in the car lighter. Seconds later the lighter popped out. With the blunt in my mouth, I lit the end of the Backwood. It sizzled, smelling of skunks and berries. The sunroof was open and the air-conditioner was set to defog as I cruised down south to school. I was indeed - high on life.

Everything was going great as I crossed the Virginia border into Raleigh, North Carolina. Two state troopers appeared out of nowhere, causing me to ease off the gas pedal. I hated seeing cops on the road; the sight of them made my skin crawl. Every time I saw the cops, I would immediately turn down my music. Within the past two years, I received four speeding tickets: two in North Carolina and two in Virginia. I had no intentions on getting another one. Determined not to let the sight of the troopers bring me down, I drove past them with no problem. About a mile and half down the road, I looked in my rear view mirror and saw one of them pulling out. *God please don't let him come after me; please don't let him come after me.* I looked in the right lane and saw a young white guy who looked to be in his early twenties riding beside me. We both saw him coming and from our facial expressions you could tell we were thinking the same thing. *Is he coming to get you or me?* Getting pulled over was the last thing I wanted to happen, especially since I still had half of a rolled Backwood left. My car stunk of weed, and my eyes were glossy red.

I looked down to see how fast I was going. Before I knew it, the sirens were on and he was pulling up right behind me. I guess the marijuana had me thinking he wasn't coming for me, so I continued to drive like nothing was happening. He then drove on the right side of me in his dark green police car and stared me down. Putting my right hand in the air, I motioned for him to keep going. *Was he giving me that look because he wanted me to pull over or because I was going too fast?* When he aggressively pointed at me and signaled for me to pull over, I knew I was doomed.

Driving over the rumble strips, my car growled as I crossed onto the side of the road. My heart dropped and my soul became filled with fear. I immediately started praying to myself. *Oh God the Backwood! What am I going to do with the Backwood? I have to get rid of this.* Looking in the rearview mirror, I saw the cop hadn't gotten out the car yet. I quickly tore the blunt in half, stuffing half in my mouth and the other half in my liquid strawberry air freshener bottle. Yuck! I loved the taste of smoking, but eating it was a totally different story. Was I chewing crumbled cotton or weed? Holding the air freshener to the floor, I sprayed my car making sure he couldn't see what I was doing through my windows.

Hopefully, this would eliminate the odor. I shook my head while I watched the cop door open from my rear view mirror.

He was tall, muscular, baldhead, and white. He resembled the WWE wrestler Stone Cold Steve Austin. *This is it! This is the end of my college career, I'm going to jail and I'm not going to live in my new house.* He's going to racially profile me and wipe his hands with me. This is the south! My mind was so clouded with negative thoughts, you would have thought my car was filled with smoke. Whenever a cop pulls me over, I always hoped he was black, so he could at least be lenient. I rolled down the window as he bent down.

"Hello, Officer. How are you doing today?" I said while grinning from ear to ear trying to appear innocent.

"Do you know why I stopped you today?" he replied in his southern country voice.

"No Sir."

"I stopped you because you were driving too close to that tractor trailer. Let me get your license and registration please." I could tell he was young, maybe a rookie, and as country as they come. As I reached for my glove compartment he sniffed around my car like he smelled fresh bacon. Then he stopped and stared at me with his nose turned up.

"Have you been smoking?"
My heart dropped to the lower pits of my stomach. He was on to me. I had to think of something quick.

"Yes, I was smoking a Black & Mild, Sir."

"Really, a Black & Mild? I'm going to ask you again, have you been smoking marijuana in this car?"

"No, sir. I don't even smoke marijuana."
He took a deep breath while holding my license and registration in his hands.

"I'm going to give you another chance. Have you been smoking? Let me know, because if you have less than an ounce in the state of North Carolina you will only get a ticket and not arrested. You know, we do have dogs that can sniff it out. I hope you know that." He explained.

I paused, looked at him, and said to myself *He's lying, and he's just trying to get me to confess!*

"Sir, I don't have any weed at all."

He reached for his radio and called for backup, "Yes, I'm going to need a K-9 on Highway 85 South as soon as possible, over. I'm going to run your tags and look up your information. Don't go anywhere alright?" He must have really thought I was a criminal. What stupid person would drive off knowing he had my license? I looked in my rear view mirror and saw him walking back towards my car playing with his handcuffs. He reached for the door handle and opened my door. "You're not under arrest, but I know you've been smoking so we're going to wait until back up arrives with the K-9. When I got out of the car, he turned me around and placed the handcuffs on me. My high was completely gone. Walking to his car with handcuffs on while people drove past was a sobering reality. They probably think I'm some thug, but they have no idea how much I have going for me. My dad was right; I should have taken my bandanna off. I was fitting every stereotype of a hoodlum.

He sat me in the front seat instead of the back. I looked around staring at his computer, gun, and the bars separating me from the back seat.

"I'm going to ask you one more time, have you been smoking?"

"No, sir." I replied. Did he think I was going to change my answer just because I was in the cop car?

"What are you chewing?"

What does he mean chewing? I wasn't chewing anything, and then it finally registered in my head. I was nibbling on the weed I tried to swallow. *What should I do? What should I do?* "My tongue, sir." *Did I really just say my tongue? How the hell do you chew on your tongue, James?* He looked at me like the stupidest person in the world, pulled out his flashlight, and told me to open my mouth. As soon as the light shined in he said, "You lied, you tried to swallow it. I know there's weed in the car now. I can see all of it in your mouth." He picked up his dispatcher and said, "Hurry up with the dogs." My mind started racing. *What am I going to tell my Mom and Dad? They know I occasionally smoke, but this will take the cake? Was this going to be on my record? Will I be able to get a decent job? Plus, I won't be able to move in my new house!*

How was I going to get out of this? I started thinking about what I could say, or what I could do and then it hit me. They're not going to find the other half and the other part was basically devoured. I'm just going to tell the truth; what's the worst that could happen?

"Sir, look! I don't have any weed in my car, hell, I barley even smoke! I was just celebrating because I got a new house and was headed back to school after a great summer. I have a job and I intern for the Charlotte Bobcats. I smoke every now and then, but I'm no drug dealer!" I confessed feeling completely exasperated. He looked me up and down for a few seconds and surprisingly started laughing.

"Man you're crazy," he said while still giggling. *What does he mean I'm crazy, he actually thought that was funny?* If that's the case, I'm just going to say what's on my mind from here on out.

"What college do you attend?" he asked.

"Livingstone College in Salisbury, about 30 minutes away from Charlotte, North Carolina."

"Oh really? I went to Fayetteville State."
I stopped, looked around the car as if I was lost and looked back at him confused. Fayetteville State and my school were both Historically Black Colleges and Universities (HBCU) and both in the CIAA division.
"Why are you looking like that?" he asked.
I hesitated on answering, but I just let it out.
"I mean, you're white and you went to an HBCU, that's different."
"Yeah you're right, but my wife is black and mostly all of my friends are black too."
I sat dumbfounded. He was cool after all. I never saw this coming.
"So who do you intern for again?"
"Charlottevibe.com. I interview celebrities. I'm also a correspondent for the Charlotte Bobcats."
"Officer Dan to Officer Williams. Yeah I don't need back up anymore, you can cancel the dogs, over," he said talking into the radio.
When I heard him call into back up, I inhaled then exhaled slowly. Only one thing helped me in the situation and that was honesty and God. He hit the top of his pen and grabbed his ticket book. I realized I would still be getting a ticket, but that was better than being arrested.
"So listen, I'm going to issue you a ticket, but it's only a warning. Don't ever trail a tractor trailer like that. As a matter of fact, just go around them," he said.
I was smiling on the inside. Did I just get out of a ticket and going to jail? The angels must really be watching over me today.
"Yes sir!" I replied.
"And stop smoking, focus on your future; you seem like a good kid. Don't let this be your downfall."

"Yes sir," I said while nodding my head in agreement. While he was walking around to open my car door I uttered under my breath "God, thank you." I shook his hand like he was one of my close friends, which made him laugh again.

I sat in my car and placed my head on the steering wheel in relief. I drove the speed limit all the way to Salisbury. The paranoia of getting pulled over was still there; I would be a fool to risk it again. When I reached the Salisbury line, I remembered that I still had the other half of the blunt in the air freshener bottle. Grabbing the bottle from the floor, I untwisted the cap, rolled down my window, and tossed the bottle out the window, watching it hit the ground with the red liquid seeping out. I wasn't carrying this habit into my junior year. I was leaving it right where it belonged - in the past.

Lesson Learned: There are good people in this world and there are bad people, just like there are good cops and bad cops. I shouldn't have judged the police officer based on the color of his skin or how he looked. Dr. Martin Luther King Jr. said "I look to a day when people will not be judged by the color of their skin, but by the content of their character." We're all human. In order to get out of racist mind state, don't focus on the color of people's skin, but simply think of them as human, just like you. It can be hard to change those thoughts with so much racial tension in the world, but it starts from within. When those negative thoughts come in your head, replace them by expressing love and thinking positive thoughts. There's no harm in that, and it creates positive energy that will carry you forward in a great way. You never know what somebody can do for you, so keep an open mind.

Never smoke on the road; the risks are too high. All police aren't nice like Officer Dan. Never give people a reason to question you or pull you over. My dad told me I shouldn't have been riding with a bandana on, which might have been the reason the officer pulled me over at first. Not giving people a reason to look at you in a negative way can be applied to your job or school. You might have a co-worker, boss, or teacher who isn't fond of you. But if you do what you're supposed to do, there's nothing they can hold against you. Stay out of harm's way and never give the enemy ammunition. Remember to always keep God first. I prayed and thanked God numerous times during this situation. It's times like these where some of us forget about the quick prayer we said before something terrible could've happened. The officer might not have been so lenient if I hadn't prayed. Prayer Works!

Chapter 5: Cold Summer

Sunrays melted into the California hills as Lisa and I drove down the dusked wooded roads to her house with Kevin, Juan, and Ralph following behind us. We were all leaving our friends Tia's graduation cookout in Baldwin Hills. Staring out the window, I realized how much I loved Baldwin Hills, a dreamland community filled with palm trees, mansions, luxury vehicles, and, the best of all, peace. Not to mention it was one of the wealthiest African American neighborhoods in Los Angeles, California; a complete difference from where I lived in Crenshaw. Parking our cars at Lisa's house, we joined the guys in Kevin's black 2001 Impala; Juan in the passenger seat, Ralph behind him, and Lisa in the middle. I was behind Kevin, whose seat was back too far. I never understood why guys drove with their seats extended. How could they see?

Kevin turned on his high beams as we headed out of the forested hills and into the city. When we stopped at a red light, a loud pop struck the air causing me to flinch. *What was that?* I asked myself looking around. More rippling sounds sliced through the air in a rapid succession. "Everybody get down!" Kevin yelled. Pop! Pop! Pop! Echoes of gunfire rang out as the back window shattered, causing tiny pieces of glass to hit my back. As I struggled to hide behind Kevin's seat, I could see Ralph trying his best to cover Lisa's head while he hid below the passenger seat. I was petrified.

The shooter wasn't letting his finger off the trigger; he was emptying the whole clip. God help us! I've seen plenty of movies like this, but never thought I would be living it. "Juan what are you doing? Get down!" Kevin yelled as he saw Juan reaching for his pistol in an attempt to fire back. Suddenly the shots stopped followed by screeching tires peeling off into the night.

"Y'all alright? Everybody good?" Kevin asked, panicking as he looked down at us hiding behind the seats. All of us seemed ok, but one of us wasn't.

"Oh my God! Brittany got shot!" Lisa screamed.

"Oh shit," Ralph uttered with his eyes bulging out, looking over at me.

"What should we do? What should we do? Drive to the hospital Kevin. Go, go!" Lisa yelled.

Kevin made a snap decision and raced back to Tia's house. The ride to the hospital was too long; we needed help now. "It's going to be ok, Brittany, it's going to be ok," Lisa said with tears coming down her eyes. Quickly putting the car in park Kevin, Ralph, Juan, and Lisa swiftly hopped out. "Somebody help us, please! Brittany just got shot, call 911!" Lisa screamed as she ran up the hill to Tia's house, leaving me alone with the car doors wide open. We had just left Tia's cookout and now we'd returned with a gunshot wound to my back right side. My white halter-top was drenched in blood. When I placed my palms against the black leather seat in an attempt to remove myself from the car, a piercing pain shot through my side. I was stuck. The more I moved, the more pain I felt. My legs, back, shoulders, and feet were immobilized, leaving me frozen.

Adrenaline rushed through my body. The gunshot wound fiercely burned my flesh as the realization that I had been shot settled in. *"Jesus, Jesus, Jesus, Jesus!"* My sight became hazy as my body weakened, causing me to fade in and out of consciousness. I could hear footsteps running towards the car. In a swift motion I felt Tia's father place his arms under my thighs and back, lifting me off the seat and out the car. Laying me in the middle of the street, he looked down at me with his glasses on never losing eye contact with me. "Stay with me Brittany; hold on, you hear," he calmly said. I could only imagine what was going through his head. Why was his daughter's friend shot and bleeding uncontrollably at a high school graduation cookout? Tia was a year younger than me and had recently graduated from my old high school. It was only my second week home from my freshmen year at North Carolina A&M College. I couldn't believe this was happening to me.

Cries and frustration filled the street as Tia's family and friends came from the backyard and into the chaos. In disarray, people begin to yell, "Where is the ambulance?" "Oh My God! What happened to Brittany?" "Somebody do something!" Nobody knew what to do or could professionally help. It was a complete nightmare! Out of nowhere, as if there was an immediate signal from God, I watched as Tia's family and friends formed a circle around me holding hands. With blood pouring out of me, I looked up at each of them while I lay in the middle of the street. Lisa, the shortest out of the bunch, stood there sniffling with her gold bamboo nameplate earrings swinging back and forth against her cocoa skin as she wiped her nose. Tia's father started to pray "Our father who art in heaven...," he continued as he added my name into bits and pieces of the Lord's Prayer. *Could this be it? Was it my time to go?* If not, the Holy Spirit needed to show himself and save me from this dungeon of hell.

Loud sirens and thunderous sounds from the helicopters above started to overpower the prayers. As the ambulance drew closer and closer, my breaths got shorter and shorter. "Oh no, not my baby!" I heard from a familiar voice. Turning to my right, I could see my mother and twin brother, Brian, breaking through the circle. They rushed to my side on bended knee.

Tears drifted down my mother's cheeks as red and blue police lights flashed across her face. "I'm here baby, I'm here. Just hold on," she cried.

"Give us some space here please!" The paramedic yelled, moving his blonde hair out of his face and placing his gloves over his pale hands.

"What's your name ma'am, and how old are you?" he asked.

"Brittany Smith. I'm 18," I softly replied after taking a deep breath.

"We have a young African American female, light-skin, long, black hair, about 5'8 and 122 pounds, shot in the lower back right near the rib, over," he said talking into the dispatch and constantly asking my name to make sure I was conscious. My mom stepped aside as the two paramedics lifted my body onto the stretcher. Placing the oxygen mask over my face, I could see searchlights from the helicopter shining into the woods and onto my friend's faces. They wept into each other's arms, consoling each other.

"Sir, I need to ride with her to the hospital. I'm her mother."

"I'm sorry ma'am, you'll have to follow behind us." Her eyes, already bloodshot red from crying, became more somber after realizing she couldn't ride with me. I watched as she pulled my brother by the hand and ran to her car. The one person I wanted by my side couldn't be there. I was alone – fighting for myself.

Racing through traffic as the paramedics applied pressure on my side, I continued gasping for air while I internally prayed. "Ouch, what the fu….!" I yelled, almost cursing as I felt a constant prick from a needle on my left pinky finger. "I'm sorry Ms. Smith, but I need to get a sample of blood in case you need a blood transfusion," the paramedic explained. After numerous attempts, he just couldn't get any blood. *Why does he need more blood? It's ounces of blood spilling from my side; get it from there.* The more he pricked, the more he grew frustrated, causing his pale cheeks to turn red. "I'm sorry Ms. Smith, but I wasn't able to prick any blood. As a last resort I will have to prick it from your vaginal area. This is in effort to save as much blood as possible," he said. Slowly shaking my head in agreement, I clenched my teeth in preparation for the pain. Proceeding to lower my blue denim Guess shorts, he lowered the finger prick near my skin. In an instant the pain ricocheted throughout my entire body. The suffering double-teamed me, it was pain on my right side and groin; and to top it off I was on my monthly menstruation cycle. I was losing blood from all over. *Had I died and gone to hell?* With all of the torture and red around me, this had to be it; the only thing missing was the fiery pits.

Upon bursting through the Centinela Hospital doors, I was met by a doctor and three nurses who rushed me through the hallways and straight into ER. With the IV catheter connected, the primary doctor injected me with medicine to numb the pain as the doctor stitched my side.

"Everything is going to be ok, Ms. Smith," he said with the surgical mask covering his brown skin as he noticed me examining my wound.

"Am I going to die?" I asked with a low hoarse voice.

"No, Ms. Smith. Actually the bullet went straight through, but three of your ribs are broken and you have a pierced liver."

"What's your name?" I asked.

"Dr. Patterson, Ms. Smith."

"Dr. Patterson do you know what kind of gun it was?"

In a look of shock, his eyes grew bigger, seemingly surprised that a girl like me would ask him such.

"I'm not sure Ms. Smith, but because of the damage I'm positive it was a smaller handgun.

As Dr. Patterson placed bandages on me, I heard a light knock at the door. The door crept open as my mom appeared with a smile on her face and light red eyes from crying. Brushing my curly hair back, she couldn't fight the tears as she stared into my eyes.

"Hello ma'am, you must be her mom," Dr. Patterson said.

"Yes, I am. Is she going to be ok?" my mother asked with a look of worry in her eyes.

"Yes, she's going to be fine. A little damage here and there. I'm going to leave you two to talk; I'll be back later with more information."

"How are you feeling, baby?" she asked.

"I'm a little sore. Mom, were you able to get my clothes I had on today? I loved my outfit."

"No baby, those clothes are destroyed; but you're here and that's all that matters," she replied smiling.

"All of your family and friends are downstairs waiting to hear that you are ok. I'll be back in a few, let me go deliver the good news," Mom said, giving me a kiss on the cheek before leaving. I could hear people talking outside of the door.

"Thank God that girl is still going to be herself. The first thing she asked me was her outfit going to be saved," my mom said to my family standing outside of the room. The hallway erupted with laughter, brightening the mood.

"Pss" I heard from the door. I looked over to find my twin brother peeping his big head self into the operating room.

"How you feeling, sis?"

"I'm ok. The doctor said I have a lot of internal damage, but I'll be fine."

"This is crazy! You're the last person on earth that should be here. It's mindboggling that there was a bullet hole in every headrest, but you're the only one who got shot!" he said. I could tell something was on his mind from how he looked around, but he was afraid to tell me.

"What's wrong, Brian? You know I can tell when you're keeping something from me."

"Man, I hate when you do that," he said with a smirk.

"Don't tell mom what I'm about to tell you because she doesn't want you worrying."

"What?"

"Uncle Jon got in an accident before coming to the hospital because he was rushing to get here."

"What!" I yelled as my stomach dropped to my knees.

"No, he's fine Brittany, he's downstairs."

"Oh, then why did you make it seem like something was wrong?" Brian glanced around the room before answering me, avoiding eye contact.

"Brian what is it?"

"Man, sis, Uncle Jon is downstairs raising hell. He got Kevin, Ralph, and Juan pinned up outside asking them thousands of questions about who shot you. No telling what's about to happen; everybody is going ballistic about this. The police are asking thousands of questions and everybody acting like they don't know nothing." I couldn't imagine what was happening in the lobby. My Uncle Jon wasn't to be played with, especially when it came to me. He was like my guardian; my father was incarcerated and he filled that void, especially when it came to my protection.

Uncle Jon wasn't the only one upset. My boyfriend, Anthony, was also at the hospital, and he didn't hold back about how pissed he was. Anthony and I were supposed to be going out that night, but Lisa persuaded me to go with Kevin,

Juan, and Ralph to the movies since we hadn't seen each other in so long. Just think, this could have all been avoided if I would have stuck to my original plan. With my mother and brother downstairs, Anthony sat beside me with a look of anguish upon his face.

"Babe, I told you about messing with them Crenshaw dudes. They can't be trusted," he said.

"Anthony, all the guys from Crenshaw aren't like that. I have no idea what they've been up to since I left for college. As far as I'm concerned, they're still the same cool guys I went to school with. They're just mixed up in the wrong crowd," I replied.

"If you was with me, that wouldn't have happened. You know we don't play like that in Compton."

"Anthony please, you know this is not the time or place for that," I said.

Sitting back in his chair, he didn't have a response. Anthony and I both went to North Carolina A&M College. It was a long way from the sunny state of California, but he knew not all guys from Crenshaw were caught up in the streets.

Growing up in Crenshaw was rough, but I had friends from the good and bad parts of L.A. The shooting took place in the glamorous community of Baldwin Hills, but only a few miles away were some of the most rugged and crime infested areas of L.A. One minute you could be riding through the fantasy town of Baldwin Hills, but right down the street was Baldwin Village or as the locals call it, "The Jungle." The same neighborhood Denzel Washington drove through in the movie, *Training Day*. Helicopters, or as we call them, "ghetto birds" filled the sky each night, flying above the apartment buildings looking for suspects. There were no birds chirping like in Baldwin Hills; only guns blazing. To top it off, my high school was right in the middle of it. My high school was a mixture of high class, middle class, and lower class students. For some, money wasn't a problem; but to others, EBT was the way to be.

With the sun shining through the blinds awakening me from my sleep, I prayed everything from yesterday was a nightmare; but as Dr. Patterson walked in the room, I realized it wasn't. Pulling up the blinds Dr. Patterson disturbed my mother and Anthony's slumber, who were allowed to stay with me throughout the night. Dr. Patterson turned to me and smiled.

"Rise and shine, Ms. Smith. How are we doing today?" he asked.

"I'm fine Dr. Patterson. Will I be able to go home today?"

"Home?"

Silence took over the room as he looked at me, placing his clipboard on the edge of the bed.

"I'm sorry Brittany, but it will be two months or so before you can go home."

Leaning my head against the pillow, I let out a deep sigh. I couldn't believe this. *Was he serious?* My 19th birthday was in two weeks and I was going to be spending it in this stupid hospital.

"Two months!" My mother and boyfriend both yelled out.

"I thought you told her the bullet went straight through?" Anthony asked.

Looking overwhelmed, Dr. Patterson took a deep breath while grabbing my X-ray files.

"If you take a look at Brittany's X-rays, you can see where her three ribs were shattered."

All three of us looked closely at the white and black X-rays, examining my broken ribs.

"Throughout the next two months, Brittany will have to be in rehabilitation. If she tries to get up right now, she won't be able to."

Flashbacks from the night before bounced around in my brain. I remembered struggling to get out of Kevin's car.

"Her ribs will heal, but they will never fully connect which, will cause pain from time to time. Ms. Smith, your ribs and lungs work together; because of that we will have to put you on a breathing machine until you can properly breathe on your own," he explained.

Warm drips of tears begin falling down my cheeks. Everyone sat in silence as the heart monitor beeped consistently in the background. My heart was healthy and thriving, but on the inside I was flat lined – emotionally dead.

Two weeks had passed and my birthday was finally here. "Happy Birthday to you, Happy Birthday to you, Happy Birthday to you!" Overwhelmed I looked around the hospital room at all of my loved ones, family and friends, as they stood around the hospital bed singing happy birthday. "I'm 19 years old, I'm 19 years old, I'm 19 Years old!" I sang as my mom stood by me holding my two-tier Strawberry Upside Down Cake, my favorite! Closing my eyes before blowing out the candles, the only thing I could wish for was a speedy recovery and to get out of this hospital earlier than expected. My room was bombarded with large birthday balloons, get well cards, and gifts. Even the Dean of my college along with the student court sent me a card with African American angel dolls. Word had spread to North Carolina A&M that the 2005 Ms. Freshman Homecoming Queen, Brittany Smith, had been shot. Thousands of students voted for me to be Ms. Freshman, so if I was receiving gifts from the student court, there was a chance the whole school knew. I may have been physically hurt, but I was loved!

"Brittany, I have a surprise for you," my mom said, hiding what looked like a plastic bag behind her back.

"What?" I asked smiling with suspicion.

"I made your favorite meal, pork chops smothered in gravy, mashed potatoes, and string beans with minced pork." My face beamed with joy when I uncovered the plate. I hated hospital food; it wasn't seasoned and sometimes it wasn't cooked thoroughly. It was just plain old nasty. Quickly pulling my tray to the bed, I devoured the food in an instant; this food didn't stand a chance. My stomach begin to growl as I grabbed my napkin to wipe my mouth. *Was my stomach just as happy as me to get a home cooked meal?* The growls then turned into pain. Holding my stomach, trying to ignore the tossing and turning, saliva started to fill my mouth.

"Honey are you ok?" my mom asked.

"No. I think I'm about to…" before I could finish my sentence I grabbed the small trashcan beside my bed and unwillingly regurgitated my food. Shocked at what she saw my mother ran out the room calling for Dr. Patterson.

"Thank God you're here Dr. Patterson," she said opening the door.

"What's wrong?" Dr. Patterson asked walking into the room.

"I bought her some food and she threw it all up now she looks weak, I don't know what to do."

"Well she's definitely running a fever. What did you give her?" he asked while placing his hand on my forehead.

"Just some pork chops covered in gravy, mashed potatoes, and string beans minced with pork."

"Well, this is what happens when Brittany consumes those types of meals. Like I stated before, her liver is damaged, that means her diet must change until she is fully recovered. We've placed her on a special diet here at thc hospital."

"So what can she eat?" my mom asked.

"Foods with protein like fish, chicken breast, potatoes, not mashed with gravy, fruits, whole grain meals, and especially milk which will help repair her internal organs. I know she's not of age to drink, but she can't drink alcohol either," he explained.

This was just getting worse and worse. I couldn't eat what I wanted to eat, I was stuck in the hospital, and it was my birthday.

A month had passed since the shooting and I was in the beginning stages of rehabilitation. I imagined this is what it felt like for a baby to learn how to walk; the only difference was I had a cane and walker. Luckily my past cheerleading experience helped me to fully recover. Every day for a full month, Dr. Patterson nursed me back to health. My walker helped tremendously as I learned how to balance myself, strengthen my core, exhale properly, rotate my hips, and stand tall like a tree. Anthony and my mom also played a huge part. On my down days, Anthony would walk with me throughout the hallways, which not only strengthened my body, but also strengthened our bond.

The hospital was understaffed and because of that, other areas of my body were neglected. Consistently the nurses would change the bandages of my roommate, who had been shot in the head, but they would forget mine, causing my wound to get infected. Peeling back my bandages, my mother's face looked gruesome as she examined the wound.

"This is unacceptable, Brittany. I mean just look at this!" she said while propping a pillow behind my back to properly dress the wound.

"I know mom, but they're understaffed and have other patients with bigger problems."

"My baby, my baby, always so understanding," she said sarcastically.

"That's not your problem, Brittany. They need to hire some more nurses. Anthony and I shouldn't have to change your bandages and clean your wounds on a daily basis. I like Dr. Patterson and some of the other doctors, but these nurses are incompetent!"

Later in the month, Dr. Patterson walked in my room whistling and smiling from ear to ear.

"I have some great news for you today, Brittany!" Dr. Patterson said showing all 32 of his pearly whites. Looking confused, I didn't know what to say. I waited for him to finish his sentence, but he was waiting for my response.

"Isn't this the same girl who asked me what kind of gun it was when she first came here? Now you're stooped for words?"

"Sorry," I replied with a slight grin.

"Well, this should make your day. You're being released! You're able to walk again, you're breathing on your own, and your ribs and liver have healed significantly."

"What! Are you serious? Should I start packing now?" I replied, imitating that I was about to gather my belongings.

"Whoa, whoa, whoa, Ms. Smith, not so fast! The proper protocol is that you have to be assisted by a guardian and wheeled out of the hospital. Also, you still have to take a few meds for the next few months, and I'm prescribing you a medicine pillow.

"Um a medicine pillow? What's that?" I asked.

"Yes, a medicine pillow. It will apply pressure to your ribs so they can heal properly."

I despised it already. I was just ready to put all of this behind me and go back to North Carolina; it seemed to be the only place I would find peace.

Rolling through the hallways as my mom pushed me in the wheelchair, I became so grateful that this would be my last time seeing these hospital walls. The strong smell of antiseptics mixed with air freshener and sometimes urine surely wasn't going to be missed. Ahhh, the sweet sounds of L.A. could be heard as the Centinela Hospital front doors opened and we exited. My brother pulled up in my mother's white Infiniti.

Walking around from the driver side to greet me, he reached for my hand to help me get in the car, but I snatched it back in a fright. Glass shattering, bullets grazing, screeching tires, and helpless screams flashed through my mind.

"Come on, Brittany, stop playing. It's time to go home. Let me help you get in the car," my brother said.

"No! I don't want to get in the car! Please don't make me, Brian!" I yelled in a panic.

"Girl what is wrong with you; stop playing. You've been in this hospital all summer and now you can go home. Come on," he said.

"I'm scared please. No!" I yelled with tears streaming down my face. My mother came to the front of the wheelchair kneeling down to look at me.

"Brittany, honey. What do you mean you're scared?" she asked.

"I don't want to get in the car. What if somebody tries to shoot at me again? I'm scared." Grabbing my hand and holding it tight she looked me in my eyes.

"Baby, nothing is going to happen to you. You're covered by the blood of Jesus and there is nobody around that will put you in harm's way. It's only me and you brother," she said. I heard the hospital doors opening behind me.

"Hey Brittany; I see you're finally leaving," said Dr. Patterson as he was leaving out of the hospital dressed in his black slacks, white shirt and medicine jacket. He instantly noticed the tears in my eyes and became concerned.

"Is there something wrong?" he asked.

"Yes, Dr. Patterson. Brittany is scared to get in the car; she's afraid something is going to happen to her again," my mom explained.

"I see." He said placing his right hand on my left shoulder.

"This happens often. Patients come here who've been shot or involved in accident and they develop a phobia about being in cars or being around certain items that were a part of their trauma. Brittany, I assure you that nothing is going to happen. I promise," he said looking me straight in the eyes. Dr. Patterson grabbed my left hand and my mother grabbed my right as they both walked me to the car, step by step reassuring me that I was safe.

I had been home for a week and I was finally getting adjusted to being back. Boy did I look good today! That's what I told myself while standing in the mirror applying eyeliner in preparation for today's events. There were only a few weeks left in the summer before I left to go back to college and I was finally back to my old self. The only thing reminding me of that dreadful night was the medicine pillow. Luckily my Uncle Jon, who knew I was a big kid at heart, surprised me with a neon fish medicine pillow that looked like Nemo. I named him Peidre. Straightening my natural ringlet hair, I could hear my mother's footsteps walking towards the bathroom. Catching a quick glance of me, she abruptly stopped in her tracks.

"Excuse me hot mama, don't you look beautiful today," she said as I smiled back.

"And where do you think you're going?" she asked.

"Lisa is coming to get me and we're going with some friends to Fridays."

"Going out! Brittany you better put your stuff down because for the next few weeks, or until I feel safe, you're not going anywhere unless you're accompanied by me or one of your family members."

"What do you mean? I've been in the hospital all summer, that's not fair! It's not my fault about what happened to me!" I yelled.

"I don't want to hear it Brittany; you're not going. If you want to go out with Anthony that's fine, I trust him; but if it's not him or your family, you can cancel it!"

Shaking my head as I looked at her, I brushed passed her slamming my bedroom door behind me. Curling into bed, I swung the covers over my head hugging my pillow tight as drops of tears landed on my sheets. Hours went by as my phone rang back to back from my friends who were waiting on my arrival. Awakening later in the night from the doorbell, I crept to my bedroom door placing my ear to it.

"Hi, Ms. Smith, is Brittany here? She was supposed to meet us at Friday's, but she's not answering her phone." It was Lisa; she gave up calling and came to my house. I wanted to burst through the doors and tell her what happened, but I couldn't muster up the courage and risk possibly getting embarrassed by my mom. I could hear the front door opening wider and in an instant it was closed, blocking me from hearing their conversation. Footsteps pounded through the apartment towards my room, causing me to dive back in the bed. Opening the door slowly, my mother peeked in as I faked sleep. Another hour went past and there was another knock at the front door.

"Brittany get the door! I believe it's for you," my mother yelled. *For me?* I said to myself. She already kicked Lisa out and I wasn't expecting any guests. Unlocking the door, I was stunned! "Surprise!" Staring into the hallway, I burst into tears as my entire high school cheerleading team bombarded me with hugs. When the girls got wind that I couldn't leave, they ordered take out from Fridays and brought it back to my house. That's what my mother and Lisa were discussing when she went in the hallway. I guess mommy dearest had a soft spot after all. In the back of my mind, I knew if I had a child who was innocently shot, I would be overprotective too; but this wouldn't last much longer. My mother would eventually have to let go once I left for school. For now, I was just grateful and blessed that I survived this cold summer.

Lesson Learned: Sometimes you're just in the wrong place at the wrong time. The night of the shooting, I was supposed to go on a date with Anthony, but I cancelled on him. From this experience, I learned that I should always keep my word; if I had, none of this would've happened. Never in a million years did I think I would be shot, but bullets have no names on them. If you think you're in a hostile environment, be keen to your instincts and be aware of your surroundings. I learned a lot during my recovery, including patience, and the power of prayer, which brought me closer to God. I learned to be grateful for the things we take for granted, such as walking, eating whatever I want, spending time with my family and friends, and extended summer vacations. If you're grateful for the small things, the universe will bless you with much more than you can imagine.

I didn't hold any grudges towards Ralph, Kevin, and Juan. Grudges only end up hurting you; it harbors anger within you that will reflect in your everyday life. It leads to stress, and stress leads to unwarranted sickness that you don't need. You have to learn to let it go. You can't help who you know, but as you mature, start building relationships with like-minded people. Align yourself with people who are connected to your purpose. All things, good and bad, work together for those that love God, which will ultimately prepare you for the future. I turned that situation around and applied it to my current circumstance. After graduating from college, I enrolled in the University of California, Los Angeles to pursue my dream of becoming a juvenile judge. My goal is to change the system for the better by creating new programs for troubled youth as an alternative option instead of just locking them up and throwing away the key. Hopefully my contribution will go to lower the staggering $174 billion dollars firearm injuries cost the United States. These costs include medical, mental, criminal justice, and wage losses all due to violent assaults and suicide acts.[4] Young adults and adolescents like the guys in my old neighborhood could benefit from this. My summer wasn't taken from me in vain because now everything has come full circle, connecting me to my divine purpose.

Chapter 6: 19 & Pregnant

"April, are you ok? You've been in the bathroom all day and some of the girls on the floor can hear you," my friend Taylor asked standing outside of the bathroom stall.

"Yeah, I'm ok," I replied while catching my breath. With the taste of Cruzan Rum still on my mouth, I could feel it coming again. Oh God! Swiftly I placed strands of my black and brown streaked hair behind my ears and let it loose.

"Ugh!" Taylor uttered as she heard splashes of last night's liquor pouring into the toilet.

"I'll be out soon and I don't give a damn about them hearing me. I saw a few of them in this same predicament after the Kappa party last month," I said while wiping my mouth. The smell of perfume and urine filled the air, causing me to regurgitate my food and liquor even more - yuck!

"This bathroom stinks!" I yelled.

"Wait a minute, April. Are you praying? What is going on? I'm coming in."

Swinging the stall door open almost hitting me, Taylor stood above me with her hand covering her mouth and nose.

"Yes, I'm praying! I'm already on my knees; might as well ask for forgiveness, maybe I'll feel better," I replied with my head in the toilet. She couldn't contain from laughing; she knew this feeling all too well. Just last week I was the one standing outside of the stall while she was on her knees acting like she was dying.

I felt horrible, and on top of that, my English paper was due tomorrow. It was Sunday morning and my freshmen year at Morgan State University was coming to an end. I wanted to ace all of my assignments and tests. My advisor always said my accumulative GPA would be based on my freshmen grades, so these grades were vital. I sprayed the toilet with Lysol, brushed my teeth, wrapped my hair, and headed back to my dorm room, plopping down on my bed in relief. Grabbing my phone after it vibrated, I smiled when I saw three missed calls from Trey. I wondered what was wrong; he never called me that much. Trey was my friend and I guess something like a boyfriend with no title. Glancing at my fingernails while dialing his number, I saw that my French manicure was still intact. Last night was vague, but thank God my nails survived.

"Are you ok? Taylor told me you were sick; too much partying last night huh?" he asked with a smile in his voice. I smiled before answering him; the fact that he was so worried was cute.

"I was a little sick, but I'm better now."

"Do me a favor?" he suspiciously uttered.

"What?"

"Are you going to do it?"

What was he up to and why was he asking me for a favor without telling me what it was?

"Umm yes, I guess."

"Look out your window for me."

Leaning over my bed, I pulled up the blinds and immediately saw his tall, lanky body standing in the courtyard holding a grocery bag, grinning from ear to ear.

"Come downstairs to the lobby, I got something for you," he said.

"Give me five minutes. I can't stay long; I'm going to the Library."

Tossing my phone on the bed, I opened my closet door, looked in the mirror and unwrapped my hair. I had to look presentable for my baby. Walking through the lobby I saw him sitting on the couch playing in his hair.

"Stop messing with your hair," I said jokingly.
He hugged me as I smiled looking up at him. Trey was 6'1 and I only came to his chest.
"Here open this. I got you a little something," he said. Opening the grocery bag I found a bottle of Ginger Ale, water and Advil. He must have been reading my mind because I really needed this. Typical of him to come save the day.

Sitting on the second floor of the Earl S. Richardson Library, I typed away on my laptop; but a few minutes later, I started to feel nauseated. Before I knew it, I was running in between the bookracks to the bathroom. Thank God my stomach finally settled and I was able to finish my paper. The following morning, I stood in front of class to present my paper. As everybody stared at me, I began to feel worse. My stomach turned and turned as I fought to smile through the pain. Burping mid-sentence, I could taste my morning breakfast - Jimmy Dean sausage, eggs and pancakes; damn that meal was good. Saliva filled my mouth as I completed my presentation. Finishing my last sentence, I sprinted to the hallway bathroom, accidently dropping my poster board behind me.
"Are you ok," Professors Howard and Taylor simultaneously asked standing outside of the stall.
"Keep an eye on her, Taylor. I'm going back to class," Professor Howard said.
"April you should go to the doctor. If you're still throwing up from two nights ago, something might be wrong," Taylor said.
"I'm fine, Taylor. I'm not sick; I know when I'm sick."
"Are you sure you're not pregnant?"

Flushing the toilet then opening the bathroom stall, I stood there staring her in the eyes. *Was she crazy?* Of course I'm not pregnant. I would lose it if I was.

"Of course not; Trey and I always use protection," I said. Walking back to class, I thought about what Taylor said. Memories of the three times the condom broke with Trey popped into my head, not to mention these ongoing migraines I've been having. I hope I'm not pregnant; that's the last thing I need on my plate right now.

Taylor's pregnancy suspicions were wearing down on my conscience; I had to be sure. Morgan State was in Baltimore, Maryland, but I was from Glendale, Maryland, an hour away. To make sure these migraines weren't the cause of anything critical, I scheduled an appointment with my primary doctor at home. My parents were out of town, so they wouldn't be asking me a million questions about why I was home. Perfect. Gassing up my 2002 blue Beetle, I hopped on 95 South praying the whole ride home. *God please don't let me be pregnant, please. I promise I won't have sex anymore.*

Dr. Lee walked in with her glasses covering her pale rosy skin and short grey hair looking happy to see me.

"April, it's so good to see you. How's school?" she asked.

"It's going good. Almost done with my first year."

"Good for you. I'll be right back to let you know what's going on with your migraines," she said after taking my vitals.

"April, I wrote out a Zorvolex prescription that will help with your migraines," she said as she walked backed in. Sitting in the chair I looked up at Dr. Lee as she leaned against the wall taking a deep breath. *What is wrong with her?* I said to myself.

"April, I ran some tests and it came back that you're 4 weeks pregnant. Is your mom here with you?" she asked.

Covering my mouth in shock, I gasped as she told me the news. Taylor was right; I am pregnant.

"No Dr. Lee, she's out of town and please don't tell her. I'll tell her myself, please Dr. Lee, please!" I begged.

"April, I couldn't tell her if I wanted to. The physician-patient confidentiality restricts me from doing so."

As I drove home in silence, it seemed like everybody wanted to call; but I ignored them all. My mom called twice, Trey once, and Taylor three times. Pulling into my parent's driveway the gas light came on and in an instance I felt just like the tank - empty, emotionally drained. Burying myself in my covers, my pillow became dampened with tears as thousands of thoughts ran through my head. *"I'm only 19." "I'm a freshman." "What is Trey going to say? "He's not even my boyfriend." "What are my parents going to say?"*

Returning to Baltimore Sunday night, I went straight to Blount Towers, the dorm Taylor and I lived in. When I walked into my room, Taylor and our friend Jazmine were trying on clothes for tonight's party.

"April! You're back; I've been calling you all weekend. How was home?" Taylor asked.

Sitting down at the desk chair, I decided I would just tell them.

"Well, I went to the doctor and Taylor you were right. I'm pregnant."

Taylor's mouth dropped to the floor.

"I knew it! Nobody continuously throws up liquor days after a party. So what are you going to do?" Taylor asked.

"I don't know yet. I think I'm going to get an abortion, but I have to tell Trey first."

"I want to be an Aunty!" Jazmine said with excitement.

Jazmine always seemed a bit slow, but saying she wanted to be aunty made it clear that she was slow and crazy.

"What if you keep the baby and get a place off campus. Then you'll be able to finish school here and all three of us, including Trey, can help," Jazmine suggested.

"What! An Aunty? I always knew you were crazy, but this takes the cake, Jazmine," I replied looking at her as if she was foolish.

"There's no way I'm depending on two of my friends to help me with my baby. Who even knows if we'll be friends this time next year," I said.

I know that sounded harsh, but I've seen females change friends like the wind.

"I'm not having it Jazmine. I've made up my mind."

"What about Trey? What does he want?" Taylor interjected.

"What if he wants to keep it?" Jazmine asked.

I sat confused; I never thought about that.

"I don't know yet, but can y'all two please keep it a secret? I don't want him to find out before I tell him."

A month had gone by and I still hadn't told Trey, I just couldn't bring myself to do it. It was a headache keeping it from him. I also didn't have the money for the abortion and I wanted to wait until school was over. I knew I would be showing soon, so I had to tell Trey or he would definitely become suspicious.

"Hey April!" My friend Charlotte yelled as she dashed across the street in her tomboy attire as I walked out of Video Production class.

"Where have you been? You don't hang outside of the dorms no more. Who you hiding from?" she said with a smirk.

"I'm not hiding from no one, silly. I've just been focused on school; it costs too much to be slacking," I said trying to convince her.

"Are you pregnant or something? You know all the girls go missing when it's cold outside then pop back up in the spring like the Easter bunny with a pregnant belly," she said jokingly. *Or was she joking at all?*
Walking beside her I quickly grabbed her arm holding it tightly.

"Who told you? It's none of your business; keep it to yourself, you hear me? I'm not playing, Charlotte," I murmured to her.

"What are you talking about, April? You're pregnant? I wasn't saying it like I knew you were pregnant; I was just joking," she explained.
I shook my head as we continued to walk. I should have known she was joking.

"Please don't tell Trey. I know you and him are cool, but I want to tell him myself, please!" I begged.

"I won't, I promise,"
Nervously walking back to my dorm, my spirit didn't feel right. Charlotte promised she wouldn't tell, but when she said it she couldn't look me in the eye.

Lying in bed, I could see Taylor pulling in the dorm parking lot from my window. I knew she was taking Jazmine to work so I rushed down the steps to ride with her. I was craving for a Kit Kat bar and smoothie. After dropping Jazmine off, I devoured my smoothie from Smoothie King and instantly my stomach started grumbling.

"Oh hell nah, you bet not throw up in my car. This is a brand new 2010 Camry, April!" Taylor yelled as she watched me cover my mouth.

In the nick of time, we pulled into the dorm parking lot. I swung the door open, vomiting on the white parking lines. Looking up, I could see a group of guys staring squeamishly at me. I cleaned my mouth, rolled my eyes, and slammed the door. *They never seen somebody throw up before?* My phone started buzzing in my purse; it was Trey.

"What's this I hear about you being pregnant?" he asked. Immediately tears flooded my eyes as I became speechless.

"Hello? Did you hear me?" Trey said.

"Yes, Trey I am pregnant. I was going to tell you, I promise I was. I just hadn't found the right time." I confessed.

"Why didn't you tell me? I thought we were supposed to be cool and we're friends; you have to let me know so we can work these kinds of things out," he said.

I was surprised at his response. I've heard so many stories about my friend's ex-boyfriends' threatening them if they didn't get an abortion; I was expecting Trey to do the same.

Glancing out the passenger window, I was startled to see Trey standing a few yards away with the phone still to his ear. Hanging up once he saw me, he started walking towards the car. With each step my stomach turned and turned as tears flowed down my cheeks in horror. Suddenly I felt it again. Opening the door, I vomited on the ground stopping Trey in his tracks. Looking up I could see his eyes almost popping out of his sockets. It was one thing to hear I was pregnant, but to actually see it was an eye opener, literally. Walking behind me, he pulled my hair out of my face making sure it didn't get wet from the regurgitation.

"April, why didn't you tell me?" he asked.

"I'm so sorry, Trey. I was scared. We already talked about what we would do if I got pregnant, so I was just going to get an abortion once I got the money. I swear I was going to tell you," I pleaded.

"April, lock the car up. I'm going to my room so you and Trey can talk," Taylor said. As she walked away Trey stood me up, embracing me in his arms.

"It's ok baby. I remember you said you wanted to be a wife first and that our education came before anything else. If you want to keep it cool; if not, I'll help pay for it,"

"I'm almost 10 weeks," I said.

Reaching down to feel my stomach, his eyes grew bigger once he felt how hard my stomach was.

"How did you find out?" I asked.

"I was walking on campus and people started congratulating me. I didn't know what they were talking about until I saw Charlotte and she told me."

Of course it was Charlotte; I knew she couldn't be trusted.

School was over and I was headed home for the summer. I was 12 weeks and still hadn't told my mother. My abortion was scheduled for the following day, so I was just going to come out and tell her. "Yes!" I said pulling into the driveway. My mother wasn't there. At least I could unload my car without her seeing me and going crazy. I was already short and slim so she would easily see if I got bigger. Lying down in bed I pulled the covers over my body with only my head peeking through. My goal was to tell her before she could see my stomach.

An hour later, I could hear the garage door opening and in an instant I started gathering my thoughts. "April, honey, you're officially done with your freshmen year of college. My baby is about to be a sophomore!" She yelled walking through the door. I didn't reply; I was too scared. Walking through the kitchen while making her way up the steps she yelled again.

"April, are you here?"

"Yes, mom I'm in my room."

Opening my door, she looked so happy to see me. I felt horrible knowing I was about to break her heart.

"How are you doing my love?" she said standing over me.

"Not so good, mom."

"What's wrong, baby. Are you sick?" she asked putting her hand on my forehead.

"It doesn't feel like you're running a fever or anything.

"Umm, not really. Mom can you sit down I have to tell you something."

"Oh Lord, what happened, April?"

Looking around at my colored pink walls, I avoided eye contact with her until I finally mustered up the strength to look at her.

"Mommy, I messed up. I'm pregnant, but Trey and I decided to get an abortion. Having a baby is not something that we want right now," I quickly said.

Taking a deep breath, she paused for a few seconds while holding her head down in disappointment.

"How far along are you? I can't believe this; you have your whole life ahead of you. Why didn't you tell me? What is your father going to say?"

I stopped her right there.

"Mom, please don't tell Dad, especially since I'm not having the baby. He won't be home until late, so he won't see me. The abortion is scheduled for early tomorrow, so he won't know." I begged looking her in the eyes.

She had to understand. I was a daddy's girl and I didn't want to disappoint him.

"I can't believe I'm doing this, but ok. April, I respect you, you're a grown adult. Even though you're 19, this will affect your life. Some mistakes you make in life won't be this easy to just wipe your hands. Obstacles will come where you just can't say forget it. You can do this, but please believe you'll have repercussions," she said.

I understood, but I was still getting an abortion.

"Do you want me to come?" she asked.

"No, Trey is coming, but I will update you as soon as it's over. He also booked a hotel room for us afterward so I can recover in peace."

It was May 7th and today was the day. Taylor was having a cookout for her birthday and I felt bad that I wasn't attending, but she understood. I couldn't wait any longer; this abortion was happening today. I was too far along and I didn't want my dad to find out. Taylor's been supporting me throughout this whole ordeal, even lending me $120.00 toward it because Trey only had $300.00 that he borrowed from a friend. I heard the horn blow outside and slowly I walked down the steps feeling shameful as I met Trey. Riding in the car, he turned the music down and looked over at me.

"Do you really want to go through with this? I don't want you to feel any kind of resentment towards me after it's done. If you think you will, you don't have to do it," he said.

Letting out a slight sigh, I said "I don't want to have this child because I had second thoughts or because I'm scared. I want us to have a child because we really want to be parents. What if we don't end up together? That would be a disservice to this child." He agreed, turned the music back up, and started singing along to the radio. Trey could actually sing, which is one of the reasons I'm in this predicament now – he was so charming.

As I walked down the hallway to the clinic, my mother's words replayed over in my head. *You'll have repercussions; you'll have repercussions.* As Trey signed me in, I gave him a kiss goodbye; the secretary explained she would call him when I was done. "Ms. Jones, right this way please," the nursing assistant said, opening the door to the back of the clinic. Deep down in my soul I knew this wasn't right, but it was the best decision for me. Telling myself a million times I was going to be fine didn't block out the guilt. I was about to kill my first child and the irony of it all is that tomorrow was Mother's Day.

Nervously walking into the medical room, I stopped in my tracks when I saw the medical bed. I was ready to leave, but before I could the nurse walked in startling me. "Ms. Jones, Dr. Suskin will be in soon. Can you please disrobe and put on the blue gown behind the door," she said. Stepping on the stool to sit on the bed I flinched as my butt touched the cold metal. Lying on my back I prayed one last time. "God, please give me the faith and strength for what I'm about to do. Please forgive me and let all my organs work after this." Listening to myself pray, I couldn't believe what I was asking for. I knew this was wrong. I was a Christian and this was clearly a sin.

In her green surgical outfit with her hair tied to the back exposing her pale features, Dr. Suskin walked in smiling from ear to ear.

"Ms. Jones how are you doing today? Are you ready?" she said with a smile.

"No, I'm not," I somberly said shaking my head. Placing her latex gloves on one by one she sat down in the chair to explain the procedure.

"April, under Maryland law and because the suction machine will overpower my voice, I will have to explain the procedure to you before we begin. This suction machine is going to be the primary use for the abortion. I will dilate your cervix and remove the baby from your uterus with this tube. This machine is powerful enough to suck the air out of a steel can, crushing it from the inside out. I usually detach all of the body parts on the first try, but because you're 3 months that may not be possible.

Tightening my legs I squirmed as I listened. *Was this abortion or murder?*

"Sometimes the head won't come out because of the size. This is rare, but if this happens I will have to use forceps to retrieve it. Lastly, I will use a spoon-shaped instrument to retrieve any leftover tissue. Any questions Ms. Jones?" she asked, seeming to show no sympathy.

"No ma'am," I sadly replied.

"Before I pump you with anesthesia, you have to sign this consent form," she said handing me the form. "The anesthesia will numb the pain, you won't be completely out, but you won't feel anything. I also have to do an ultrasound, so lay back for me, please." *An ultrasound?* My friends who've gotten abortions never told me about an ultrasound, this was just getting worse and worse.

The ultrasound gel tingled my belly as she smoothed it around my abdomen and pelvic area. "Here we go Ms. Jones. If you look at the screen I will explain what you're looking at." Black and white images appeared on the screen while I tried to make out what I saw. "Well it looks like you have a cyst on your cervix that I'll have to remove," she said pointing to my 4cm cervix that I could hardly see. *How much more bad news can I get today?* Within the next minute, I heard a light thumping from the screen. I quickly looked down at Dr. Suskin; she cut me off before I could say anything. "Yes, Ms. Jones, that's the heartbeat you're hearing." Slowly I turned my head away from the screen; I couldn't bear to watch. As the machine went off, tears poured down my cheeks. That was my child's heartbeat. That was my soul, my flesh, and my blood.

My mind was scattered with thoughts as my legs laid propped open on the medical bed. I fought to take my mind off what was happening, but with every crank of the stirrups opening me wider and wider it was impossible. My lower bottom slowly became numb as the sound of the machine blasted throughout the room.

"Can you feel anything Ms. Jones?"

"No ma'am," I replied as I started to fade in and out of consciousness.

"You can sit up Ms. Jones."

"We're done?" I asked.

What seemed like a quick ten minutes was really 45 minutes.

"Yes ma'am," she replied while taking off her gloves.

"Ms. Jones, while extracting the fetus there was more blood than expected. So I'm going to run some tests to make sure everything is ok."

Immediately looking down after hearing what she said, I saw a pool of blood splattered into the machine. Going into a panic tears filled my eyes, I was horrified. Looking at the bloody stirrups, forceps and embryotomy scissors almost made me sick. *What did I just do?*

I was sick of crying. I never felt so emotional in my life. Every day for the last four months I've done nothing but vomit and cry. As I wiped my eyes, Dr. Suskin returned to the room.

"April, we're going to keep you for a little longer. One of the assistants will be transporting you to the intensive care unit. You're bleeding pretty badly, so we're going to monitor you. We don't want you to hemorrhage."

"What! What do you mean bleeding excessively?" I replied.

"Ms. Jones, I assure you that everything will be ok. This happens often, not to mention your blood pressure shot through the roof because you went into shock. In a few hours everything should be ok."

All alone, I waited for hours as the doctors monitored me. Staring out the window as the night fell, I heard a knock at the door. As it opened, I could see Trey's reflection in the window as he walked in.

"Hey, baby. Are you ok?" he said rubbing my hair.

"Yeah, for now."

"Do you want me to call your Mom?"

"No! Are you crazy? That's the last person I want to talk to right now." Realizing I was yelling, I quickly calmed down. I didn't want to deal with her. It would just prove that she was right.

After nine gruesome hours, I was finally released. "We're releasing you, Ms. Jones. The nursing assistant at the front will have the medications I prescribed for you. The medicine should help with the pain and fight off any possible infections. Also, no sex for 4 to 6 weeks," Dr. Suskin said while looking at me and Trey.

She didn't have to tell me twice. Sex was the last thing on my mind.

"Here are a few depends that should help with the bleeding, Ms. Jones."

"Wait a minute are those diapers?" Trey asked as he laughed.

"You think this is funny? I have to wear this partially because of you."

"Aww, baby, I'll still be with you, diapers and all," he said embracing me.

Trying not to smile, I couldn't help but to laugh.

Lesson Learned: It never crossed my mind that I would end up pregnant my freshmen year, but sometimes you can't prepare for life lessons. Trey and I practiced safe sex, but we didn't fully practice it. Not only should we have used condoms, but I should've been on birth control. If you're going to be sexually active, please takc cvcry precaution that is comfortable for you. If I didn't have a mind of my own, I could've been persuaded to choose the option that I ultimately didn't want. Never let anybody influence you to do something that you don't want to do. Do what feels right in your heart. Numerous people said they would've been there for me, but I knew in the back of my mind that probably wouldn't have happened. I not only would've needed help from my family and friends, but I also would've needed help financially. Millennial women are reproducing at the slowest rate ever due to the economical turmoil from the Great Recession.[5] In 2014, fertility reached a record low.[6] Finances play a major role in raising a child. In recent years, many women have chosen to pursue education and careers over having a child. I still feel guilt and sorrow from aborting my child, but I had bigger goals to obtain. I have to live with that, nobody else.

We're all built differently, some women might have chosen to have their baby and that's good, but I know what I can handle. I'm also adopted; my outlook on family and love is different. After I graduated, I wondered what would've happen if I had the baby. Trey and I shouldn't have had sex, we weren't married and he wasn't my boyfriend. You have to learn to cancel out certain things and people in life that may hinder you. When I was in high school, I told myself I wanted to be in love when I had my first child. I didn't want to bring a child into this world with high chances of his or her father being absent from their life. I didn't want to be a single mother.

Now, years later, Trey and I aren't even together. My child would be another lost soul in this world with no father; I didn't want that. If you happen to get pregnant and make the decision to have your baby, don't give up. Having a child at a young age isn't a road block; it's just a delay and there are still pathways to success. There are numerous colleges that help with single mothers and there are also scholarships geared specifically for your demographic. Do your research and pick a school that will benefit you and your child. There's still hope.

Chapter 7: Big Man on Campus

Thunderous rain pelted against the van as my parents, sister, and I drove south on Interstate 95. I always thought this day would be bright and sunny, but it wasn't. Sitting in the back seat, I saw my mother mumbling in the rear view mirror. Her only son was going to college, she was supposed to be elated, but the look on her face matched the glum skies. "Listen up Chris, we need to talk," she said with her face flustered in emotions. I knew she was proud about me leaving the rough streets of Brooklyn, New York, but nervous that I might take that mentality to college.

"Yes, mom," I said letting out a deep sigh. In the back of my mind I knew this conversation was coming.

"Please don't make me regret this. I need you to par the course and leave all that nonsense behind. The streets will only leave you with two choices - jail or death. But with a college education your options are unlimited. You have the opportunity to change your life, but you have to stay clean. You've gotten in enough trouble. I know times are hard, but just try," she said.

"Ok mom, Ok!" I yelled cutting her off, as I grew frustrated. This wasn't her first attempt of keeping me out of trouble, but this time it was different. I had the opportunity to change my life; I would be a fool not to try.

"Give it your best and make momma proud," she said with a smile on her face. Looking out the window, I noticed that the weather had adapted to her joyous expression. The clouds were gone and the sun was shining brighter than ever.

My mother wanted me to go cold turkey, but she deserved it. I put her through enough when I was in high school. In 10th grade I was apprehended twice for a blunt of marijuana. Then during my 11th grade year security seized multiple bags of marijuana, I was charged with intent to distribute, and the courts sentenced me to a year of probation leading into 2005. From the outside looking in, I appeared to be a problem child; but I wasn't. I was on the football team and maintained a B average. I didn't sell drugs because I wanted to; I did it because I had to. It was a way of life. I was raised in a single parent household and didn't come from money. I was a product of my environment; selling drugs came easy and fast. I could've gotten a job, but that wasn't enough. I liked nice clothes, living comfortably, traveling, pretty females, and even more, helping my family. It took every ounce of energy to give it up, but I wanted to see her happy. I hated to see her saddened with disappointment.

Looking out the window, I noticed a green sign that said 100 miles from Memphis, Tennessee. In a few hours I would officially be a student of Doris University. I didn't know anything about Doris except that my two cousins, Shannon and Jamar, were also going. I was more excited when I first received my acceptance letter - until I saw the price tag. That's when my mom had to convince me. Applying for loans that would leave me in debt was absurd.

I didn't see the point. We were already struggling and taking out a loan would leave us in deeper debt. It wasn't feasible to me. My mom would be in debt, I would be in debt, and with my sister attending Shaw University next year, she would too. I wanted my family to flourish in money, not diminish in it. I frequently heard stories about the hindrances of college students; but one thing was for sure, I knew how to make money and not the legal way.

Driving on campus I couldn't believe it. *Was I, Christopher Williams III, really about to attend college?* The boy that grew up in East Flatbush, Brooklyn, New York, 95th Street and Clarkson Ave. to be exact, was a college student. It was surreal. I could see fathers carrying their daughter's refrigerators into the dorms, mothers hugging their son's goodbye, and the head resident assistant telling everybody "hi." There were license plates from all over. Tennessee, Louisiana, Florida, North Carolina, South Carolina, Georgia, Maryland, Washington D.C., Pennsylvania, Virginia, New York, and New Jersey. College was a complete melting pot.

Sitting in my dorm room, I attempted to open my duffle bag, but abruptly stopped before opening the bag. Peeking out the door, I made sure my mom, dad, and sister were down the steps as they had just left my room to grab my remaining bags. Swiftly I pulled out a zip lock bag full of marijuana to make sure it was intact. If my mom saw this, she would kill me. She just asked that I change my ways and here I was doing the exact opposite. I opened the bag to take a whiff; it smelled awfully great. The light green buds mixed with orange hairs were soft and sticky, just how I liked it. This weed was grade A. I promised my mom that my smoking and drug dealing days were over, but not before I finished smoking this bag. I bought as much as I could because I didn't know if I would find any down here. Little did I know college was a drug smorgasbord.

Hearing my parents voices as they walked back up the steps, I quickly hid the bag of marijuana under my mattress. Walking them downstairs, I couldn't believe this was it. I wouldn't be seeing them again until the Thanksgiving holiday. With a stern look on her face, I knew exactly what my mother was thinking, *boy don't you mess this up*. Giving her a kiss goodbye and hugging my dad and sister, I watched as they drove off campus. I was all alone, ready to embark on the next phase of my life. I waited until the deadline to file my admission papers and because of that I ended up on the upperclassmen side of campus. A long fenced-in bridge stretched from the freshmen side to the upperclassmen side. It was safer for students to walk across the bridge rather than Berkley Road, one of the busiest streets in Memphis.

Exploring the campus, I walked across the bridge and noticed smoke in the air. To my surprise I saw my cousin Jamar, and a sophomore named Maurice, who was also from NY. Upperclassmen weren't due on campus until the following week, but Maurice had come down early. They were leaning against the bridge smoking a Black & Mild. A smirk appeared on my face; it felt good to see Jamar. He was from Harlem, NY. We were cousins, but slightly different. I was the aggressor and he was the socialite. I was the seller and he was the consumer, but we had some of the greatest times together.

"Cuzzo, I see you finally made it," Jamar said.

"Man, I been here. I'm on the other side of campus."

"You got a room on the upperclassmen side? Man you lucky," he said.

"Lucky? Nobody's over there. Y'all the lucky ones; look at all the girls over here," I said pointing to a group of girls walking on campus.

"Yeah for right now, but next week all of the older women are going to be on your side. Did you hear me? I said women," Jamar stated with a smile. I guess he was right, I was the lucky one.

"What are you two majoring in?" I asked.

"Communications," Jamar replied.

"Business Management," Maurice said.

"What are you majoring in?" Jamar asked.

"Criminal Justice," I replied as he started laughing.

"What's so funny?"

"Man, all of the criminals major in Criminal Justice," he said with a grin referencing my past.

He had a point. One of the main reasons I chose Criminal Justice was to help change the system. I've been locked up before and know firsthand how the justice system can be - corrupt.

A month into the school year, I always looked forward to Friday evenings on campus, it was a spectacle. Robin Hall, an all-girl dorm, was the place to be. The marching band and football team practiced behind the dorm while half of the campus gathered and partied in the dorm's parking lot. The Southerners were dancing to T.I, Young Jeezy, and Lil Jon. The DC, Maryland, and Virginia sections were blasting Go-Go, a popular music sub-genre created in Washington D.C. associated with live drums, keyboards, rappers, and singers. But we, the Northerners, were partying to Dipset, Jay-Z, and 50 Cent.

Jamar, Maurice, and I left the parking lot and headed to Charles' room to buy a cigar. Charles was a super duper senior who sold everything; rolling papers, candy, juice, pills, and, most of all, weed. He was making so much money from selling drugs that he put off graduating every year. To him, college wasn't a place for education, it was a goldmine.

"Why don't we go smoke on the bridge?" Jamar said.

"Too many people are always on the bridge, we might get caught."

"But we can see who's coming and easily escape them," Jamar stated as we walked behind the football field and into the woods.

"Just trust me cuz, its safer back here," I assured him.

111

Jamar wasn't a heavy smoker, often becoming paranoid until the high subsided. I was used to it. Smoking was illegal in New York, but the cops were looking for bigger fish to fry. If they locked us up for smoking, it was petty. Their focus was the dealers. As I broke down the cigar, I could tell we were camouflaged. We had a clear view of the football team. We could see them, but they couldn't see us. After about five puffs we were laughing and checking out the cheerleading team. Suddenly the sound of a car door slamming interrupted our giggles. Looking to the right, we saw two heavyset security guards looking directly at us.

"Are they staring at us?" Jamar asked.

"I don't know, but I'm not about to stand here and find out," I murmured. Creeping back slowly I made a quick dash out the woods and onto the terrain. With Maurice and Jamar in my peripheral, I was sprinting faster than the running backs on the field. "Hey, come here!" One of the security guards yelled. Abruptly Maurice slipped and fell, but quickly got up as we continued past the football field and into the crowd. The overweight security guards were left in our dust; they didn't stand a chance.

"See I told you," Jamar said as we laughed at Maurice's stained jeans. Walking into my room, I pulled out my zip lock bag to roll up another joint and immediately their eyes grew bigger.

"Chris, is all of this yours?" Maurice asked.

"Yeah. I had more, but it's almost gone. I'm quitting after this though."

"You're quitting smoking or selling?"

"Both."

"Good luck with that. Almost everybody on campus smokes and you could make a killing." Immediately my antennas went off. I could probably sell out right now if I wanted to. Looking out my window at the parking lot and it was filled with students who smoked. My dorm was in a prime location and they probably would purchase from me before anybody else. My mother's voice kept replaying in my head "make me proud," but all I kept seeing was dollar signs.

"Man, your friend Bria is crazy!" Jamar said as he walked into my room the following week.

"Why you say that?" I asked.

"Yesterday when you told me you were thinking about making her your girlfriend, I thought I would introduce myself. I asked her where you were and she yelled at me saying "none of your business!" I told her I was your cousin and she still didn't care."

"When I first met her she did the same thing to me" I said. I couldn't control my laughter after Jamar explained what happened. That sounded just like Bria; I loved it. She probably didn't mean any harm, but she was protective. Bria was from Wilmington, North Carolina. We met during the first week at school through Maurice and clicked right away. She smoked, had brothers who'd been in jail for the same crime as me, and was a no nonsense type of woman. We were a modern day Bonnie and Clyde.

As the weeks went on, I wanted to quit smoking weed, but the pressures of class deterred me from quitting. I needed a smoke reliever. College wasn't a game; the work was piling and piling, but I still didn't sell. My bag was dwindling away bit by bit and I went straight to Charles' room once I ran out. His roommate let me in and when I looked at his bed, I was shocked! It was filled with pounds of marijuana! "Hold on man! You can't just be letting people in here! What's wrong with you," he yelled at his roommate. Immediately I started calculating numbers in my head. It was at least $7,000.00 worth of marijuana on his bed. I couldn't believe it. Temptation was right in my face, I could smell the money. All I had to do was ask, but again, I resisted.

With no job, I didn't have much money and I hated being broke. The more I smoked, the more people asked if I had any marijuana for sale. I had possibly missed out on a thousand dollars worth of sales. It took everything in me to call home and ask for money, but to my surprise the funds were expedited right away. The amount was only $100.00, but I was only buying snacks and toiletries, so I made it work. I was trying to be frugal and only buy things I needed. But the following weeks, $100.00 went from $80.00 to $50.00 to eventually nothing. Again, I was broke.

I couldn't take it anymore. I had my sister send me some cash from the money I had stashed away at home for emergencies. I felt like I had no other choice. Seeing my bank account in the negative and asking for money drove me back to my old ways. I felt like a bum, plus I had a girlfriend now and I didn't want Bria to know I couldn't afford to take her out or buy her nice things. That went against everything I knew. Day-by-day I was starting to think college life wasn't for me. I promised my mom I was done, but times were hard. I felt even worse that I couldn't send my younger cousins money. When I was in high school, I use to always give them money, but they hadn't received any this year. I took my money and went to see Charles.

I had everything figured out. I would make my prices lower and take the other distributors' customers. Charles' weed was a lower quality then the kind I had from NY. It was darker and filled with seeds, making it cheaper on the market. I started off with a pound, sold three nicks for $10.00 and repeated that same step every week until my customers increased. The pound would cost between $600.00 - $800.00 and I would make $300.00-$400.00 a week off of that. I could have made more, but selling lower meant a quicker turn around. My dorm was in the perfect spot, so it wasn't hard for my customers to find me. As I made more money, I started buying 3 to 4 pounds a week, equaling $1,500.00 in profits. *If I was making this much, how much was Charles making?* Calculating my revenue, I contemplated on being a super duper senior myself.

As I sat at my desk weighing and filling the bags up with marijuana, my cell phone rang; it was my mother. Answering the phone, I tried to sound as innocent as possible.

"Hey, mom!" I said cheerfully.

"What you been up to, Chris? I haven't heard from you lately."

"Nothing, just going to school. You know, doing the college thing. It's going great, real great." I sarcastically said as I continued to stuff the bags.

"You haven't asked for any money lately. How have you been?"

"I don't really need any. I got money for snacks and I eat at the cafe," I said trying to downplay the situation.

"Chris, do you think I'm stupid? I birthed you, boy. I told you to at least try!"
Pausing from filling the bags I held my head down letting out a deep sigh.

"Mom, I can't keep asking you for money when you don't really have it. I can't stand that! That's not a man!"

"You're a student. Stop making excuse and get a job!" she yelled.

"A job where? How am I going to get there? I don't have a car."

"The bus comes right in front of your school. They have grocery stores and fast food chains up and down that street!"

"Fast food chains and grocery stores? I'm not working there!"

"You know what Chris; don't call me when your butt is behind bars. Jesus what is wrong with this boy!" She yelled in frustration. I didn't have anything else to say. Why would I suffer financially if I didn't have to? My mind was made up; there was money to be made, and I was going make it!

It was Valentine's Day weekend and a plethora of my friends were outside loading their cars to go home. Little did I know trouble was brewing right outside of my dorm. My cousin, Shannon, came to my room and was perturbed by what Charles said to her. "Don't buy it from Chris, he gets it from me and my bags are bigger," she said. I was confused and couldn't believe that my own supplier was jealous. I was putting money in his pocket, but he was envious. I was starting to see that college life wasn't much different from the streets. I became skeptical of Charles, but let it go; after all he was my connect. A wave of bitterness was sweeping across campus and I could feel it. Charles was a backstabber and the twins Mike and Melvin who were in the band, kept inquiring about me to my friends. I didn't know why they were asking about me, especially since they never purchased from me. It worried me that people were asking so many questions. That's usually when the trouble started.

I was up all night again weighing and bagging up two pounds of marijuana I had purchased from Charles. I didn't like the comments he said to Shannon, but until I found another supplier I had no choice. A lot of the other dealers were leaving this weekend and this was my opportunity to supply their customers. The following day Bria and I were in my room watching a movie and Mike appeared at my door wanting to buy a bag. I didn't think twice about it, besides he was on the phone not paying me any mind. Closing the door behind him Bria started yelling. "Why would you have your bags, scale, and weed out? I don't like Mike; he's suspicious and weird. Next time serve him outside."

After walking Bria to her dorm, I came back and went to the bathroom. Standing in the hallway, I could see my door slightly open. I raced to my room thinking somebody was trying to steal from me. Slowly, I pushed the door open to get a clear view of the perpetrator. Suddenly, the door swung open from the inside and the police and I were standing face to face. "Damn," I murmured to myself. Two campus security guards and Officer Bradley, a real Memphis Police Officer, looked me up and down. "What's this," Officer Bradley asked while holding up the pounds of marijuana. I held my head down in disbelief. *How could I be so stupid?* Officer Bradley turned me around placing the handcuffs on my wrist then sat me on my bed. I watched as the officers searched under my bed, drawer, closet, ceiling, and air conditioning ducts; I could tell this wasn't new to them. I was caught red handed.

While in the back of the police car, I became mad at myself. *How could I be so careless? What was my mother going to say?* "You have your whole future in front of you and you're just going to throw it away?" Officer Bradley said as we pulled into the Shelby County jail. "We've been watching you for a long time and we finally got our tip," said Officer McCullough, who was one of the campus security guards. Officer Bradley slightly tapped his leg, giving him a glare as if he was telling him to shut up.

Sitting in my cell, I pondered on what Officer McCullough said. What did he mean "finally got our tip?" My suspicions were up; somebody told and I had a feeling on who it was. I avoided calling my mother the first night; I wasn't ready to hear her mouth. The following day I was allowed to make one phone call, so I sucked it up and braced myself for her wrath.

"Hey, mom," I said letting out a deep sigh.

"Boy, don't hey mom me. I know all about what happened, your school called me."

"I know, mom, I know," I replied.

"How do you feel? How much did you have? You couldn't last a year, Chris!" she said yelling into the phone.

"Mom, I'm sorry," I somberly said.

"Chris I don't want to hear it! I wanted a better life for you, can't you see that! They expelled you Chris! Now I have to come down there and get your stuff because it can't stay in the dorm. I don't want to drive down there! I'll talk to you at another time!"

My own mother didn't want to talk to me, making me feel worthless.

On Monday morning I stood before the judge in an orange jumpsuit with handcuffs around my wrist. "Mr. Williams, I don't know what you were thinking bringing illegal drugs on a college campus. You had your whole future in front of you," the judge said. *"Your whole future in front of you"? This must be everybody's favorite line, but I'm sick of it.*

"Mr. Williams you're being charged with possession with intent to distribute. Bail will be set at $20,000.00" the judge said.

"Your honor, that's too much. My client is a college student; he can't afford that," my lawyer argued.

"Apparently he's not, he's a drug dealer. The bond will stay as is," he said banging his gavel.

I asked my sister to send me some money from my stash, but it wasn't enough - I was stuck.

Throughout the next week, the Memphis locals kept me company during my down time.

"Where you from blood? I know you not from around here." one of the inmates asked.

"New York" I vaguely replied.

"New York? What you doing down here. I'm Donald by the way."

"I got caught with a few birds on Doris University (birds was slang for pounds).

"Doris University! You were the big man on campus huh?

"Yeah, something like that."

"My little brothers go there, you probably know them. Mike and Melvin, they're twins. My grandfather works there too; he's the chief of security, has a mix of grey and black hair and drives a white Caprice"

"Nah, I don't know them," I quickly replied hoping he would leave me alone, but then it hit me.

"Wait, what are they names again?" I inquisitively asked.

"Mike and Melvin, and my grandfather is the chief of security."

"Yeah, I know your brother, Mike; he's the one that got me in here! He's a snitch!" I yelled causing the other inmates to look at us.

"And did you say your grandfather is the chief of security, the one that drives the white Caprice? Oh yeah, your brother definitely told on me," I said looking him in the eye.

"Man, I don't know what you're talking about," he murmured as he walked off.

It all made sense now. When Mike came in my room, he was probably talking to his grandfather on the phone - a true informant. Speaking with his brother was all the confirmation I needed. Later on that day I called Bria, I knew she would get a kick out of this.

"You won't believe what happened today, baby. Remember you told me not to serve Mike?

"Yeah I remember. What happened?"

"I met his brother in here and do you know that Mike and Melvin's grandfather is the head security guard on campus?"

"Are you serious? See, I told you! I knew it was something funny about him. I can't believe this! I'm going to tell everybody, but Chris I have to tell you something," she murmured.

"What's up?" I asked as I braced myself. From the tone in her voice, it sounded like bad news.

"Everybody knows you were arrested. What's even worse is they're posting pictures of your mug shot around campus," she said.

I wasn't surprised or upset. Every time a student got arrested a few rejects would plaster their mug shots around campus for laughs and giggles. It was the norm.

After being in jail for a week, I finally had my court date. With my mom and dad by my side, we sat with my lawyer as he explained my options. "Chris has a good chance of getting out of here; I'm golfing buddies with the judge, so more than likely he will let you go. Your charges will be possession with intent to distribute and two paraphernalia charges with two years unsupervised release. This means that Chris isn't allowed to get into any trouble for the next two years." My parents and I signed the documents consenting to the agreement. If I didn't have the funds to pay my lawyer, I would have served time, but money makes a huge difference. I held my head down in shame as my parents paid for my release. Bria also helped with the payment. I told her she didn't have to numerous times, but she insisted. I was expelled from Doris, my rap sheet was getting longer, and I had disappointed my mother once again. Driving back home, I started having second thoughts. I didn't want to leave Memphis. Losing the opportunity to gain a higher education just to make a few bucks wasn't worth it; now I was back at home feeling trapped.

Lesson Learned: Drugs are addictive, but so is money. I was accustomed to having cash on hand, lots of it. I complained about paying for school, but I should've thought about my future. I might have struggled financially the first year, but once I fully became adjusted, I could have gotten a job or possibly been hired as a paid intern. When my mother sent me $100.00 it lasted for 2 weeks, but if I had a job, the money I made would've lasted way beyond that. If you're like me, try to fight the urge to sell drugs. Your education is more important than a quick buck. You may think selling drugs is the only thing you're good at, but that's far from the truth. If you can sell drugs you can own a business. You have the mindset for it and you don't even know it. To sell drugs you have to advertise it, you have to manage your supply (inventory), and keep your customers happy, which is customer service. Those are some of the steps to owning a business. I was already doing it, and you can too. Drop the drugs, find your passion, and make a way for it to be profitable.

I was also against taking out a loan because I didn't want to be in debt; but, as I look back, there were numerous options that would've avoided that. There are plenty of scholarships and programs geared towards helping students. Even if you're not a top student, there are still options for you. After you graduate, you don't have to be broke. There are income-based payment plans, consolidated plans, and programs that will forgive your loans depending on the stipulation.

I should have been smarter about selling drugs. My intuition told me something wasn't right about Mike. I should have avoided him at all cost. I made a promise to my mom and I didn't keep it. My cousins Jamar and Shannon went on to graduate, but I didn't. I thought if Charles could do it, so could I, but years later his ways finally caught up with him. He was arrested by a confidential informant for trying to buy 100 pounds of marijuana. That just further confirmed what my mother said "the streets will only leave you with a few choices – jail or death." You choose.

Chapter 8: iRacist

What does she mean I'm in the wrong class? Looking down at my schedule, I stepped back into the hallway to make sure I wasn't mistaken. The room number was correct and the professor's name matched. With my heels clicking the floor, I walked to the doorway interrupting her lecture.

"Ma'am my schedule says I belong in this class," I said.

"I'm sorry, my name is Professor Murphy and you shall address me as such. The fashion classes are on Farmers Street. I believe you've come to the wrong building; this class is for Video Production students," she said.

Is she hard of hearing or something? Maybe she misunderstood me or I didn't properly introduce myself.

"No, I'm sorry, my name is Angel Gudger. My schedule say's I belong in Freshmen Orientation for Video Production taught by Professor Murphy. Now am I in the wrong class?" With her smoke-grey hair covering part of her white seasoned face, she lowered her glasses looking me up and down.

"Really, interesting…." she uttered. I was confused; first she said I was in the wrong class, now she seems baffled that I belong here. I didn't think much about it, she was old, maybe senile, but she was also lucky. It was my first day of class and it was too early to display my impulsive temper.

Walking back to her desk I stood there waiting for her response as she grabbed the student roster. "Have a seat young lady. I'll figure out what to do with you later." *What to do with me later?* Out of all days, the devil wants to test me today. I don't know what her problem is, but she's taking this orientation class way too seriously. I wasn't receiving any credits for this class, but it was required for all incoming freshmen. Freshmen Orientation was the least of my worries; I was more concerned with Video Production 1 and Mass Media, so she needed to calm down because nobody was taking this class serious. "Enjoy the rest of your day students," Professor Murphy said as the class came to an end.

Walking around campus, I started to smile on the inside. I always wanted to attend The College of Arts in Philadelphia, Pennsylvania and I was finally here. The outside of the building was reminiscent of a vintage theater. I loved my new school plus my friend Courtney is here with me. She's a sophomore majoring in Fashion Merchandising and we both were from Newark, New Jersey. I dreamed about someday leaving Newark for a better life; even though Philly wasn't far, it was perfect.

Walking in the Cafè for dinner, I spotted Courtney sitting down with her friends. "Hey y'all this is my friend Angel from Jersey. Show her some love," Courtney said to her friends as I sat down. Surprisingly, a lot of her friends thought I was a Fashion Merchandising major too. I was puzzled and didn't understand why.

"My professor thought I was a fashion major and now your friends think I am too. Why is that?" I asked. Courtney giggled, "Look at you. You have style, you're trendy, and always on point. Some days you'll wear the newest sneakers, denim jeans, and cap it off with a high-end shirt. Or you'll throw on a pair of six-inch heels, a dress that fits every curve with your hair flawlessly shining down your back. Plus, you're a cute little chocolate thing." I never looked at myself like that. To be honest, I didn't care about clothes; I just wore what I thought was hot. I was a tomboy at heart, but I also loved looking like I stepped out of the latest issue of Vogue. I received "Best Dressed" in high school, but didn't really care to. I didn't think that would qualify me to be recognizable with fashion. I dressed how I felt – it was natural.

As we sat at the table, Courtney and her friends tried to convince me to change my major so I could have classes with them, but my passion was Video Production and I wouldn't trade that for the world.

"What professor thought you were a fashion major, Angel?" Courtney asked.

"Professor Murphy."

After taking a bite of pizza, she instantly rolled her eyes with a look of disdain.

"What was that look?" I asked, tilting my head to the left.

"Girl, I've heard so many stories about her, but the worst thing I heard is that she's racist. A few people I know had her class and she gave them hell." I thought about what she said and didn't get too worried. I dealt with racist cops in Newark all the time. As long as I minded my business and did what I was supposed to do, they left me alone. I was going to apply that same method to her class. If I do all of my work and complete all of my assignments, there's no way I could fail.

Months went by and the end of first quarter was right around the corner. I couldn't wait to see my grades. I met with all of my professors to make sure I was on the right track, but never thought to meet with Professor Murphy. After all, it was only Freshmen Orientation. I turned in all of my work and doubled checked everything to make sure there wouldn't be any excuses. Besides, her class was all about getting adjusted to college life; by this time, I was more than adjusted. Courtney said she was racist, but I only noticed one problem with her. She never called on me to answer questions even when I raised my hand. Sometimes I'd raise my hand on purpose to see if she would call on me and she never did. It was a bit excessive.

Courtney and I sat on the top floor of the Library near the window, with a view that overlooked downtown Philadelphia. While I was doing my work, an email popped up from the academic department stating that grades were now available online. I anxiously signed into my student account. I saw my first grade and smiled from ear to ear.

"Read them out loud, girl," Courtney murmured.

"I received an A in Video Production, a B in Mass Media, B in Audio Production, A in Communication History, and a B in Writing." As I got to my last class, my eyes bulged out and my right leg started shaking nervously. "An F in Freshmen Orientation; It must be something wrong!" Courtney stared at me shaking her head.

"See, I told you. I wish somebody would get rid of her. We pay too much money and nobody should fail a class that doesn't count. It's just so stupid," she said.

Courtney was right, we did pay too much for school. The financial process of getting in college was a struggle. I didn't have the money to pay for school. My mom, uncle, and dad applied for loans, but all of them were denied. They eventually scraped together what little money they did have and paid for my tuition I didn't understand how I could fail. I did all of my work and to top it off, I'm going to have to tell my mom. I could hear her voice now, full of disappointment. Slamming my laptop, I left the library and retreated back to my dorm.

Plopping down on my bed, I stared at the ceiling filled with anger. Grabbing my iPhone, I noticed the battery was almost dead and I felt just like it - powerless. Plugging the charger in, I scrolled to my mother's number, calling her as my hands shook nervously. I prayed she didn't answer. If she didn't pick up by the second ring, I was hanging up, but before I could she answered.

"There's my college baby, I was just talking to my co-worker about how proud I am of you," she said. My heart sunk even further; not only was she happy to hear from me, I was about to drop the F bomb on her, literally.

"Hey, Mom," I replied in a low voice.

"What's wrong?" she asked noticing something was off.

"Well, I got my grades and I got all A's and B's." Before I could finish telling her my grades, she started yelling.

"That's what I'm talking about, baby! I'm so proud of you; I'm going to have to get you something nice when you come home!"

"Mom, that's not it."

"You have more good news, honey?"

I put my hands in my face letting out a deep sigh. Why was she getting so excited? Jesus, make it stop.

"No mom, I got all A's and B's, but I got an F in Freshmen Orientation!"

"Freshmen Orientation! How in the hell did you get an F in your easiest class, Angel?"

"To be honest, mom, I don't know. I turned in all of my assignments and I'm always on time. But a lot people have told me Professor Murphy is racist."

"Racist? Its 2015, Angel. I doubt she's racist. A lot of black students go there."

"I know mom, but this is what everybody has been telling me. The first day of class she assumed I was a Fashion Major because of the way I was dressed."

"Because of the way you dress? I don't know what's going on honey, but you need to talk to her and your advisors. I know you're not going to receive good grades all the time, but an F in this class is ridiculous."

Before speaking with Professor Murphy, I sent my advisor, Mr. Carter, an email about my grades. Mr. Carter was a younger black man in his mid-30s. I felt more comfortable telling him about my problem. Responding to my email right away, "Ms. Gudger come to my office so we can talk," he wrote. Mr. Carter reminding me of my Uncle Jay; tall and a bit chubby.

"So, Ms. Gudger I see you got all good grades except for Freshmen Orientation. I understand your frustration; but if you fail her class again, you'll be placed on academic probation." *Academic Probation, are you kidding me? This isn't the streets. Who knew they had probation in college?* He stared at me as if he knew I was yelling profoundly in my head.

"But I did all of my assignments and passed them. This isn't fair," I said.

"I'll speak with Professor Murphy, but I think you should talk with her first." Instantly I frowned; just the thought of speaking with her made me cringe.

Maybe I dressed too fancy for Professor Murphy; after all, my major was Video Production, not Fashion Merchandising. I decided from here on out I would wear nothing but jeans and a t-shirt to her class. I sat in her class and didn't raise my hand or converse with the other students. I was too worried about what her response was going to be. When class was over, I stayed behind to speak with her. Sitting down at her desk looking at papers, she completely ignored my presence.

"Excuse me, Professor Murphy, can I speak with you?" I said.

Letting out a deep sigh, seeming irritated while taking off her glasses, she looked up at me from her desk.

"What can I do for you today, Angel?"

"Well, I wanted to know why I received an F in your class."

Looking through her papers she pulled out her assignment sheet.

"See right here? You missed one crucial assignment that was worth 70% of your grade," she said pointing at her paper.

"I turned in that assignment and you gave me a D, which I didn't deserve."

"In that case, you still would have failed. Now please, I'm trying to grade some papers. You will have to take the class again. It happens in college, I'm sorry," she said showing no compassion. *Did she just dismiss me like I didn't pay thousands of dollars for this class? I swear she's lucky we're in a professional environment.* Frustrated with her response, I barged out her class slamming the door behind me.

Mr. Carter spoke with Professor Murphy, but to no avail; my grade still didn't change. I couldn't even switch to another class because Professor Murphy was the only Professor available for that class. I felt defeated. I was trying to better myself and develop my skills in Video Production, but this class was holding me back. I barely made it to college and now this lady was trying to take me out. Throughout high school my GPA was never above a 2.0; I was involved in numerous fights and occasionally suspended. I started taking Video Production my senior year and fell in love with it. I finally found my purpose, but it seemed like I was taking two steps back instead of two steps forward.

Throughout the following months, I made sure I was never late to her class and turned in all of my assignments. I begged my mom to pay for the class so I made sure everything was in order. Returning to Philadelphia from visiting Newark at the end of the semester, Courtney got a text from her friend, Robin, saying grades were online. I started to grow anxious, as the only grade I was concerned about was Freshmen Orientation. Hopping off 95 South, Courtney laughed as I rushed to park the car and ran up the steps to my dorm.

Opening my laptop, I logged right in to my account. "A, B, B, A….what the fu..! Another damn F! I can't believe this!" I yelled out. I wanted to slam my laptop on the floor. Courtney sat on the edge of my bed with a look of disgust on her face. "She is the worst!" I yelled. Throughout the night I couldn't sleep; I was furious. I made my mind up; I was going to have a serious talk with her tomorrow and get to the bottom of this.

As she dismissed class her auditorium style seating classroom became empty. I sat in the front row, contemplating if I should speak with her or not. I watched as she flipped through papers totally ignoring me, which seemed to be her ritual. I looked over at my friend, Sarah, who was placing her brown hair in a ponytail; she looked at me concerned, as if she could feel the tension in the room. She was one of the only white students I talked to in class. She was Caucasian, but was so down to earth. She loved hip-hop more than me and was very stylish. Gathering my belongings, I walked towards Professor Murphy's desk with my iPad in hand, hoping for the best.

"Excuse me, Professor Murphy, do you mind if I could have a word with you?" I asked, standing in front of her desk.

"I guess, Angel. How can I help you?"

"Well, as you know, I received an F in your class again and I wanted to know why."

The wrinkles in her forehead appeared as she became visibly agitated while her right pinky tapped the desk in annoyance.

"Well, Angel, because you deserved it."

"Professor Murphy, I didn't deserve an F. I didn't score anything below a C this semester," I said calmly. Reaching in my book bag, I started pulling out all of my assignments from the semester. I knew she would say something like this, so I was ready. Before I could finish pulling papers out, Professor Murphy stopped me.

"Please stop pulling your papers out, Angel. You need to get out of my class and take this up with your advisor," she said dismissing me. I paused and immediately looked at her as if she reeked of garbage because at this point she was trash, pure filth - leftover slops. I told Courtney before I came to class that if this talk didn't work, I was taking this up with the Dean and that's exactly what I was headed to do.

Storming towards the door, I could hear Sarah talking with Professor Murphy, and just before leaving, I stopped as I heard Professor Murphy talking. "It's bad enough I let these black girls think they're going to be the next Karl Lagerfeld. Now I'm supposed to let a black girl think she's going to be the next Steven Spielberg. Are you kidding me? She'll never pass this class," said Professor Murphy. Did I really just hear that? Is it 2015 or 1962? Slamming the door, I turned around in a rage, walking towards her with my iPad in hand. "What the hell did you just say!" I yelled as I walked faster towards her. Her eyes widened as she stood up from her desk, attempting to fix her blazer. Before she could say anything, a loud smack from my iPad going across her face stopped her. Her glasses flew to the white tile floor as she fell to the ground. Her salt-n-pepper hair lay dismantled across her face, as I stood over her ready to deliver another powerful blow. Only this time, my six-inch heel would administer it. Loudly Sarah gasped, "Angel, oh my God, get out, just go. I can't believe you just hit her!" she yelled.

Looking down at Professor Murphy, I couldn't believe it either. I didn't even have time to think before I hit her – I was in a rage. Grabbing my book bag, I ran out of class and into oncoming traffic, nearly getting hit by multiple cars as the drivers blew their horns ferociously. Tears drenched my pillow as I lay in my bed; I knew I was finished at this school. I packed my clothes and went to Courtney's room to tell her what happened.

"You did what? Angel, you're crazy as hell. What are you going to do?" she asked.

"There's only one thing to do, Courtney, and that's go back to Jersey. I'm not about to wait around for the cops; I'm not going to jail," I replied.

"I'll ride with you home. It's Thursday and I don't have any Friday classes; plus, I need to get my hair done," she said.

The lights from the Philadelphia Eagles Stadium shined in the air as we headed towards the highway. I wiped my eyes as I realized I had just ruined any chance of making it out of Newark.

"What am I going to tell my mom," I murmured to Courtney.

"Angel, if anything, she should understand. Professor Murphy is a racist; about time somebody slapped her," she said laughing. "You hit her with an iPad? Those things just came out. Professor Murphy should have a sign on her head that reads iRacist. Get it?" I giggled at Courtney; at least she was trying to lighten the mood, but the fact still remains that I possibly wasted thousands of dollars for a single year in school. My phone started ringing, and, to my surprise, it was my mom. I must have talked her up.

I answered the phone with tears coming down my eyes. She could hear the sniffing and sad tone in my voice as I said,

"Hello."

"Angel, what's wrong with you, why are you crying, baby?" she asked.

I couldn't bring myself to tell her as I sat quietly on the phone.

"Angel, answer me, tell me what happen."

"Mom I....I messed up."

"You what, honey?" she said in a soft tone.

"I was talking to Professor Murphy about my grades and she said she'll never let a black girl become the next Steven Spielberg."

"She what!" She said cutting me off.

"That's not it, mom. When she said that, I lost it and smacked her in the face with my iPad."

"You did what, Angel!"

"She was blatantly being racist, mom!"

"I don't care what she was doing. I told you about controlling your temper! You can't take that same mentality from high school with you to college, Angel. You're probably going to need a lawyer. God! What am I going to do with you? I'll just talk to you when I get home." Placing my phone on the car console more tears ran down my cheek while Courtney rubbed my back consoling me. Arriving home, I knocked on her door, but she wouldn't answer, only yelling from her bed "I'll see you in the morning, Angel." I haven't been home in months and she didn't even want to see her own flesh and blood.

Walking into the living room the next morning, I could hear my mother on the phone. "Yes, Dean Robinson, I understand, but from listening to you I realize that you haven't heard the other half of the story. Are you aware that Professor Murphy made a racist remark to my daughter?" Leaning against the wall in her work clothes, her honeycomb skin was beginning to turn red as she grew frustrated. Noticing me standing in the hall, she started shaking her head while pointing at the phone.

"Yes, she's right here; I'll let her explain," she said while signaling for me to pick up the phone.

"You tell him everything you told me, Angel. You hear me," she uttered.

"Hi Dean Robinson."

"What is this I hear about Professor Murphy making racially charged statements to you, Angel?"

"Yes, I was talking to her about my grade and she said,

"It's bad enough I let these black girls think they're going to be the next Karl Lagerfeld. Now I'm supposed to let a black girl think she's going to be the next Steven Spielberg. Are you kidding me? She'll never pass this class."

"Are you serious?" she asked.

"Yes, Ma'am."

"Angel, I had no idea that was the reasoning behind your actions. On behalf of the school and myself I'm so sorry that Professor Murphy would say such harmful remarks about one of our students. We will be investigating this matter. In the meantime, if you have any witnesses or any proof to those allegations, we will need them as soon as possible," she said. The first person that came to my mind was Sarah. I prayed and hoped she would be on my side, and that the color of my skin wouldn't deter her from the truth.

After talking to Dean Robinson, I decided to call Sarah right away. I prayed while the phone was ringing. Sarah and I were cool, but I didn't know what she would do in a situation like this.

"Angel! Oh my God, I was just thinking about you. I saw Courtney and signed the petition she has going around about getting Professor Murphy fired," she said.

"Petition, what do you mean petition?"

"You don't know? Courtney has everybody signing a petition for you about Professor Murphy. Everybody's signing it. It's totally unfair what they did to you; she should be the one gone not you."

Courtney was the best! She had a petition going around for me and I didn't even know it. After hearing Sarah say she signed it, I knew she was going to help, which she agreed to do. I was slightly starting to feel out of harm's way.

Months went past as I sat day-by-day applying to numerous colleges and internships, but my high school grades weren't good enough and I had to be enrolled in college to start an internship. I had dreams of working for BET or MTV that summer, but they were shattered because of this case. While surfing online, I came across a five-month program from the Connecticut School of Broadcast, but there was one problem: the price was $5,500.00. I asked my family and again they agreed to help, but I had to pay for half. Five months later I passed the Connecticut School of Broadcast with flying colors and was awarded with a letter of credit.

My mom, father, and I prayed in my dad's black Suburban before walking into court. I was a nervous wreck. Walking into the building entrance, my lawyer who resembled Jennifer Aniston, greeted us. "I have some great news for you today, Ms. Gudger. We won't be going into the courtroom; instead follow me into the conference room. I was confused when I saw that we were the only ones in the room. Where was Professor Murphy, Dean Robinson, and anybody else representing the school? Sitting at the large wooden table adjacent from my lawyer, I begin to ask questions.

"So, where are the other lawyers, Professor Murphy or Dean Robinson?" I asked.

"Well, I'm glad you asked, Angel. Your school has decided to drop the charges."

My heart caved into my chest with relief.

"But you're still expelled. Given the evidence from Sarah Parker, the emails that you sent requesting to be removed from Professors Murphy's Class, and the 250 signatures from the petition, the school decided there was no reason to take action," she explained.

My mother and dad smiled from ear to ear knowing that their baby girl would be safe.

"Will Professor Murphy be terminated?" I asked.

"I'm sorry, Angel, the school has decided to keep her; but she has been placed on administrative leave until the new semester."

Administrative leave? How could they let a known racist work at their institution? I felt like I won the battle, but I lost the war; either way I was I grateful. I was leaving out of the courtroom a free woman.

I started sending out resumes right away, but nobody was responding. *Had I failed? Was this it? Was the universe punishing me for what I did to Professor Murphy?* I applied to numerous companies, but still nothing, until one Sunday afternoon my mentor, Ms. Simmons, who was the Public Relations manager at BET and youth counselor at my church, said she had something for me. She told me to apply as an intern at BET; the following week, I was in D.C. living with my cousin and working for the *BET Now* television show with Alesha Renee. Every day I worked from 9:00am – 5:00pm for free. In between working for *BET Now,* I also logged in videos, documentaries, and TV shows to the BET library. The end of my internship was nearing and I started to wonder what my next step would be. I got my certification from the Connecticut School of Broadcast, but still no official degree.

On my last day at BET, the show's producer, Allen, told me to come in early. When I arrived, he was sitting in his office in front of the TV. "Grab a seat and relax," he said with a smile. We started watching *BET Now* and I immediately got excited. As the credits started to roll, I saw "Producer and Editor Ashley Gudger." *Ashley Gudger?* Why the hell would he say my name is Ashley Gudger? Allen has been calling me Ashley for the last three months, but I didn't want that as my name on the credits. Why would he use my middle name when I told him beforehand what I wanted? He's lucky I didn't have my iPad because he would've become my second victim.

"There are three things I want to go over with you. One, do you know why I call you Ashley?" With my lip turned up I stared at him confused. *No I don't know why you call me Ashley. Do I look like a psychic?* "Well my ex-wife's name is Angel; I hate her, but I actually like you. Two, you received an overall grade of a D because you have to work on your edits and transitions more, but I really believe in you. Three, here is your form to fill out your application. You start on Monday and you will report to the BET Library for video logging." I paused looking around the room as if I was lost. Was I just offered a job? A huge smile came over my face as I rushed to hug Allen. "Thank you, thank you, and thank you! You don't know how much this means to me," I said. The pay was only $12.00 an hour, but that was more than the internship, plus I knew this was my foot in the door to one of the largest television networks.

Lesson Learned: In life, you will come across people who will discriminate against you, laugh at you, talk behind your back, and much more. Your only job is to love and pray for them. God will not let their talents take them where their character can't keep them. Always think before you act and never let someone have control over you. I saw the signs that Professor Murphy was a racist, but the way I responded was a mistake. I could have gone to jail and possibly had a criminal record that would have ruined my career. I hope that one day racism is no more; there is progress, but we're a long way from it being completely abolished. The Generation Z and Millennial demographic are a mix of different racial and ethnic backgrounds and we also interact with people from different backgrounds more than the older generations.[7] Because of this, the future may be promising, but again this will take time.

I wasted valuable time for my actions. I regret what happened, but that incident prepared me for the real world and made me work harder. I've worked with a plethora of television networks and it's shocking to see that racism still exists. Instead of hitting Professor Murphy, I should've reported the incident to the Human Resources department. It would have been properly handled and karma would have taken its course.

Life is funny and really does come full circle; a year later I was promoted as the Production Coordinator for BET. My position consisted of hiring new interns and lo and behold my old college was pitching their students for internships. I denied all of them. I explained to BET what happened and that they employed racist professors. Everything happens for a reason; if I wasn't expelled from college, I might not have been in the position to get the job at BET. I'm a firm believer that every place you end up is where you're supposed to be. It might set you back, but it will set you up for something better. Always do what you know is right morally and you will have favor.

I still haven't had the chance to graduate from a credited university. I've worked for numerous TV shows and movies, such as BET's *The Game*, Tyler Perry's *Madea Goes to Jail*,

The BET Awards, The BET Hip Hop Awards, MTV Music Awards, Dr. OZ, Love and Hip Hop Atlanta, and much more; but those are all freelance jobs. Freelancing is not a bad thing, it allows me to travel and I've worked on several sets. But one day I want to have a family and stability; a corporate position will provide that. I've applied to a plethora of corporate positions, but a Bachelor's or Master's degree is always required. I've reached a lot of goals in life, but receiving my degree is still one that I want to achieve. Remember to always keep a level head and the enemy will never be able to get you. The cat only catches the bird because the bird comes to the cat's level.

Chapter 9: Passion for Fashion

I swear the Dominicans do it every time; my hair is flawless. My blow out makes each curly blonde strand look polished to perfection. My bathroom countertop was cluttered with makeup, toiletries, jewelry, and hair accessories. After I finished my makeup, I pouted my lips, shifted my right leg creating the perfect arch, and snapped several selfies of my caramel complexion. Ugh! Those eight pounds I lost earlier this year came right back. Jumping around my bedroom to fit in these jeans shouldn't be this hard, but, hey it's worth it. Today when I walk down the runway, all eyes will be on me, magnetizing every person in sight, especially the way my curves are filling these Zara jeans. My black patent leather plexi pumps I got from Nordstrom's, ASOS white blouse with the French cuffs, and Ruby Woo lipstick from MAC should do the trick. Being one of the founding members of the Sheek Fashion Modeling Troupe, I have to set the standard. If we want to win the annual Homecoming Fashion Show Gala this year, we have to show the newcomers that we're coming for blood.

I could hear Rachel blowing the horn and calling my name from outside of my dorm window. "Ava, would you hurry up! You've had all day to get ready; we're going to be late, girl!" Rachel had some nerve yelling my name. Hell, we were already late and, to be honest, tryouts didn't start until we got there. Rachel and I were the founders of Sheek Fashion Modeling Troupe. We became friends instantly during our freshmen year and we're both from New York. Rachel's from the Bronx and I'm from Queens, but one thing we had in common was our passion for fashion. During our freshman year, we visited Rachel's friend at Florida A&M University and she was a part of FACES Modeling Troupe. Intrigued by what we saw, we decided to start our own troupe the following year at Carolina City State University located in Greensboro, North Carolina.

Walking out my dorm towards her green Ford Taurus, I could see her green eyes, rosy red cheeks with her hair tied in a bun. A true redbone. "Oh, you showing off today, Ava. I'm loving that hair color boo!" she said, screaming out the car window smiling. I could feel the jealousy from the other female students standing outside. The animosity was still in the air from a few girls who tried out for Sheek before. Hopping in Rachel's car, we both couldn't contain ourselves from laughing, but who cared. If you wanted to join Sheek, you had to be stylish, photogenic, trendy, vintage, have personality and confidence. Sheek isn't some high end modeling agency, but, at the end of the day, we want to be the best.

This year's prize for the Fashion Show Gala was $2,000.00 and I'll be damned if we weren't going to win. I was a senior and even though I wasn't going to be here next year, the money could go towards the troupe. If we won, Sheek would have numerous props, outfits, and special effects for next year's show. Rachel and I spent countless hours putting together fashion shows and teaching our team the basics. We didn't owe anybody anything, so if someone was upset because they weren't picked, then so be it.

"Girl, look at all these people," Rachel said while staring at that long line outside of Douglas Hall. Walking into the auditorium the lights were dim as the spotlight shined down on the stage. We held a meeting with the other members of Sheek before the auditions started. Chris, who was one of the first members of Sheek, looked irritated while we discussed the rules of the audition.

"I really think we should incorporate dancing, singing, and different talents into Sheek," Chris said while rudely interrupting Rachel.

"I told you before, this is a modeling troupe not a dance group, choir, or anything else, Chris," I said. Sucking his teeth, his attitude visibly grew stronger. This wasn't the first time I told him this, but I guess something wasn't registering in his thick skull. Or maybe his bifocals weren't allowing him to see the vision everybody else saw. Don't get me wrong, Chris was of value. He was tall, muscular, and clean cut with midnight brown skin. He was Sheek's Creative Director and his ideas were usually great; but this dancing and singing thing wasn't going to cut it.

I stood at the beginning of the runway while Rachel stood at the end explaining the key points of modeling to the contestants. In her New York accent and authoritative voice, she held nothing back, giving it to them cut, dry, and clean:

"Today we will determine if you have what it takes to be a model for Sheek. First things first, modeling is an art form and it should almost become second nature. The basics of walking are learning to keep your feet straight while positioning your weight with your hips. Your arms should be to the side or you can place your hands on your hips giving pizzazz. Keep your neck and shoulders straight and always remember you're showing off clothes. This may sound easy, but, once you're walking, it can become difficult. You want to give off the illusion that you're gliding and never, I repeat, never sing the words to the song. If you're chosen, I would advise you to practice every day in front of a full-length mirror in a variety of high heels. Ava will demonstrate how to walk the runway. Please pay close attention; you can take some of what you see and make it your own style. Be creative."

As Rhianna's "Fresh Off The Runway" blasted through the speakers, I could feel everybody's eyes piercing at me as I walked the runway. "Yasssss, you better work!" Rachel yelled through the microphone while snapping her fingers. After my demonstration I took a seat in the front row. I became distracted by a group of people laughing and making noises. I turned around and saw Chris and his friends talking loudly, interrupting the models who were trying out. "Cut!" I yelled from my seat. Slowly getting up while trying to maintain a smile and not show my frustration, I walked over to Chris.

"Could you and your friends be any louder? Stop being rude! Why are y'all in here anyway?" I sternly asked.

"My bad, Ava, me and my friends was just checking out the auditions," Chris replied.

"I'm confused, Chris. You know these are closed auditions."

"See, I told you," whispered one of his friends.

"Told you what? Chris, you got something you want to say?" I replied with my head cocked to the side waiting for a reply.

"I think it's time for your friends to leave."

"You don't own this auditorium." Chris snapped back.

"Excuse me? I don't own it, but I requested it for two hours and I can do as I please."

"You got it, Ava. We don't want any trouble. We were just on our way," Chris said.

"You don't have to leave, but your friends do. You're a part of Sheek."

"No, I'll leave too; I'll catch you later, boss lady," Chris said.

Boss lady? What did he mean by that?

Once Chris and his rude entourage left, we were able to finish. Sheek selected 30 new models out of 100 contestants -

20 girls and 10 boys. I was happy about the new contestants, but I was puzzled. What did Chris's friend mean "See I told you?" *What were they saying about me?* This was so unlike him. *Was I too aggressive? Was I rude?* I told Rachel what happened and in true New York style she suggested that we stop past his apartment. "Let's go past his place, let's really see what's good. He stays right around the corner in the Commons."

Knocking on his apartment door, we could hear laughter and what sounded like a group of people talking. "Oh, he's having a party and we weren't invited huh?" Rachel said jokingly. Chris opened his door and when he noticed it was us, he quickly stepped outside as if he was trying to hide something. I couldn't see everybody, but I did see a few females sitting inside having drinks.

"Don't worry, Chris, we're not trying to ruin your little party," I said.

"It's not a party, Ava. We're just having a meeting about a few things," he replied looking nervous.

"A meeting about what?" Rachel quickly interjected.

"A meeting about minding your business, Rachel. What's up? Why did y'all come here; you two don't never come to my place."

"I just wanted to apologize. I didn't mean to be rude to your friends, but what did they mean I told you so?" I asked.

"That was nothing. I don't know what my friend was talking about, but I'm busy right now. I'll see you two later. Can I go now?"

"We have practice tomorrow, will we see you?"

"Yeah, you'll see me."

Something didn't feel right about Chris; he was acting suspicious. I wasn't that rude to him, plus he was from New

Jersey, he was used to the "up north" attitude. Walking back to the car, Rachel must have been thinking the same thing. "Was that awkward to you? Chris was acting mad funny, and he doesn't usually act like that," Rachel said.

The following day at practice was hectic. The gym was filled with new members running around in sweatpants, tank tops, and high heels. We wanted them to be comfortable, but also prepared. We treated practice just like the show. Chris was missing, which was so unlike him; he's always the first one here and the last one out. We needed him here to explain the concept of the show. As I looked around, I noticed Chris wasn't the only one absent, 10 other members were noticeably missing too. "Look at this, Ava, I can't believe this! I've seen a lot of disloyal things in my life, but this takes the cake!" Rachel said as she came barging into the gym with her heels pounding the floor. I had no idea what she was talking about; I just wanted to get practice started. Pulling her to the back of the bleachers so we wouldn't distract the others, I asked her what was going on.

"Girl what the heck is wrong with you running in here like this?"

"Read this!" Rachel said with her arms crossed and a vicious frown upon her face.

👑 **"Hear Ye, Hear Ye!"** ♟

Royal Modeling Troupe wants
you to audition to be Carolina
City University's next best
model, dancer, singer or poet.
Our first show will be October
31st, so be prepared to show us
what you got!
Auditions – 8/29/2014 at
Douglas Ballroom
Contact:
Chris.Davis@carolinacity.edu

"Chris Davis! I can't believe he would do this," I murmured in a low voice so the others wouldn't hear me.

"Right, I told you he was up to something; I could feel it from the way he was acting yesterday." Rachel said.

"You know what, I'm not even worried. I bet you no one will show up. Who actually has a modeling troupe with dancers and singers?"

A devious smile appeared on Rachel's face. Right then and there I knew she was up to no good.

"You know what, I have an idea. Let's go to their auditions tomorrow and confront him. Nobody is going to show up anyway."

Since Chris and his friends rudely interrupted our auditions, Rachel and I will gladly return the favor, but it will be much worse.

The following day, Rachel and I drove slowly towards the Ballroom in Rachel's green Taurus. We couldn't believe our eyes. Not only was the line wrapped around the corner, but we saw numerous people in line that we knew.

"There he go right there," I said as I saw Chris walking towards the ballroom.

"Look at this idiot; with his mustard color chinos, brown boat shoes, and white Henley smiling and talking to everybody like he's some god. He must have forgot who made him." As me and Rachel started walking towards the entrance, we could hear other students mumbling.

"What are they doing here?" one girl murmured.

"Uh oh, here comes the drama!" another guy yelled out. Rachel quickly turned around as if she was about to charge the guy.

"What did you say?" she asked standing face to face, but the heckler was speechless. Rachel had a reputation for embarrassing anybody and from the looks of it the guy didn't want any problems. Going in the side entrance of the ballroom, Rachel and I sat behind Chris where he couldn't see us. "Wack! Wack! Wack! She's terrible, try again!" Rachel screamed from the seats. Chris turned around with a frown upon his face, which quickly changed to shock once he saw it was us. We were looking directly at him, waiting for him to reply.

"Yes! You honey! Try again next year; this isn't the right troupe for you," I continuously yelled to the model while Chris was walking towards us.

"Ava and Rachel, how may I help you?" Chris asked.

"How may you help us? Are you serious right now? How can you be so disloyal, you didn't even have the balls to tell us that you were starting another troupe?" I replied.

"For what? I tried to tell you a million times that we should incorporate dancers, singers, and models, but neither you nor Rachel wanted to."

"Yeah because it's stupid, just like this Royal Modeling Troupe," I said while putting my hands in his face.

"See! That's exactly what my friends and I were talking about! You two don't know how to compromise. Goodbye, ladies. We will see you at the Homecoming Gala. I hope you're ready because that $2,000.00 is ours." he said with a smirk.

"You must of slipped and bump your head!" I said while placing my finger on his forehead. As I walked closer to him, he started stepping back.

"You're not winning anything; we've been doing this way longer than you!" I said as my voice filled the ballroom. All eyes were on us as I continued to yell, but I didn't care. As friction grew, Rachel started pulling me away, but I wasn't having it.

"Let me go!" I said yanking myself away from Rachel.

"Ava, boo, you have to calm down," Rachel said.

"I am calm! We've worked our butts off these last years and now Chris thinks he's going to take it during my last year. I'm not going to let this happen and you shouldn't either!" I completely threw out Chris's ideas for the gala. If we kept them, he would surely use it against us. I didn't want him to know anything.

Me, Rachel, and two other founding members, Monique and Thaddeus, sat in my apartment all night thinking of concepts for the show. They sat on the couch watching *America's Next Top Model* while I sat on the floor painting my toenails.

"I wonder what Chris' troupe is going to do," Monique said.

"I don't care what they're going to do. They could roll over and die for all I care. Please don't bring that name up," I replied.

"Sorry," Monique replied.

"I got an idea," Rachel said.

"Let's do a Graduation theme, where everybody walks up to receive their diploma, then rips off their gowns and walks the runway in college prep attire. The boys would wear cardigans, chinos, and loafers; the girls would wear skirts, high heels, and mixer dresses."

"Or let's do a Harlem Renaissance theme. All of the models will wear vintage clothes and act as if we're having a fun night at the historical New York Cotton Club. Sequined dresses for the ladies and suits for the males, and we can end the show by recreating the famous "A Great Day In Harlem" picture that was in Esquire Magazine," Monique said.

"That is a great idea!" I said.

"But that would be so expensive. We would have to buy every girl sequined dresses and every guy a suit. We're college students; you know we don't have money like that," Rachel said.

After *America's Next Top Model* went off, VH1 started showing reruns of the famous rapper 2Pac's *Behind The Music*. Flashes of Notorious B.I.G's and 2Pac's funerals appeared on the screen.

"Let's do a funeral theme," Thaddeus suggested. We all looked at him like he was crazy, but he was dead serious.

"A funeral? I don't know about that, Thad." I said.

"With the money we have from petty cash, we can afford to go to the costume store, especially since its Halloween season. It won't be your typical funeral. It will be a woman in the casket and she will come back to life. There should also be a good side and a bad side; one girl dressed as a sexy angel and the other as a sexy devil. I'm sure every model has some dress clothes they can wear. Rachel and Ava I know you two have some lingerie. We can create a whole scene based on that. It's just an idea, we can add on other scenes as well.

Everybody agreed with Thaddeus; his idea was inexpensive and genius. We didn't have any time to waste, so we hopped in Rachel's car and headed to the costume store. Last year we raised over $1,000.00 from fundraising, so we had more than enough for props and costumes. I had no idea how we were going to get a casket, but, to my surprise, there were fake cardboard caskets in the Hot Topic store. We purchased a smoke machine, face paint, makeup from MAC Cosmetics, costumes and stayed under our budget by only spending $450.00.

We practiced every day. On weekdays from 4:00 p.m. to 12:00 a.m. and sometimes we would go until 6:00 a.m. on the weekends. It was do or die. Practice lasted so long, some models even brought sleeping bags. I loved how dedicated they were, even when I made them run around Douglas Hall in their high heels. They thought I was crazy, but I just called it passion. Taking a brief break from practice I had my boyfriend, Jason, bring me some food from the popular fast food restaurant Cookout. Sitting in Jason's car, he laughed as he watched the girls and guys run around outside.

"You're crazy, Ava. Why do you have these girls running around in high heels? It's 2 o'clock in the morning. You're worse than the Greek organizations."

"Shut Up! You're just mad because I never ran around in heels for you." I flirted.

"That's because you know better than to run from me," he said as I smiled back.

"Look over there. Who are those people sitting in the white Camry across the parking lot?" he asked.

"Where?"

"To the right of the building in the parking lot. It looks like they're recording or something."

"What in the hell," I said curiously as I saw the flash from the phone they were holding.

"You know what, drive over there." I said

Whoever was in the car couldn't see us sitting on the side of the building. Once we got closer, I couldn't believe my eyes. It was Patricia, Patrick, and Kelly, three of the old members of Sheek who left to join Royal.

"Are they spying on us?" I said.

"That's what it looks like. Man, y'all are taking this fashion show thing way too serious. Does he really have his cell phone out recording?" Jason said jokingly.

"Oh, they're about to see who's really serious," I said.

Pulling up behind Patrick's car, Jason blocked them in with his black Tahoe. I immediately got out, slamming the car door behind me. All of their heads quickly turned around, except Patrick who was still recording. I could hear Jason yelling as he rolled the window down, "Yo, Ava, chill!" I stood in front of the driver's door with my hands on my hips, then abruptly opened Patrick's door.

"What the hell are you doing? Y'all spying on us now?" I yelled.

"Nah, Ava, it's not even like that," Patrick replied.

"That's what it looks like to me!"

In the blink of an eye, I grabbed his phone as he quickly tried to grab it back. When he heard another car door slam, he looked back and saw Jason getting out of the car. Patrick knew Jason wasn't going to take any disrespect. Jason was 6'1 and had a reputation for ending parties early, so Patrick wouldn't dare try anything. Looking through his phone, I saw that not only was there footage of the girls running outside, but there was footage from us practicing our routine. They've been scheming for the last 2 weeks.

"Really, Patrick, really? You've been recording us for the past week, how pathetic."

"I didn't want to do it; Chris made me do it, I swear," he pleaded.

"Aww, he snitching, he snitching," Jason said while laughing.

"Well, you tell Chris that I just deleted all the footage and he better hope I don't see him until the gala."
Jason started laughing hysterically; he couldn't believe the lengths Chris' troupe went through to spy on us. Eventually, I handed Patrick back his phone and he apologized, driving off looking humiliated.

It was Halloween night and today was the day that Carolina City would see who would reign supreme. Just like every year, Garvey Auditorium was packed to capacity and the gala was sold out. The rising tension between Sheek and Royal even caused a spike in ticket sales. Unlike the previous years, where we battled Virginia State University and North Carolina State, this year it was just between Sheek and Royal. Royal was slated to go first and I wasn't going to miss this for the world. There were rumors that their theme was going to be based on the 18th century Royal Kingdom. When I walked into the auditorium, I looked at their stage props and the rumors were true.

There was a mural in the back of the stage painted like a European castle, similar to the Palace of Versailles in France. Right in the middle of the stage was a King's Chair. The lights dimmed and people started to cheer in excitement as the host, Terrance J from BET's 106 & Park, introduced Royal.

"I said Carolina City are you ready! I said Carolina City are you ready! Let me hear you scream!" Terrance J yelled to the crowd as they screamed back.

"Carolina City, please help me welcome to the stage, the newest modeling troupe to grace this campus, Royal Modeling Troupe!" he yelled as the name echoed throughout the auditorium.

The speakers started knocking as the 808 drum kicks from the rapper T.I.'s song "King Back" blasted throughout the auditorium. As the lights shined on the stage, there Chris stood basking in all of his glory. With a crown on his head, black slacks, white button up shirt, sunglasses, a king's staff and robe to match, I couldn't deny it, he did look good. He walked down the runway with so much confidence as a plethora of girls screamed his name boosting his ego even more. He sat on his throne with the palace behind him as all of the models came out in different 18th century costumes. The guys came out as knights, butlers, princes, and chaplains all dressed in slacks, khakis and dress shirts. Chris sat on the throne the entire time - how arrogant. He should have just told them to kneel down and kiss his feet. Ashia, one of our old members appeared in the audience and slowly walked on stage singing Beyoncé "Sweet Dreams." As she sung, the princess, queen and different dancers graced the staged to walk the runway. I was disgusted, if you're going to sing Beyoncé, you have to sing it right. My confidence grew stronger as their show came to an end; they weren't going to beat us. Although Ashia's singing wasn't up to par I started to have second thoughts about having singers and dancers because that part was a nice touch.

It was our turn and before heading out I lead our troupe in prayer. I could hear the crowd starting to chant Sheek's name. "Sheek Troupe! Sheek Troupe! Sheek Troupe!" My stomach filled with butterflies as the chants got louder and louder.

Luckily, a lot of our models were majoring in art and theater, so the art department designed a huge mural of a church for us. Stained church windows, the pulpit, the pastor's podium, and a choir were all carefully drawn into the picture. There were chairs on the stage so the models could sit while the other models viewed the casket. A doorway was also cut in the middle of the mural where the models would come in and out during the show.

Jay-Z's and Kanye West's "No Church in The Wild" played as the male models elegantly walked through the church door, all dressed in a mix of suits, blazers, and slacks. Heading straight to the casket, they viewed the body then immediately walked the runway showing off their outfits. After each guy sat in his seat, the female models graced the stage in their black and white dresses to the sounds of Rhianna's "Disturbia." The crowd started going wild as the girls twisted, turned, and flipped their hair as they sashayed down the runway. "Yassssss," "Go off!" "Come through!" "You better slay!" could be heard throughout the auditorium. Six muscular models came out with their shirts off, dressed in black dress pants and red bow ties. Instantly, screams were heard from the females in the crowd. The smoke started to fill the stage as the muscular models lifted the black casket above their shoulders, with three of them on each side, walking slowly towards the beginning of the runway.

As the guys walked to the front, I appeared from behind the mural as a sexy devil dressed in red lingerie topped with horns. As I walked the runway, the guys in the crowd went wild. I could hear Jason in the audience yelling, "That's me, that's all me! That's my baby!" in true New York fashion. Next, Rachel slowly walked in from the crowd as the spotlight shined on her. She was dressed as a seductive angel in all white lingerie with a white halo over her head. With the muscular

155

men still holding the casket, Rachel directed them to lower it then tapped the casket with her magic white wand. Monique popped open the casket, shocking the audience as one of the muscular models helped her up. As Monique stood there in her white fitted sheer gown, the crowd erupted in applause as Fabolous' "You Be Killin Em" started playing through the speakers. I smiled on the inside watching from backstage as Monique worked the runway in her all white heels, turning, posing, and flipping her hair. We were killing it! The crowd went wild as the entire audience was singing Fabolous' song word for word. *"I dead them all now, I buy the caskets, they should arrest you or whoever dressed you, ain't going stress you, but I'm going let you know, girl you be killing them, you be killing them."* As Monique finished walking, we all took one last stroll down the runway as the crowd cheers grew even louder.

On stage, Royal Troupe and Sheek Fashion Modeling Troupe were face-to-face as the judges tallied up their votes. The crowd was still chanting "Sheek Troupe! Sheek Troupe!" They were so loud that Terrance J had to tell them to calm down so he could announce the winner. Opening the envelope, a smile beamed from Terrance's face, "For the third year in a row, Sheek Fashion Modeling Troupe wins the Carolina City Homecoming Fashion Gala and the grand prize of $2,000.00 dollarsssssss!" We all erupted in excitement as the DJ replayed Fabolous' song. The entire trouped cheered, modeled, and vogued down the runway one last time. This was our victory lap. Royal Troupe quickly exited the stage as we taunted them, giving them the wave goodbye. Jason and his friends came backstage while we were celebrating, but, in the midst of the excitement, quietness fell over the room. Turning around to see what everybody was looking at, there stood Chris staring at me in front of everybody.

"What do you want? You cheater! As a matter of fact you loser!" I yelled to him.

"I don't want any problems, Ava," he said.

"Oh yeah, I hope not!"

"Look, I just wanted to apologize. I know what I did was wrong and I should have talked to you about it first. We've been friends for three years and you're leaving this year. I don't want it to end like this."

I stood there looking at him then looked at Rachel asking,

"What you think, girl? Should we forgive him or not?"

"Hmm, I guess we can be cool. After all we did win!" Rachel replied giving me a high five as we poked our tongues out at Chris.

"That's fair, that's fair." Chris said.

I leaned in and gave Chris a hug. I was so happy that I even poured him a glass of Champagne. Toast to the winners!

Lesson Learned: In most organizations or companies you might not see the other person's vision, but it's important to have an open mind. In hindsight, Chris's idea wasn't bad; when Ashia sung "Sweet Dreams" I thought to myself this is really creative. I should have been more open to his ideas; most college modeling troupes have dancers, singers, and poets. It's all about teamwork, which reminds me of the quote "alone we can do so little, together we can do so much," written by Helen Keller. I shouldn't have been so narrow minded on just having models. Through this experience, I learned to be graceful. Just because you have leadership responsibilities doesn't mean you have to yell or be disrespectful. Some people are intimidated and become passive when met with aggression, causing them to shut down and not express their true feelings. Be calm and hear them out.

I got flack for having too much confidence mixed with my attitude; in return some people didn't like me. I've learned that when I see people who don't like me, I still speak to them. It makes them uneasy, but eventually they will come to like you. They have no choice, it's like burning hot coals on their heads, and eventually they have to let it go. Always show respect and watch your words when working with others. We all come from different backgrounds and others may not react the same, but you have to show compassion. I changed my attitude because I knew I couldn't take it to corporate America. If I did, I would surely get fired. Chris and I were both flawed. He didn't talk to us about starting his own troupe; he did it behind our backs. Have no fear in telling your friends exactly how you feel. If they're your true friends, you'll come to a medium. Communication is key in any relationship. People who are deceitful and cut corners rarely end up on top and if they do it doesn't last long. What's done in the dark always comes to light.

Chapter 10: Draft Day

All of the hard work, all of the sacrifices, late night practices, staying focused and consistently improving my game is about to pay off. That's what I told myself as I sat in my mother's living room in Winston-Salem, North Carolina. I dreamed of one day moving her out of this apartment; we've been here for too long. If things go as planned, I might finally get my chance. Surrounded by my closest family members and friends, we were patiently waiting for Commissioner David Stern to call my name for what was about to be one of the best days of my life. It was Draft Day; not just any draft day, the National Basketball Association (NBA) Draft. I was so nervous I could feel the sweat dripping off my hands. Thank God I didn't get nervous during my games - the ball would slip right through. But that would never happen; once I got on court it was show time. All week I watched ESPN and read numerous articles about me. Some analysts said I was a shoo-in, but there were some who said I might not get picked. I know a handful of guys who've entered the draft and weren't chosen, and I know others who hurt themselves during their first year. I definitely didn't want to be a one-and-done statistic. I didn't come this far to fail.

I sat on my mother's couch that was still covered in plastic and crunched every time you moved. Time grew closer and closer to David Stern announcing the beginning of the draft. I could see my grandmother staring at me from the corner of my eye. She could see the worry on my face. Just before I could turn towards her, she leaned in whispering, "Josh, no matter what happens, I just want you to know that I'm proud of you, honey. You've come a long way." Those few words comforted me for a few moments, but the ongoing media quote kept replaying in my mind. "Joshua Howard is 6'7, 210 pounds and does everything good, but not one thing great." I couldn't believe people were saying that about me. I guess it was hard for some NBA teams to see how I was going to pan out during the season. Hell, if I was a general manager, I would try to get a guy that does everything good and not just one thing great.

This draft was considered "The Draft of a Generation." It was the year Lebron James, Dwayne Wade, Chris Bosh, and Carmelo Anthony were all picked. Pictures of New York City and Madison Square Garden, where the draft was held, flashed across the television. I wasn't there because I wasn't thought to be a first round pick, but the energy was felt throughout my house. Looking at the TV, I imagined that someday I would be playing against the Knicks in Madison Square Garden. Slouching down on the couch, I quickly sat up as David Stern made his way to the microphone. "For our first three picks the Cleveland Cavaliers will have the first pick, the Detroit Pistons will have the second, and the Denver Nuggets have the third," he said. All of the teams I practiced with weren't in the top ten, so I knew my chances of getting picked in the first round were slim. I trained with the Memphis Grizzlies, Utah Jazz, Charlotte Bobcats, New Orleans Hornets, and the Milwaukee Bucks. They worked me out all day and night; it was intense, but, throughout it, I maintained my momentum.

It was a long process, but a great learning experience. Just how basketball scouts recruit high school players, there were basketball agents scouting college players. I had agents coming at me from every angle, offering me all types of deals. It was overwhelming; but thankfully my coach assisted my mom and me with picking the right agent. Not only did I work out with the teams, I also interviewed with them. The recruiting process made me realize this was more than just playing basketball, this is a job, and you have to meet the standards that the franchise sets.

It was July, and it had only been two months since I graduated from Wake Forest University. Everything happened so fast; I never had the time to digest that I graduated from one of the top colleges in the country. Right after graduation I was traveling from city-to-city, training with the best and biggest athletes on the planet. I watched as more and more players were getting called. I watched as the Cleveland Cavaliers chose LeBron James, the Denver Nuggets chose Carmelo Anthony, and the Miami Heat chose Dwayne Wade. Seeing the newly drafted players jump for joy, hug their families, and place their new teams' hats on made me anxious. Not to mention my mother's living room seemed to get quieter and quieter as each name was called.

Glancing at the screen door, I could see my friends standing on the balcony. I decided to join them; I needed a breath of fresh air. All of them were leaning against the guardrails holding white paper plates in their hands chowing down on some of my grandmother's famous macaroni and cheese, cabbage, and bar-b-que chicken. Once I stepped outside, they all looked at me and could tell the doubt was starting to kick in.

"Josh, don't come out here looking like you just lost your favorite puppy. It's not over until it's over. There's no way that you were unanimously selected as the Atlantic Coast Conference (ACC) Player of the Year and you're not going to get picked. Not only that, you were Basketball Player of The Year over Dwayne Wade, so stop tripping," said my childhood friend, Derrick, as he continued to stuff his face full of chicken. He was right, but hearing Dick Vitale and all of the other commentators talk about the accomplishments and accolades of the other players was a bit discouraging.

My cousin Rob, who's almost as tall as me, stood there looking at me with a smirk on his face. I could tell he was about to say something funny. He was the jokester out of the crew, always lightening the mood.

"What are you about to say? I already know you got something on your mind," I said, smiling at him. He started laughing before he could even talk.

"When you came out here looking all sad, it reminded me of the time you were dating Tiffany during your freshmen year. She had your nose wide open. You were in love for real! You had to be the tallest person I've ever seen in love like that," he jokingly said.

"Hell yeah he was!" Derrick added.

"You were driving back and forth from Winston Salem, NC to the University of North Carolina, Charlotte (UNC) to see her every weekend. But you know what? Karma is something else. If she's watching the draft right now, she's probably trying to hang herself. She knows you're the one that got away," Rob said making everybody laugh.

If you asked me, she probably wasn't thinking about me, especially since I hadn't got picked yet. He was right though, my nose was wide open. I remember it like it was yesterday. We went to different high schools. We both knew of each other, but never got the chance to talk. The stars aligned one day and we finally got some time alone. She was a light skin, sweet southern girl who could cook and ride a dirt bike just like the fellas. I couldn't avoid falling for her even if I tried.

We started dating during my freshmen year. I was so blessed to attend an ACC school with a full endowment scholarship, but almost blew it messing around with Tiffany.

Like clockwork, every Friday after practice, I would drive down Highway 85 to Charlotte, North Carolina. We spent almost every weekend together during my freshmen year. She was slowly becoming my favorite pastime instead of basketball, and it was showing. My grades were slipping and my professors weren't easy on me about it. Professor Knight, my Statistics teacher, stayed on me about study hall; it seemed like she wanted me there everyday, but I wasn't having it.

There were only two things that mattered to me: basketball and Tiffany. Forget study hall. I had just gotten my freedom back from attending Hargrave Military Academy. I transferred from Glen High School to Hargrave so I could get my SAT score up. If I didn't do that I wouldn't have been accepted into Wake Forest. Everything they were trying to instill in me at Wake Forest was already done at Hargrave. I was disciplined, had morals, and knew how and when to study, all because of the academy. I didn't need Professor Knight all on my case. I had it under control, or so I thought.

"Wake Forest was a whole new ball game," I said to my friends. "For one, Wake Forest was a private college and athletes were required to have higher GPAs and SAT scores than other colleges. Basketball practice was daily, sometimes twice a day, plus I had to have my grades in order. With Tiffany in the picture it just didn't add up. I was more focused on what she was doing than my schoolwork. I can't believe I was caught up like that. Then later on that year, she ended up dumping me for another guy. I guess she wasn't getting enough attention."

"I'm glad she dumped you. We might not be here today if you would've kept trying to follow behind her," Rob yelled out interrupting me.

"Yeah I guess, but who did she think she was dumping, me?" I sarcastically replied.

"Speaking of girls, you know who I did like for you?" Rob said.

"Who?"

"Erika, your other girlfriend that went to Winston-Salem State University."

All of my friends immediately chimed in saying how much they liked and admired her, too. I looked around at them, thinking was she that good? Erika was a different type of woman. She was a year older and a little more seasoned than me. She kept me in check and made sure I had my priorities in order. If I had a test coming up, she would make sure I was studying and never distracted me. If I had an upcoming game, she would encourage me to practice more; but the most important quality about Erika is that she listened. After a stressful game or when I thought my coach was coming down on me too hard, she was always there to talk. She didn't hold back one bit, she always told me the raw, uncut truth.

"She sounds like wife material." Rob said.

"She was. Those are the type of women you need around you; a true support system and somebody who would shoot with you in the gym," I replied.

"You went through so much these past four years. I'm just happy you didn't enter the draft two years ago; you might not have made it," Derrick said. I flirted with the thought of not graduating, entering the draft, and playing for the Philadelphia 76ers; but God had a different plan for me. I sprained my ankle that year and there was no way I was going to the NBA without a full recovery. You hear stories all the time about players not finishing college, getting hurt their first year, and never hearing from them again. People refer to them as a "one-and-done."

Spraining my ankle that year actually worked out for me. I was able to properly heal, train for the next season, plus have one of my best games ever against North Carolina State. I'll never forget that game; everybody doubted us and had us at the bottom of the barrel for the tournament. We knew they were going to play us hard, and they gave us a fight. They were beating us by 10 all the way up to the last five minutes of the game, but then something came over me that said: *It's either now or never!* I started thinking of what Coach Poser always told me when he decided to make me the leader of the team. "Don't just be a 3:00 p.m. - 6:00 p.m. leader, which was the time we had practice, but be a 6:00 p.m.-3:00 p.m. leader," meaning to be a leader on the court and off the court. During halftime I explained to my teammates what we had to do if we wanted to win this game because N.C. State was killing us.

The Reynolds Coliseum was packed to the capacity and the energy was all in favor of N.C. State. But in a blink of an eye, the last five minutes of the game became the Josh Howard and Wake Forest show. I scored 27 points, including six free throws in the final 1.7 seconds. The New York Times said *"Howard was clutch once again, going for 8 for 10 from the field and 8 of 8 from the free-throw line."* The crowd got so upset, they started throwing trash on the floor during the game. It was insane. It was the most intense college game I ever had. Thinking about that game made me think about the ongoing quote again. How can they say "I do everything good, but nothing great" with a game like that - it was unfair. "Josh when you get picked, remember to keep some of your thoughts to yourself; don't forget about when the Winston-Salem Journal misquoted you about the war in Iraq," my teammate, Brian, said while still eating on the porch.

That was probably one of the most controversial things that happened to me at Wake Forest. My big mouth got me in trouble with our coach and the whole Winston-

Salem city. I remember the day Coach Poser called us in for a meeting. I thought it was a meeting about our next game or how we performed in our previous game. "Yeah, I remember that day we walked into the gym and coach just came out and said it," Brian said. *"So team, Josh made a few comments in the paper that has the town up in arms about him right now, so everybody try to avoid giving any interviews."*

I was shocked and confused. I read the paper and it said a lot of great things about me, but when I got to the bottom it said "Howard Opposes War!" It was in reference to the 9/11 attacks and the ongoing war in Iraq. After the article was printed, I couldn't believe all of the comments and hate mail I received from people in Winston-Salem. This was my hometown. *"You're not supposed to say that," "We need to fight," "You should stay an athlete and not a student,"* were a few of the statements. You can't put me in a box. I'm a student too and I happen to attend one of the best universities in America; I have an opinion. Reading those comments drove me to study even harder.

Just before the article hit the newsstands, I coincidently changed my major to Religion. I grew up in church and the 9/11 attacks made me interested in other religions. I just couldn't wrap my head around somebody committing a heinous crime like that. A lot of athletes majored in Sociology or Communications and I didn't want to be a part of the big pile up. Brian chimed in, "Now that I think about it, you'll probably have media training and they'll teach you how to deal with journalists and their sideways questions." I wasn't that upset with the media because they covered a lot of my greatest moments, even the ones that weren't basketball related. Before graduating, my coach called me into the athletic department to sign a few papers for graduation, but it was all a ploy. When I arrived in his office, news cameras, my mom, friends and a few others surprised me with a "Joshua Howard Day" at my school. It was surreal.

It seemed like all of the moments we were discussing was preparing me for my future. Something told me to go back in the house to see what was going on with the draft. "Glad you came back in baby, they just cut to commercial, but the last pick of the first round is coming up," my mom said. It was down to the last straw. What was I going to do if I didn't get picked? This can't happen to me. But I still wasn't losing my faith. I know God didn't bring me this far just to leave me stuck at this point. Finally, it was back on. The lights were shining down on David Stern as he walked to the podium in front of the energetic audience as he prepared to announce the last pick of the first round. He took a deep breath as the camera's zoomed in on him. "With the last and 29th pick of the 2003 NBA draft, the Dallas Mavericks have chosen Joshua Howard of Wake Forest University!"

Before Stern could even say "Howard," shouts from my family erupted throughout the house. Pictures were falling off the wall and food was spilling off of plates as everybody screamed with joy. You would have thought it was an earthquake in the middle of Winston-Salem. The first thing I did was hug my mom and grandmother, not wanting to let them go as I embraced them. They've supported me since I was a child playing basketball. They kept me grounded throughout these last years and helped me decipher all of the fakes and phonies that were coming my way because of my status. Thank God I went to a school in the city that raised me. My friends were there to keep me humble and my Grandma was always there to tell me the truth no matter the circumstance.

My whole life flashed before my eyes that day. I remember as a child my legs were so severely bowlegged that my doctors had to break them in order to reset them and make them grow straight. It was a possibility that I would never play basketball and now I was about to play in the NBA. To this day, I still think the doctors put some sort of power in my legs because after that surgery, basketball was all I thought about. I never would've thought I would go from almost being handicapped to being a professional basketball player.

The next day I packed my bags and headed to the Greensboro airport. I couldn't believe my eyes, Mark Cuban sent out a private jet just for me. Once I entered the plane and realized my life was about to change forever I decided I was going take everything I learned in college and apply it at Dallas. This was my gift to them for giving me the gift to play professional basketball. If it wasn't for the Dallas Mavericks there's no telling where I would be.

Lesson Learned: When you're the star player, remain focused because distractions can appear from anywhere. Those four years in college can really make or break your future. The choices you make can be so easy, but can be so devastating if you make the wrong ones. Your morals and values are going to form you to be the person that you are. I was never disrespectful to anyone and I never went looking for trouble, that's how I stayed out of it. Don't let anybody run over you. Always think about your goals when making a choice and if it might hurt your goal, try your best to avoid it. You have too much to lose.

There will be a lot of people coming in your life who don't belong there; if you see they're deterring you from your purpose, let them go. They're nothing but wolves in sheep's clothing. My relationship with Tiffany could have deterred me from making it in the NBA. Be careful in your relationships, only a few are golden and the others are just lessons. Keep positive people around you because, believe it or not, there are people who want to see you fail. Negative thinking does nothing for you; when a negative thought comes in your mind block it out and replace it with a positive one. I did that when I kept hearing the analyst say negative statements about me during the draft. Experts can be wrong. Experts built the titanic and it sunk, but amateurs built the Ark and it floated. Don't let those negative labels seep in. Your thoughts eventually manifest, so always keep the positive outcome in your mind.

Coach Poser told me to be a 6:00 p.m. - 3:00 p.m. guy and that has stuck with me since. Don't just do your best in school, basketball practice, work, or your career, but be paramount all the time. With that mindset, you will get much farther than you can imagine. I was blessed enough to have a "Joshua Howard Day" in my hometown of Winston-Salem, North Carolina, a street named after me, and much more. Always remember where you came from and give back to the community. Once you give back, it will come back to you tenfold. The greatest gift I ever gave was starting my Joshua Howard Foundation in my hometown; no amount of money can compare to the smiles I see on those kids' faces. Never be selfish because it will only hurt you. There's enough room in the universe for everybody to be successful; you just have to find your purpose.

Everybody is not meant to be a professional athlete, so make sure you have a Plan B. Only 1.3% of college basketball players make it to the NBA,[8] so you have to work extremely hard if you want to make it. Never give up; if it keeps you up at night and stays on your mind from sun up to sun down, then that's your purpose. Learn all of the ins and outs of your passion until it's manifested in your life. I've been extremely blessed to play for the Dallas Mavericks and go to the 2006

NBA championship with them. I was an All-Star in 2007, invited to be on team USA for the Olympics in 2008, and also played for the Washington Wizards, Utah Jazz and the Minnesota Timberwolves, which all came from hard work and dedication.

Chapter 11: Co-Sign

Sitting patiently in the financial aid office, I prayed a miracle would happen. I watched as the secretary scrolled through my files. Pushing her gray locks away from her glasses, she looked me straight in the eyes.

"I'm sorry Cameron, but without a cosigner for your Sallie Mae loan, you won't be able to enroll for spring semester."

"What!" I yelled.

"I'm sorry, baby."

"Are you serious? So, after two and a half years of attending Florida A&M (FAMU), there's a chance I may not graduate?"

"Well, you have one option. Last semester you received a $1,986.00 refund check. Do you have any funds left from that? If so, we can put it towards next semester."

"Refund check? I wish I did, but that money went to bills," I replied, knowing I was lying. I didn't spend my refund check on bills. I spent it on clothes and taking trips to other schools for homecoming.

"I understand, but I'm sure you can find somebody to cosign. Can't you?" she asked.

I barged through the financial aid office. It was only 9:00 a.m. and my world was upside down. Tiny drops of rain trickled down my face as I walked on campus thinking about my options. *Should I move back to Miami? Work at a local retail store or maybe trade school?* I didn't plan on leaving Tallahassee until I graduated; this couldn't have come at a worse time. I had recently spent $600.00 to self-publish my second book *Farewell to the Game*. Not to mention, my friend;

Antonio and I were almost done with the day-to-day hurdles of joining the Alpha Phi Alpha Fraternity. If I wanted to sell any books, Florida A&M would be the best place to start. With over 12,000 students, I could make a killing and possibly pay for school.

I had a total of five loans, three in my name and my father cosigned the other two. So maybe this time he'll cosign for me again. He wasn't the easiest guy to convince, especially when it came to money. Every time I asked him for something, it was like pulling teeth. He cosigned all of my sister's loans, but wouldn't cosign mine. Elena was his favorite child and I was an outcast. She graduated from Florida A&M two years prior with no financial obligations. Her loans were approved every year, but for me it was a constant struggle. Elena had a house off campus and a brand new Altima, but I lived in an apartment and drove a Dodge Intrepid that was close to breaking down.

I was too depressed to drive home. Classes were letting out and I didn't want everybody staring at my car as I drove by. The muffler was so loud you could hear it before you saw it. My sister always said nobody cared about my car; I was in college so it was understandable. Plus, I was 6'2, with waves in my low haircut, so that made up for it in the female department. Making a quick detour, I stopped past Antonio's room to deliver the bad news.

"Why do you have fake flowers in an empty Grey Goose bottle? Is this your idea of a vase?" I asked with a grin while sitting at Antonio's dining room table.

"That's how I impress the ladies, you know I'm smooth with it," he said with a snicker.

Antonio glanced at me and I knew he could see the frustration on my face.

"What's wrong with you? Your dog just died or something? You should be happy. Finals are over and tomorrow it's back to Miami for winter break! We're going back to Overtown for the holidays." Overtown was the neighborhood we grew up in.

"I know, but I might be going back for good."

"What do you mean for good?"

"I didn't get approved for my loan because I don't have a cosigner."

"Did you ask your dad or mom?"

"Not yet, but I have a feeling he's going to say no and my mom isn't in the position to do that."

"Try to think positive, you never know what he's going to say. We're supposed to be pledging in the spring and I don't want to be alone. There's no telling what they might do to me," he said. I laughed at Antonio, but on the inside I was hurting. I really wanted to become an Alpha. My sister was an AKA and my girlfriend was in the process of becoming an AKA. Everything seemed to be going great. The Alphas invited us to parties, football games, and basketball games. I had hope, but in the back of my mind I knew my dad would probably say no.

Rain poured into the streets as I left campus. Luckily, the thunder and lightning made everybody stay inside, relieving me of my car embarrassment. My stomach was in knots as I scrolled through my iPhone searching for my dad's number. How was I going to convince him? I hated asking him for money; now I was asking him to cosign a $9,000.00 loan.

"Hey, Cameron. To what do I owe this phone call?" he asked.

"Nothing, just ran in the house to avoid the rain. It's raining cats and dogs out here."

"Why are you in the house, shouldn't you be in class?"

"Yeah, I actually wanted to talk to you about that," I replied.

"I'm listening," he said in a weary voice. "Cameron, are you there?"

I gathered my thoughts.

"Yes sir. Well, in a nutshell I didn't get approved for my loan because I didn't have a cosigner."

"I see."

"I wanted to know if you would cosign for me?"

"I'm sorry son, but you know I can't do that."

"Why not, you cosigned everything for Elena!"

"Elena is a different story, Cameron....."

"What do you mean a different story? Last time I checked, we had the same mother and father. You cosigned her loans and paid for her to have a house off campus, but wouldn't let me live there after she graduated. That doesn't make any sense!"

"Cameron, you just don't get it. You're not mature enough and I can't trust you."

Hanging up the phone, I didn't want to hear anything else he had to say. The hell with him.

What does he mean I'm not mature enough? I've been in college for three years and haven't failed once. I didn't get anybody pregnant, well, let me take that back. I haven't had any children or gotten in trouble. He still hasn't gotten over me getting locked up in high school for selling drugs. I did my time, learned my lesson, and now I was trying to change my life for the better. Sure, I made a few mistakes here and there, but I've been on a straight path for three years.

I didn't go to any classes that day, but I did go to work. At least Bank of America was paying me. When I got home from work I dropped my books on the floor, put my cell phone on the nightstand and collapsed right in my bed. I was exhausted, but before I could attempt to close my eyes my phone rang. *Was this my dad calling back? Did he change his mind?*

"Hello," I answered.

"Eww, I can smell your breath from over here."

"Amber?"

"Yes, its Amber, who else would it be? You didn't look at your caller ID?"

"I'm so tired I didn't bother to look."

Amber was my girlfriend who I met at Spelman University's homecoming in Atlanta, Georgia during our sophomore year. She went to Auburn University in Alabama, but she was from Miami too. Tomorrow she was meeting me at my school, so we could follow each other to Miami for winter break. I could tell she was in a good mood. I didn't want to bring her spirits down, but I had to tell her what was going on.

"So, ah, I have to tell you something," I murmured.

"What is it now Cam? (Cam was my nickname that a few of my friends and family called me for short)

"Relax, it has nothing to do with us. Well, I don't think it will affect us."

"I'm listening."

"I don't have a cosigner for my loan, so I won't be in school next year."

"Are you serious? Please tell me you're joking."

"I wish I was joking."

"I wish I could do something. Let me guess; your father said no?"

"Yup, but I'm not even surprised."

Unexpectedly, the phone disconnected. Before I could call back, she was FaceTiming me on her iPhone. I accepted the call and there she was, with her beautiful brown skin, favoring a young Kerry Washington. Saddened by the news, she sat on the bed in her all pink Victoria Secret onesie with her bottom lip poked out.

"Babe, I don't want you to go home," she replied in a baby voice.

"Wait a minute, does this mean you're going to be in Miami next year?" she asked.

"Huh, yeah," I somberly replied.

"Cam, we're already three hours away from each other, but Miami is 10!"

"I know, I know, but at least we'll have December and some of January together," I replied, trying to downplay the situation.

"Don't be messing around with none of them girls! I swear, if I find out something, it's over," she said jokingly, but deep down inside I knew she was serious.

Arriving in Miami, I could smell the beach in the air as we drove on I-95 South. Riding through the city, I missed the bright lights and tall skyscrapers. It was beautiful; but my side of town was far from glamorous. I lived in the slums of Miami, where some people wouldn't dare to go. Unloading my bags from the car, I still couldn't believe I was back for good. Amber helped me unpack while my grandparents prepared dinner. When I was 13 I moved from my parents house in Opa-Locka, Florida to live with my grandparents in Overtown. At a young age my parents and I didn't see eye to eye, but Elena still lived with them. My grandmother and I were like best friends. Grandma's living room was filled with pictures, and biblical paintings. With only two bedrooms and one bath, our house was far from big; but it was home.

"Grams you didn't have to cook for us," I said.

"Yes I did, now sit down and eat. I cooked your favorite: steak with baked potatoes and salad. It looks like you've been starving yourself; eat up," she replied while laughing with Amber.

"So how you been?" my grandmother asked.

"I've been good, Granny."

"Look at your boyfriend, Amber. He's worried sick that he won't return to school. I can see it all over his face."

"I know, I feel so bad for him," Amber replied.

"Don't you feel bad for him; he's going back to school. Everything will work out."

"Grams," I uttered.

"Don't you Grams me. I've told you time and time again that you got to have faith."

My grandmother was a firm believer in God. I never understood how her faith was so strong when right outside of her door were drug dealers, murderers, and racist police officers. Not to mention my uncle, who lived around the corner was addicted to drugs. When I was younger, I sold my cousin and uncle crack cocaine, which didn't allow me to have much faith. Maybe my grandmother knew something I didn't. But, being back in Miami, what little faith I had was vanishing.

The next morning, I walked around the corner to visit my uncle. I hadn't seen him in a few months, but much hadn't changed. He was still sitting in his favorite chair watching reruns of *Sanford and Son*, drinking moonshine out of a mason jar. He wasn't a man of many words. He asked about school, but that usually led to him asking me for cocaine. I hadn't sold drugs in three years, but yet he still asked. If I wanted to make some extra money, I always knew I had two loyal customers, my uncle and cousin. I remember telling Amber about my drug dealing past and she didn't understand how I could sell my family poison. If they were dumb enough to destroy themselves, then why not; but deep down inside, I knew my reasoning was ridiculous. While I was sitting on the couch, my phone rang; it was Antonio. This must be important because it's 8:30 a.m. and he never calls this early.

"Man, you won't believe this. You know grades came out today?"

"I completely forgot. How did you do?" I asked.

"I did good. I got a 3.5, but I thought my cumulative GPA would rise to a 3.0. It only went to a 2.87."

"That's not bad, why are you stressing? Everybody knows it's hard to get your cumulative GPA up if you didn't do good your freshmen year."

"Yeah I know, but you have to have a 3.0 cumulative GPA to join the fraternity, so I won't be able to join this year."

"Dang, so you and I are basically in the same boat with the Alphas."

"Yeah, basically," he replied.
Antonio didn't have the grades and I wasn't in school. The chances of me joining the fraternity were getting slimmer and slimmer by the second.

Leaving my Uncle's house, my friend Rashad pulled up in his 1972 red Chevrolet Impala convertible with 26-inch Donk rims. This car was a classic, a staple in Miami. If you had one, all the guys admired you and all of the ladies wanted to be with you.

"Cam!" he yelled as his pipes roared from the car. "You back in town for the holidays?"

"Man, I'm back for good."

"Are you serious? What happened?"

"My student loans didn't work out, so I'm back."

"My man back in town. Hop in, I'm about to go over one of my girls house. She got a roommate too if you want to go."

"Nah man, you know I got Amber. We're going out tonight and I don't want to hear her mouth."

"Lover boy, Cam! I respect it. Just hit me later," he said. I hadn't been home for a full 24 hours and temptation was already knocking at my door. Rashad was my sister's ex-boyfriend, but he was like a big brother to me. When I was in high school, he taught me everything; from girls, drugs, sports, and much more. I even lived with him for a few years during my troubled high school days.

During the next few weeks, I was with Amber almost every day and in between I was with Rashad helping him hustle a plethora of things. I didn't work at Bank of America anymore, so I needed money and I needed it fast. My uncle was my first customer once I got back in the swing of things. It was so easy to sell drugs; I asked myself why I ever stopped. Amber never knew when I was with Rashad. If she did, she would completely flip. She knew the type of things Rashad was into, but I kept her far away from that. In her eyes, the only thing I was selling was my book, not drugs or any other schemes Rashad had up his sleeves. Amber and her mother were my biggest supporters. When I had my book signing at Dadeland Mall, they stayed from beginning to end. I was even able to place my book in three stores.

Amber was set to leave for college in two days, so I treated her to dinner at Prime 112, a high-end restaurant on South Beach. Sitting on the outside patio, the candles burning created a romantic ambiance for us.

"You didn't have to do this, baby," she said.

"It's ok, I wanted us to enjoy our last days together."

"You're acting like we're breaking up or something," she said.

"Breaking up? We're at Prime 112, we better not be breaking up. Do you see how expensive this menu is?" I said as she laughed.

"This is interesting," she said inquisitively.

"What is?"

"Where did you get the money to pay for this? You haven't sold that many damn books. You've been taking me out frequently and you don't have a job. You don't have to waste your money on me."

Her response is one of the main reasons I fell in love with her. She was selfless and never scolded me for not having enough money. I knew she was on to me, but I wasn't going to tell the truth. She may call things off if she found out I was back selling drugs. But before I could explain she let me have it.

"I hope you're not going back to your old ways, especially to impress me," she said. "You don't have to do that." Taking a bite of my steak, I looked down at my plate avoiding eye contact.

"Of course not, I've just been using my credit card," I replied nonchalantly.

"Your credit card! Why would you do that when you already owe American Eagle and Nordstrom's? Cam, stop lying to me!" she yelled.

"What are you talking about?"

"I'm not stupid. These Aldo shoes, Bond #9 perfume, and everything else you bought me wasn't purchased with a credit card. Hell, the Bond #9 perfume was at least $250.00."

"I didn't hear you complaining when I was giving you the gifts."

"That's not the point! I don't want you behind bars! You're going to be in Miami for a while and I don't want you going down the wrong path. It's only been a month and you're already making bad decisions."

"What do you want me to do? Get a job at Target or something? Do you know how that's going to look? First I'm in college, now I'm working at Target."

"You don't have to work at Target; you can transfer to a Bank of America. Your book signing was just a week ago. Are you giving up that quick?"

"I'm not giving up, but this money is coming quicker than my book sales!"

Amber shook her head in disbelief. I tried to apologize on the way home, but she didn't want to hear it. She stayed with me that night, but we hardly talked. The next morning, she packed her bags, only giving me a kiss goodbye.

Our conversations became shorter and shorter throughout the next months. There was already tension, but adding to that was our conflicting schedules. While she was in class, I would be running the streets with Rashad. Even though Amber and I didn't speak often, we were still a couple, so I resisted the urge of dating other females. Rashad consistently had females around; every time I turned one down, he looked at me like I was crazy. Sometimes I asked myself was I crazy?

Spring break was here and South Beach was packed with college students from all over. Seeing the students having the times of their lives made me miss Florida A&M. While Rashad and I were walking on South Beach, we spotted our friend Carrie and my ex-girlfriend Mya. Mya wasn't in college, but whenever Carrie came home from school, we would occasionally run into each other. I could see them smiling and laughing with a look of shock when they realized it was us. "What are the chances of us seeing Mya right here on the beach? Seems like destiny to me," Rashad said with a grin on his face. I was face-to-face with my ex, one of my first loves. *What was I to do?*

"Mr. Cameron, what a surprise. I didn't expect to see you here," Mya said smiling

"You two still up to no good huh?" Carrie said with a grin.

Without notice, Rashad grabbed Carrie's arm and walked off, leaving Mya and I alone. *Dammit Rashad, this guy won't stop until I'm caught and Amber has me six feet under.* Mya still looked good. Her long black hair with brown highlights lay perfectly over her brown skin. She also gained weight in all the right places. Her black and white bikini showed off every inch perfectly. We talked for hours, reminiscing about old times and drinking frozen daiquiris from Wet Willie's while sitting on the beach. It seemed like we were picking up right where we left, but Amber was still running rampant through my mind.

We all decided to party at Club Mansion that night, but the club was filled to capacity. The line circled the corner, but Rashad and Carrie were determined to get in. I looked at Mya and could tell she didn't want to stand in line, so I saw the opportunity and took it.

"You and Carrie go in; I'm going to take Mya to one of the other bars," I whispered to Rashad.

"That's what I'm talking about, handle that," Rashad said.

"Let's go to The Clevelander," I said to Mya.
Sitting down at the bar, it seemed like she had a whole list of questions ready.

"So, what's been up Cameron? I know a handsome guy like you isn't single."

"Actually I am." *I couldn't' believe I lied that quick.*

"That's not what I saw on Facebook. What's her name, Amber right?" she said with a smirk.

"You're on Facebook? I've never seen you on there. Are we friends?" I calmly asked, but on the inside I was shook.

"That's not what I asked you, but no, I'm not on Facebook. I logon to Carrie's page sometimes."

"Oh, so you're stalking me?"

"Boy, please! Nobody is stalking you. You're a great guy and I still think you're cute, but if you have a girlfriend, we can only be friends."

"It's complicated."

"Mmhmm, whatever," she said with a smile.

"Enough about me, what about you? What have you been up to?" I asked.

"Nothing really. I work at Best Buy for now. I wanted to go to college, but it's too expensive."

"Yeah believe me, I know. Didn't you have a baby?"

"Yeah, he's 2 now; you should come meet him one day."

Almost choking on my drink from the thought of playing daddy to another child made me realize Mya might not be the one for me. I thought I would give it a try, but now I wasn't sure. She has a child, still lives at home, and works at Best Buy. She was the exact opposite of Amber who works at Victoria Secrets part-time, is a full-time student majoring in Accounting, and now a member of the AKA sorority. There's no way I'm letting her go. We could remain friends, but that's it. If Amber knew we were friends, she would kill me. I dropped Mya off at home and called Amber immediately.

"Babe, we need to talk."

"About what? I can't really talk right now, what's wrong?" she replied seeming distracted

"I don't want to lose you, I miss you."

"I miss you too. I'm sorry I have to go, babe" she replied while rudely hanging up the phone.

Did she just hang up on me?

Amber's new behavior was becoming a pattern; she never had time to talk until it was late and when we did she would fall asleep. Depression started to come over me. It seemed like I was losing everything, college, my girlfriend, and the future I thought I was going to have. *Did Amber think less of me because I wasn't in college? She probably wasn't thinking about me at all.* When I walked into the house after talking to Amber, my Grandmother was sitting on the couch watching reruns of The Golden Girls. Flopping down on the couch, I let out a huge sigh.

"Don't worry baby, your time is coming," my grandma said.

"Grandma, please, not now. Not the church speech."

"Just be patient, baby. Stay on the right track and don't slip. They say just before you're about to break is when everything begins to work itself out. Please be careful," she said grabbing my hand.

Did she have a sixth sense? Did she see me selling drugs? I lay in bed pondering about my future and Mya being a possibility. Mya was cute and the chemistry was there, but would she add or subtract from my life? Does she have goals? Does she have ambition for anything greater? What's her passion and does she realize her purpose? Leaving Amber for her would be one of the worst decisions ever, just stupid. I felt embarrassed. My friends in college were progressing while I was stagnant. Every time I talked to Amber, I felt like the biggest bum in the world. Riding around with Rashad every day, smoking weed, selling drugs, and not doing anything with my life was counterproductive. That night, I got down on my knees and let it all out. I told God everything on my mind and asked for total forgiveness.

God must have heard my cry. The following week the financial aid office from Florida A&M called to let me know that classes were being offered this summer and I could pay in cash. *Was this the blessing Grandma was talking about? Was she telling me to be patient for this?* I started weighing my options. My roommate Joseph was still at our two-bedroom apartment, so I could move back in. I was in good standing with Bank of America and could possibly earn my job back. Amber also got an internship in Tallahassee and needed somewhere to stay that summer; of course she was staying with me. But there was one problem. I could pay for summer classes with cash, but how would I afford the following semester?

Summer time was here and I was back on campus, working at Bank of America part time and living with my favorite girl, Amber. I took Statistics, Computer Technology 1 & 2, and Business Management, which were the core classes for my major, Computer Science. Sallie Mae wouldn't approve my loan without a cosigner, so I started researching other loans. To my surprise, my own bank, Navy Federal, approved my loan without a cosigner. To top it off, during the summer I moved in with Antonio and our other friend Rico in a three bedroom, one car garage house. The following year, I completed all of my classes and graduated that summer. I endured my semester off and the weight had been completely lifted off my shoulders-and I did it all without a cosigner.

Lesson Learned: If you haven't graduated from high school yet, please study and work hard. I promise it'll pay off. In retrospect, if I had better grades in high school, I could've received a scholarship and paid for college. It might have been partial or a full scholarship, but any amount helps. Scholarships ease the stress of having to apply for loans and the obligations of paying them back. The only reason I got accepted into college was because of my sister. When I received my acceptance letter my father said he would handle it, but I didn't know the loans were in my name. I thought he was being a great dad and paying for it himself; but no, I was. Do your research when applying for loans and ask as many questions as possible. When Navy Federal approved my loan, I sat in the bank for hours, so I could fully understand the process. Google anything you may not understand and don't hesitate to ask the financial aid office any questions. A few student loan terms to know are forbearance, deferment, loan consolidation, default, loan forgiveness, income driven payment plans, and interest rates. For example, my loan was $9,000.00, but because of the interest, my total was $14,000.00.

If I would have saved my refund check, I could have paid for part of my spring semester. Refund checks are the amount of excess financial aid remaining after your total cost for college (tuition, fees and books). In short, it's the money left over from your loan after everything has been paid for. Students can receive checks that range from $1.00 to $3,000.00 or more. That's still money you owe, so the smart thing to do would be to pay it back. Know your options and cause and effects, and do not get tangled into the credit card lifestyle. It will only hurt you in the end. I had an American Eagle and Nordstrom credit card that both ended up on my credit report along with my student loans.

Co-Sign

Always keep God at the forefront of your journey. My grandmother told me everything would work out if I had faith and it did. To this day, I still believe that and everything always works out in the end. I slipped back to my old ways once I went back to Miami. Making mistakes is a part of life and with each trial you'll learn a lesson, but you have to make an effort to get back on track. Please know that you're not alone; there are more people in college now than ever, which means debt is also high. Student debt surpassed $1 trillion by the end of the second quarter of 2014, making it the second largest category of household debt.[9]

Get a support system if you don't have one; mine was my grandmother and Amber. She was such a great girlfriend. I didn't have to impress her with gifts during that time because she understood my situation. Make sure your significant other is somebody who's there for you during the ups and downs and pushes you to be the best you can be. Amber is now my wife and we have two healthy kids together. I'm still paying on my student loans, but I've paid off a significant amount. I'm more than blessed.

Tips:
1. Choose the best repayment plan that works for you.
2. If you can't afford to make payments when you graduate, choose to defer or forbear your loans. When you defer, your repayment temporarily stops and the government pays the interest on your loans during that period of time. Forbearance requires you to pay interest on your loans no matter which loans you have.
3. Join a loan forgiveness program where you can volunteer for certain programs that will reduce part of

your loans. The Peace Corps, military, or working for low-income school districts or hospitals are all a part of the loan forgiveness program. You also qualify for loan forgiveness if you work for a public service.

4. Utilize the grace period. You have six months before you have to make payments, so create a strategy for your payment plan. Those six months will be over before you know it.

5. Consolidate your loans; this puts all of your loans together into one lump sum with one interest rate, which means you will only have to worry about checking one payment and not several like I did.

6. Make sure your payments are on time. A delinquent account can affect your credit score, cause your wages to be garnished, and lead to the IRS withholding your tax refund.

7. Always pay more when you can; this will eventually add up and you'll be thanking yourself for doing so once you've finished paying off your loans.

8. For more info, go to studentaid.ed.gov.

Chapter 12: Quarterbook Sneak

"The Dean and Board of Student Services have decided to expel Wayne Barnes, Kent Davis, and Ronald Lyons from the Texas Smith A&M University (TSAM) football team until further notice, including a full withdraw from your athletic scholarships. You can enroll back in school the following semester, pay the full price, and potentially earn your scholarship back; but it's not guaranteed." When Dean Johnson read the final decision for our fate as college students and football players, only one question came to mind. *How the hell did I end up here?* Me, Kent, and Ronald were sitting in front of the Dean, The Board of Student Services, our parents, and the chief of security for stealing some damn books. Listening to the Dean was like hearing nails on a chalkboard. I glanced at Kent and couldn't believe this huge 5'11, 300-pound lineman was sitting in his wooden chair crying like the biggest Cabbage Patch doll I had ever seen. It was his idea to begin with. I went from being the star football player in high school to one of the best running backs at Texas Smith A&M. Now, I'm being expelled during my junior year for a petty book crime. I guess attempting to steal over $10,000.00 in book money wasn't petty at all.

I stood there in shock as my parents held their heads down with disappointment. I couldn't bear to look at my mom once the tears started to come. I remember standing in the middle of the Texas Smith A&M football stadium, talking on the phone to her on the first day of practice. "Good luck today, son. You've come a long way and you're finally getting your chance, so make it count," she said. She was right; it had been a long time coming. I've been playing football since I was 10 years old and I almost didn't make it into college due to my C-average and 800 SAT score. Those stats alone made me unqualified to attend TSAM; when I found out I wasn't accepted I was more than devastated.

I was the star running back at Lamar High School in Houston, Texas and we were good; actually, we were better than good. We were great! Our record during my senior year was 12-1. College recruiters came from all over to see me play. I had opportunities to attend other colleges, but I wanted to attend Texas Smith A&M from the first time I visited. I remember taking a tour of the Texas Smith A&M sports facility in the 12th grade, I noticed a vintage photo of Wayne Barnes, a Texas Smith A&M football hall of famer. We had the exact first and last name, so I took it as a sign from God that I was meant to go there. I was a key player at my high school and I was unstoppable on the field. I was Wayne "The Animal" Barnes, standing at 6'0, 215 pounds all muscle. I was an untamed beast.

The only thing stopping me was my academics; if my grades were up to par, I would've received a full athletic scholarship. But my grades were average, so I had to settle for Billin Community College. I was determined to play football for Texas Smith A&M. With persistence, I lead Billin to the playoffs; combined with my 3.5 cumulative GPA, I was accepted into Texas Smith A&M the following year with a full scholarship.

Coming in as a sophomore made me ineligible to start, so I was placed on second string. I wasn't disappointed; I was just happy to make it out of Houston, Texas. My biggest fear in life was succumbing to the environment around me and not amounting to anything. Growing up in Sunnyside, one of the most dangerous neighborhoods in Houston, was no joke. I was more than grateful to receive a full scholarship; lord knows if I didn't, I wouldn't have attended. My parents barely made enough to pay the bills; taking out a $38,000.00 loan was out of the question. The head coach watched my highlight tapes over and over; he knew, with a little practice, I would go on the field and dominate. I didn't have any real problems; my only concern was football and keeping money in my pocket. Yearly, TSAM makes over 100 million dollars in revenue due to their sports teams. You would think we would get an incentive for our talents, but we received nothing, not a dime.

Kent and I were like brothers; we both started off at Bellin Community College with the purpose of attending TSAM the following year. I knew about Kent in high school; he played for Westfield High School as the star center and was from the 3rd Ward neighborhood. We both started on second string and eventually worked our way up to starters. When you saw him, you saw me. We were like Frit and Frat, Batman and Robin, or, even worse, Pinky and the Brain. Sadly to say, I was Pinky in most of Kent's schemes.

We were cut from the same cloth, poor and willing to go the extra mile to make a few dollars. We couldn't afford to get jobs, especially during football season. Classes were all day, practice wasn't over until 7:00 p.m., we had homework, and, even worse, we were on curfew. We didn't need money to buy clothes or materialistic items; we needed money for minimal tasks, such as washing clothes, buying food, or bus fare to the mall. We were broke!

I remember the day all of the foolishness started. Kent created the "Young Men of Empowerment Organization" (YMOEO) on campus, but it wasn't a legit organization. We never registered the organization with the college. We created the organization as a way to make money and it was genius. Twice a month we would walk around the dorms asking for donations towards YMOEO. We called them "Penny Drives."

All of the organizations, including Fraternities, Sororities, and The Student Government Association held "Penny Drives." It didn't matter how much you donated as long as it was at least 1 cent or whatever you felt you wanted to give. We made $212.15 during our first penny drive. We only walked through the female dorms because we played football, so we knew the girls would donate a lot more than guys. It was also a chance for us to meet hundreds of females in one day.

Kent and I did so well our sophomore year playing football, we were put as starters our junior year. We both had jobs over the summer, but once school started we were broke again. But Kent had another grand scheme up his sleeve. I sometimes wondered where he got these ideas from, but I never asked. If his ideas were putting money in my pocket, I went along with it.

Lying down with my girlfriend, Lauren, in my gigantic black beanbag, looking at pictures on Facebook, Kent came bursting into my room.

"I got it! This is the plan," he yelled.

Oh lord. I said to myself while staring at him pacing back and forth in my room.

"We're going to steal books from the bookstore and return them to get cash," he said.

"Wayne, remember when Texas Tech tried to pull that quarterback sneak move on us, but they couldn't even make a first down?"

"Yeah I remember, but what in the hell does that have to do with this?" I asked.

With a devious smile on his face while rubbing his hands together, he turned and looked at Lauren and me and said, "I'm calling this scheme 'QuarterBook Sneak!'"

Lauren and I couldn't stop laughing; he had taken it too far this time.

"Wayne before you look at me crazy, remember Vivian use to work in the bookstore. She told me everything about how the store works."

"Yeah, so," I said, still looking at him like he was crazy. Vivian was his girlfriend, but that still didn't mean this plan would work.

"I know you think I am crazy, but remember there are no cameras in the book store. This will work!" I wasn't sure if it would work or not, but I knew the last time I checked my bank account, it was only $20.00 in there. That wasn't enough for gas!

Kent was a nut, but I trusted Vivian's word; during our summer break she worked at the local Whole Foods market and we would get free groceries regularly. It was easy. Vivian would scan a few items and skip over the others. Juice, candy, cereal, steak, shrimp, and even lobster were stacked in our baskets every time we went. We never paid $20.00 for our groceries. She and Kent were a match made in klepto heaven. It was only the second week of school and we were already conniving, but in order to get full price for the books, we had to strike now.

The following day I walked into bookstore dressed in a pair of Texas Smith A&M blue basketball shorts, my white tee, and a pair of black Adidas. Walking by the bookstore staff they smiled when they recognized who I was.

"Wayne! It's so good to see you. How was your summer? Are you ready for the season?" the bookstore clerk asked as she patted me on the back, happy as ever to see me. I smiled and shook everyone's hand, hoping it would throw her off.

"You know I am! I've been practicing all summer. I think it's going to be a good year," I replied.

Browsing through the store, pretending to look at jerseys, I stopped and held up my own jersey. "Barnes," I said softly while holding up the blue and white jersey.
I was startled when I noticed the store manager staring at me. She smiled and moved closer.

"It's a beauty isn't it? To have your name on the back of a jersey, one day it might be on the back of an NFL jersey," she said in her country accent.

"Yeah, I guess," I replied softly. Honestly, I couldn't believe my jersey was being sold in the store and I wasn't getting any money for it. It made me furious.

My book bag was filled with plain white t-shirts, so it would appear that my bag was full from when I walked in the store. Looking around to make sure the coast was clear, I quickly dumped all of the white shirts into the trash bin. Walking over to the book section, I looked around and quickly I grabbed the biggest and newest books I could get. One by one, stuffing them in my bag, mainly grabbing the books on the top shelf because they were worth more. With my book bag stuffed, I headed straight towards the exit.

"I hope to see y'all at the games this year. Take care," I said to the employees while leaving out the store.

"You didn't see anything you wanted, Wayne?" The store manager asked.

"Nah, I'm good thanks though," I replied.

Small ounces of guilt came over me, but swiftly left when I remembered I wasn't stealing from them. I was stealing from the same university that had my jersey up for sale and I wasn't getting a dime from it. Frequently looking behind me as I walked out the store, I began to power walk once I made it outside. The further I got, the faster I jogged, until I ended up in full sprint mode, like I was running for a touchdown. Cheesing from ear to ear after making it safely to my dorm, I paused as I walked up the steps to catch my breath, laughing as I stood there realizing what I had just done.

Only half of the battle was done. The following day Kent returned to the bookstore with a drop slip stating that he was dropping the class the book was intended for. No ID or receipt was needed. Depending on the price of the book, we would receive between $200.00-$300.00 per book. To not make things obvious, we also used Lauren and Vivian as accomplices. Kent was a genius; by September we had made over $3,000.00.

I was content; I was becoming the star football player, had money left over from the books we returned, plus Kent and I were still doing the "Penny Drives." I rushed for 1286 yards and made 13 touchdowns. I was making a name for myself at school and loved every moment of it. My mom and dad were so proud to read about me in the Houston Chronicle newspaper. But what was about to happen next would leave them in shock.

The end of spring semester was on the horizon and Kent was planning on hitting the bookstore one last time to close out the year, but it was one small difference. We wouldn't be getting the full price for the books because they depreciated over the year. We also would have to steal from other students because the bookstore was usually out of stock during close out.

Kent, Vivian, Lauren, and our teammate Ronald who Kent brought along, were all prepared for the next "Quarterbook Sneak." An eerie feeling came over me when Kent decided to bring in Ronald. Vivian was Kent's girl and Lauren was mine so I trusted them. Ronald was an offensive lineman and I swear it felt like he would let the defensive team get through to me, so I was skeptical about him. Kent said we needed him if we wanted to get half of what we got during our first book transactions, so I agreed.

Like clockwork, students started partying uncontrollably as the school year was ending and finals were almost over. If we wanted to steal the books, now would be the perfect time. With a pair of black jogging pants on, a white t-shirt, all black tennis shoes, and Dallas Cowboys hat, I walked through the freshmen dorm as loud music blasted from multiple speakers into the hallways. Guys were running through the hallways excited like a bunch of models had just walked in. I giggled as I walked the hallway; they were so drunk and hyped about finishing school, most of them didn't have a care in the world. Looking from room to room, it was complete chaos. If they weren't ripping and yelling through the hallways, they were passed out on the floor. Glancing in one of the rooms, I saw two faces submerged into trashcans as they regurgitated the last bit of liquor they had just chugged down. It was a mess and it smelled terrible; luckily nobody was paying attention to me. The perfect set up.

I was on the fifth floor and Ronald was on the fourth. Checking out the floor, I walked back through the hall and started my first attempt. The first door to my left was wide open. Stepping directly over the guys who were passed out, I stole their Political Science, Statistics, and Educational Psychology books. Looking down at him, he was out cold, even snoring. I accidentally tapped his foot while leaving out; he didn't even budge. He laid there lifeless in his jean shorts, flip-flops, and black t-shirt. Room-by-room, I filled my backpack with numerous books. I was totally surprised some rooms were unlocked and completely empty. I decided to take the stairs instead of the elevator so nobody would notice me.

Rushing down the stairs, I heard a commotion that sounded like a group of guys arguing. Without entering the hallway, I turned my back to the door and peeked through the glass. "It was you! I saw you walk in three rooms and steal books," one of the freshmen said, yelling at Ronald. Ronald was surrounded by three freshmen looking like they were about to pounce on him if he didn't give up his book bag.

"Man, I don't know what y'all talking about; I don't have any books." Ronald said.

"Look, you're not going anywhere until you open your bag!" one of the freshmen said.

I became filled with rage when I saw what was happening. I almost screamed, but caught myself so nobody could hear me. I wanted to choke Ronald right now; how could he be so dumb.

Ronald's face was looking towards the door, but the freshmen's back was toward me. Ronald noticed me peeking through the door and his eyes widened as he nodded his head toward me signaling for help. If I didn't help him, these guys were going to destroy him. I didn't care for him that much, but he was my teammate. I turned around, gathering my thoughts. Reaching for the doorknob, I could hear the elevator doors opening and out walked campus security. There was nothing I could do now; if I tried to help, they would want to search my bag. Rushing down the steps, I dashed across campus to Kent's room.

"Ronald just got caught with the freshmen. I knew we shouldn't have brought him in with us. I told you! Campus security probably searching his bags right now!" I yelled at Kent while he stood there in shock.

"Baby what are we going to do? Vivian asked Kent.

"He better not tell! If he gets caught, it's on him, not us." Lauren said.

"Ronald wouldn't do that. He's cool; he's going to take his loss like a man." Kent assured us.

I tossed and turned all night, thinking about what happened, what excuse Ronald told security, and, most importantly, did he rat us out. The following morning, I woke up to an intense knock at my door. "Mr. Barnes, open up; it's campus security!" I paced back in forth in my room before opening the door. The books were at Lauren's place, so they would have no immediate proof. I opened the door so slow you would have thought it was a serial killer on the other end. There stood Officer Dunkin, Chief of Security, at my door. *Jesus, help me.* His 6'2, muscular frame looked me up and down. Waiting for him to say something, I looked at him confused.

"Can I help you Officer Dunkin?"

"Wayne, we want you to come down to the security facility. We need to ask you a few questions. I'm sure it's just a misunderstanding."

Being that I was one of the star football players, campus security always made sure I was in good hands, so I wasn't too worried. As I arrived in Officer Dunkin's office, I looked around slowly as he stared me up and down. "Have a seat Wayne. You might be here a while," he said. *A while?* This doesn't sound good. I sat slowly in the reddish-brown leather chair that sat in front of his desk while he tapped his pen.

"Mr. Barnes, we have reason to believe you were part of a group who stole books last night in attempt to turn the books in for profit," he said.

Avoiding eye contact with him, I looked around the room before answering.

"Stealing books, nah, you got the wrong one sir. I don't know what you're talking about. I was with my girlfriend last night," I replied.

"See, Mr. Barnes, I want to believe you, I really do; but our witness is telling us a different story," he said. Shaking my head in disbelief, I couldn't believe this was happening.

"Sir, I swear I don't know what you're talking about; and what do you mean witness?"

"Bring Mr. Lyons in here please," he yelled. Ronald came in and I immediately frowned at him. He looked redder than ever as his pale cheeks turned into fire when he saw me. I couldn't believe he told. He didn't have to bring me down with him; what a sucker.

"Ronald, is it true that you and Mr. Barnes attempted to steal multiple books last night from the freshmen dorm he said."

"Yes, sir," he nervously said.

"I'm so disappointed in you two. I mean, what were you thinking!" he yelled.

"Do you know how much of an asset you are to the team? Now the school will have to suffer the consequences next season."

Ronald's eyes grew bigger after Officer Dunkin said "we" would suffer the consequences.

"I thought you said I would go free if I told you who was responsible for this?"

"That's just something we say to bribe the suspect into telling the whole truth. You're done here at Texas Smith A&M. We will not tolerate theft at this college!" the officer yelled.

Ronald's face grew angry as he looked at Officer Dunkin. "In that case, Kent Davis was a part of this too!" I immediately looked at him, slowly shaking my head. If security wasn't in the room, I would have knocked his head right off his shoulders. Kent arrived an hour later and didn't say a word; he just looked at Ronald the whole time as if he wanted to kill him. Officer Dunkin grabbed the book bags the officers confiscated and poured them all out on the floor. "I really can't believe this; it has to be over 30 books in these bags. This University gives you a chance to make something of yourselves and this is how you repay them? You should be ashamed of yourselves!" he yelled.

We all sat there with nothing to say.

"I'm going to let you three go. Since it's the end of the year, continue to pack your bags and the Student Board will make their decision within 48 hours.

After two days of packing and worrying about our fate, our parents arrived in student court as Kent, Ronald, and I stood before the Dean, Student Board, Campus Security, and coaches. The Dean looked us straight in the eyes. "I don't understand how our top football players have gotten caught stealing books. Really, books?" You guys disgust me. You're lucky we didn't call the police because, if it were anybody else, we would have. Do you have anything to say? Do you? Huh?" What did he mean he wasn't calling the police? Were they going to give us some slack? I decided then and there I was going to tell him why we did it.

"To be honest sir, we all come from nothing. Well, me and Kent come from nothing; Ronald is privileged. We practice all day every day and have curfew, leaving us unable to get jobs. We needed money. We're broke. How are we supposed to survive?" I said.

Dean Johnson stood there with his sleeves rolled up as sweat dripped down his pale skin.

"Survive? Are you kidding me? All three of you have full scholarships to attend this school. Everything is paid for! Books, food, transportation; you name it. I don't want to hear those excuses. There have been thousands of football players who came before you and they didn't steal. If they didn't make it to the NFL, they were still successful at something else. They weren't only disciplined on the field; they were disciplined in life, period! I remember you told me about Wayne Barnes, the football Hall of Famer here at A&M, and how he was the reason you chose this school. He didn't steal to get ahead; he paid his dues like everyone else!"

"You can enroll back in school the following semester, pay the full price, and potentially earn your scholarship back; but it's not guaranteed." he said. Kent started crying like a baby. I had never seen anything like it; a 300-pound lineman crying his heart out. I shook my head while looking at him. Wiping his eyes, he noticed me shaking my head.

"You're shaking your head at me, but you know I can't afford to go to school," Kent said.

"Yeah me too," Ronald chimed in. Quickly, I turned towards Ronald.

"I don't care if you can't afford school or anything else in life. If it wasn't for you, we wouldn't be here." The Dean banged his gable, causing complete silence in the room.

"Enough Mr. Barnes. You guys have a week to decide what you're going to do."

I turned around to walk out the courtroom; there stood my mother and dad with the most disappointed look on their faces. I couldn't bear to look at them; I knew I had blown any chance of getting my family out of the slums now.

"I can't believe you would be so stupid to steal books from school, Wayne. How could you? I didn't raise you like that! And you know we don't have $38,000 to send you back to school," said my mom as she looked at me in disappointment. That was the main problem, we never had any money. I only had one school year left and I knew there had to be a way to finish.

Coach McCrae, my lineman coach, was like my uncle; we had a great relationship. He was disappointed with me, but I knew, if anything, he would have some words of wisdom for me.

"Wayne when I look at you I see myself. I never stole books, but I did a lot of things I wasn't proud of. You have to understand that the choices you make now are going to affect your future in more ways than one. You have to learn to sacrifice in this world, because nothing is going to be handed to you," he said.

"I'm starting to understand that now, coach. Dean Johnson said the same thing when we were in court," I replied.

"Yeah, I heard he let you have it," he said laughing at me.

"Dean Johnson can put a hurting on somebody when he's mad."

"Oh yes he can," I replied.

"You only have one year left here at school. If you really want to continue school you might have to get a loan. At least you didn't have one your first three years of college. This is where being disciplined comes in. The pain of discipline weighs in ounces, but the pain of regret weighs in tons. I bet you regret stealing them books now don't you?"

"Regret isn't the word. I can't believe I was so stupid." Coach McCrae made me change my perspective and enroll the following semester. His quote "The pain of discipline weighs in ounces, but the pain of regret weighs in tons," stuck with me for a long time.

Neither Kent nor Ronald enrolled the following semester. I wasn't able to play the first five games of the season. That was the agreement between the Dean, Student Board and coaches. In return for not calling the police. To avoid questioning from the students and staff about why I was sitting out I told everybody I sprained my ankle in practice. My dreams of going to the NFL were dead, but I still got to graduate and put a smile on my mom's face. A year after I graduated, a recruiter from the Greensboro, North Carolina Revolution Arena football team contacted me and said he was interested in me trying out for the team. Coach McCrae put in a good word for me and sent them my highlight reel from college. I was paid $3,000.00 per game for a 14 game season. I also had a full time job as a web developer. Arena Football wasn't the NFL, but I was getting paid to do something I loved.

Lesson Learned: Focus on your sole goal and don't let anybody take you off task. Kent and I got greedy after doing our Penny Drives. We could've gotten part-time jobs after the season was over, but we didn't. Kent wasn't a bad guy, but he wasn't great either. Keep positive people around you and execute your dreams until you hit your target. Block negative thoughts from entering your mind and when they come replace it with a positive one. Your first thought is usually the right one. Before every scheme my conscience always got the best of me. I knew it was wrong, but once I remembered how much money I had, I didn't care.

If you're in a predicament where you're struggling financially, take out a piece of paper and write down your goals. Take the necessary steps to manifest that goal in your life. Study hard at it, do your research; in time you will reap your rewards. I know it's a struggle not having the money to do what you want, but it helps you appreciate the small things in life. You wouldn't appreciate the sun if it didn't rain. You have to trust that everything is going to work out and have faith in God. Especially if you're an athlete in college - all eyes are on you. A prime example is the 2015 NFL first round draft pick, Jameis Winston, who came under fire for being accused of stealing crab legs while he was in college. This incident almost cost him his future in the NFL. Winston stated that the crab legs were given to him for free from a Publix employee, but he was still scrutinized by the media for this small act of youthful ignorance.[10]

No matter how small or how big the problem, always think twice before every decision, not only in school but in life. I understand that everybody isn't privileged, but after my experience I would rather suffer for the cause instead of risking, and possibly losing, everything. You have to be grateful for everything in life. Do you know how many people would have loved to be in our shoes with a full scholarship? Remember, the pain of discipline weighs in ounces, but the pain of regret weighs in tons. Be disciplined and make the right choice.

Chapter 13: A Different World

Looking in the bathroom mirror, I couldn't believe it. My hairline resembled the squiggly lines of a road map, reminding me of the GPS images on Interstate 20. I put my wave cap on, took a deep breath, and shook my head in disbelief. That was one of the downsides about being away in college; it was a struggle to find a decent barber, especially at Grambling State University. My barber, Kenny, always told me to wait until I returned home to New Orleans, Louisiana, but I didn't visit often. There were too many beautiful women on campus and walking around with a nappy haircut is something I couldn't do.

Walking back into my dorm room, I threw on my black Adidas tracksuit and finished packing. "Come on, Kevin. Anthony is downstairs and I'm ready to go!" my roommate Terrance yelled from the hallway. He had some nerve rushing me; for once in his life he's ready and I'm not. We weren't allowed to have cars during our freshmen year, so we rode with our friend Anthony, who was a sophomore and went to high school with us. My door opened as Terrance poked his head in looking confused.

"Come on, Kevin, hurry up!"

"Why are you rushing me? You're not driving," I replied.

"Man, just come on. I'm ready to go home. I miss New Orleans."

"I miss home too, but waiting an extra five minutes isn't going to make a difference."

Terrance paused while looking at me with a smirk on his face.

"That's why your hairline is messed up now. You're not fooling anybody with that wave cap." Instantly slamming the door, he took off running. His footsteps and laughter echoed through the hollow stairwell like an evil villain in a movie.

I loaded my bags into Anthony's Expedition, hopped in the back seat, and was slowly reminded of my hairline when Anthony pulled up his GPS. I touched the top of my head to make sure I still had my wave cap on. It was a four-hour trip from Grambling to New Orleans, but my iPod was fully charged so I was at peace. We were headed home for Thanksgiving break and I couldn't wait. Home cooked meals, family, a comfortable bed, and partying with our friends were on the horizon. Terrance and I have been friends since elementary school. He lived a few blocks down from me in Little Woods, our neighborhood in New Orleans. We both applied to Grambling State and got accepted the same year. We were some of the lucky few that made it out. While some of our college classmates were going home to bigger than life houses with rich mommies and daddies, we were headed back to the bottom of the map, literally. Don't get me wrong, we weren't poor; but once we started Grambling and saw our classmates driving Mercedes, Lexus, and top of the line SUV's; it was a completely different world for us.

I quickly learned that I couldn't relate to some of my college peers; my experiences as an adolescent were different. I shared stories with my college friends that they couldn't imagine, like the reoccurring problem with rival gangs that resulted in occasional group fights. Or the few times we had to dash in between houses and hop fences to dodge gunshots while walking home from school. I know people who've been shot and I know the shooters. It wasn't rare for people to have guns in school. I remember in 8th grade my friend got caught with a handgun and the local newspaper reported it. My mother was shocked when she read the story. Her instincts went into overdrive, like a mother bear protecting her cubs. She tried her best to keep me out of trouble and it worked; if it hadn't, I wouldn't have been in college. But for some reason I did get a weird rush whenever I participated in the mischief.

New Orleans was going to be packed this weekend because of the annual Bayou Classic football game between Grambling State University and Southern University. A few of my friends played for both teams, so I purchased my ticket before I left. A lot of our parents attended the games faithfully. They loved to see our friends doing something positive. Anthony dropped Terrance off, then drove six blocks to drop me off. "Be safe this weekend, Kevin. You know it's going to be extra crazy because of the holiday," said Anthony. He wasn't lying; every year around this time three things were for certain-drunk drivers, drugs, and violence.

Before I put my key in the door, I could hear eight furry feet pounding up the steps to greet me. King and Diamond, my two dogs, almost knocked me down with excitement as I walked in. My mom and dad were just as happy. The genuine feeling of being missed by your loved ones was something I always looked forward to. It made me feel right at home. As much as I missed them, I left out as quickly as I came. Before I could get in my car my dad stopped me.

"Son, put some air in your tires. While you were gone, I had problems with my car so I drove yours; when you leave I'll probably drive it again," he said.

"Ok."

If you're driving my car, why didn't you put air in the tires? I didn't bother asking him. I had too much respect for my father; plus I was in a rush to Terrance's house. I hopped in my 1999 black Maxima with tinted windows and drove off.

Terrance had a long driveway that led to his 2-acre sized backyard. It was our private place to kick back and relax. Girls came back there to visit, we played our music at high levels, laughed loudly, and nobody bothered us. As I pulled into Terrance's gravel-filled driveway, I could hear my friend Larry talking on the phone. "He did what, Whitney? He said what? Oh hell nah! Tell him next time I see him it's on! Point, blank, period! It's not going be no talking," he said to his girlfriend while pacing back and forth between the gravel. With anger in his eyes, he quickly paused when he noticed me getting out of the car. After hanging up the phone, he pulled his dreadlocks in a ponytail as his demeanor changed from livid to happy.

"What's up Kevin! Welcome home. What you got hiding under that wave cap huh? They still messing up your hairline down there?" I guess my hairline was the topic of discussion before I came; Terrance couldn't hold water if he tried.

"Who were you talking to Whitney about on the phone?" I asked.

"That fool, Eddie, won't leave her alone. You know he's liked her since high school and hates the fact we're together. He's been threatening her and talking bad about me. It's been going on for 3 months and I'm sick of it," he said.

"Sounds like a fatal attraction to me," I said jokingly.

"If Eddie doesn't stop, he's going to be fatal."

Terrance and his cousin, Corey, walked out of the house mid-conversation. It still amazed me how much they looked alike but acted totally different. They were night and day.

"I'm surprised you haven't confronted him yet," I said.

"Man, if something else happens, we're all going around there, forget all that talking!" Corey said interjecting.

I didn't know who was crazier, Larry or Corey; but I didn't come home for this, so I quickly changed the subject. I told them about the numerous Bayou Classic parties and that I had tickets to the game. But before they could get excited, Larry's phone rung; it was Whitney again. I could hear her screaming in the background and Larry was starting to look even more upset than before. "We're about to come around there, it's about to be handled. Don't worry about it, baby," he said before hanging up.

"Can you believe Eddie had the nerve to drive past Whitney's house and curse at her in front of her mom!" Larry yelled.

"Let's go, come on! All of us are going around there right now. I don't care what you say!" Corey said.

All four of us ran to Larry's 1997 white Crown Victoria, but Larry stopped us! "We need a car that's not recognizable. He knows my car. Kevin let's take your car," Larry said. Without thinking I agreed and headed towards my car.

"Kevin, let me drive," Terrance said

"Why do you want to drive?"

"I don't know. I just do," he said as I looked at him confused. *Why did he want to drive my car?*

"I don't care who drives, but let's go! This can't wait any longer," Larry said.

I threw Terrance the keys and got in the backseat behind him. Larry swiftly grabbed his black Smith & Wesson 9MM gun and black gloves out of his car. I watched as he inconspicuously ran to my car, as if he had already committed a crime.

"Terrance, stop past a gas station so I can put some air in the tires. If we want to get away fast, the tires should be full." I said. Pulling into the Shell Gas Station, I quickly filled each tire like a mechanic at a pit stop in the Daytona 500. After we put air in the tires, Whitney arrived at the gas station and got in with us. I started to feel that weird rush of excitement going through my veins again. The smell of trouble was definitely in the air; it felt just like old times. Terrance was cruising through the back streets and alleys of Little Woods while Larry was in the passenger seat loading his gun. One-by-one he put the bullets in the clip making sure he left no fingerprints. I was behind Terrance, Whitney was in the middle, and Corey was behind Larry. I hadn't seen Whitney since August and I could see why Eddie wanted her. She was beautiful. Her jet-black, naturally curly hair flowed down her back, touching her golden skin. I was 5'7 and she was two inches shorter than me with a figure eight shape. Out of curiosity, I wanted to know more about the situation, so I asked Whitney.

"What's really going on, Whitney? Why won't Eddie leave you alone? He knows you and Larry are a couple?"

"Kevin! I'm so sick of this! Eddie knows that Larry's my boyfriend, but he doesn't like him because of their rival neighborhoods. When he found out Larry was my boyfriend, he couldn't deal with it and he's been making threats ever since. Every week he tries to convince me to leave Larry. I've told him a million times that I love Larry, but he's still so persistent. When I mention Larry, he always disrespects him. Always mentioning that he has more money than him and if he sees him, it's on."

I laughed at the thought of Eddie knocking out Larry. He was 5'5, all skin and bones and Larry was 5'11 and easily weighed 200 pounds.

"So this whole thing is about his Napoleon Complex?" I asked.

Everybody in the car laughed.

"I always defend Larry and, when I do, Eddie starts disrespecting me. He's a nuisance and it's very tiring."

Whitney was wild and aggressive just like Larry – they were like Christian Slater and Patricia Arquette in True Romance. I've seen her demolish girls and hop in brawls while we were fighting. She would be the only girl fighting with the guys. She took the phrase "ride or die" to another level. We were finally in Eddie's neighborhood, but he was nowhere to be found. We searched the Circle K gas station, the neighborhood park, local convenience stores and still nothing.

"Whitney, call Eddie and tell him to meet you at the Circle K; and don't sound like you have an attitude either," Larry said.

"I know how to talk to him, Larry. I'm not stupid," she replied.

"Man, just call him; you always have something to say." It amazed me how they could argue in a situation like this, but before they could finish arguing, Eddie answered the phone. Everyone became silent.

"Where are you? I want to see you. Can you meet me at the Circle K Gas Station in your neighborhood," Whitney said. Before he could answer, Whitney put her phone on speaker.

"Why all of a sudden you want to see me? That sucker boyfriend finally kicked you to the curb? See I told you it was only a matter of time," Eddie replied.
Glancing at Larry's face it was flustered with anger as it took everything for him not to respond.

"Can you just come, please?"

"Yeah, I'll be there."
He sounded reluctant, but when he said he would be there Larry's face said it all. No one was stopping him; this was his shot - literally.

Pulling into the project homes parking lot adjacent from the Circle K, we sat and waited. The tall trees and bushes partially camouflaged us from any onlookers who were in the Circle K parking lot. Eddie wouldn't see us coming from a mile away. We sat there, waiting and waiting. Whitney called his phone numerous times, but he didn't answer. Larry huffed and puffed and became frustrated like the big bad wolf; he couldn't wait to get his paws on Eddie. Feeling anxious, he took his ponytail out of his dreads and cocked his gun. He was ready. Gazing out the window it was then that I realized I shouldn't be here. This has nothing to do with me and I'm in the back seat of my own car. I was willing to have my friends back, but I didn't have a gun myself. Why was I here? It doesn't take five people to shoot a gun.

Then it dawned on me. My father stated he would be driving my car while I was at school. If Eddie retaliates, he will probably be looking for this exact car. In New Orleans there's no telling when somebody will retaliate. If my Dad's driving my car, he might get caught in the middle of this. My windows were tinted so Eddie wouldn't be able to tell if it was his enemy or just an older man with the same exact car. I started praying to myself, hoping God would get me through this. I had too much to lose.

"There he is right there!" Larry yelled as I lifted my head and opened my eyes. I guess my prayers were too late. Looking out the window, I saw Eddie pulling into the Circle K parking lot in a white construction van. I started praying again. *God please get me through this so I can make it home safely.* It was cloudy and dusk was approaching as the wind blew the fall leaves through the streets. There wasn't a soul in sight. Just us, Eddie, and the Circle K store clerk standing behind the cash register. The coast was clear. Larry unrolled his ski mask covering his face, grabbed his gun, opened the door, and left us hidden behind the tints of my Maxima.

I watched as Larry crept through the bushes while holding his gun down to his right side. His black pants and black shirt hid him even more. I could see Eddie sitting in his van, parked parallel to the street. Larry ran to the sidewalk hiding behind a tree that was out of Eddie's site. Standing from across the street, he quickly turned towards the passenger side of the van and let off 6 rapid shots aimed directly into the passenger side. Pop! Pop! Pop! Pop! Pop! Pop! Instantly, Eddie ducked down. I could see his eyes bulging out of his sockets in shock! *Did I just witness the facial expression of a man getting shot?*

Whitney nervously grabbed my arm as she watched Larry rush back to the car. Holding his gun down, he sporadically looked behind him to make sure no one was chasing him. Larry leaped into the car as Terrance sped off before Larry could even close the car door. In a panic and without thinking, Terrance drove into a dead end. "What are you doing? This is a dead end! Turn around, turn around!" I yelled. Immediately putting the car into reverse he drove backwards into the main street full throttle. Abruptly slamming on breaks, Terrance yanked us back and forth as he put the car in drive and sped off like a thief from the movie *Gone In 60 Seconds.*

My adrenaline was rushing as I looked out of every window to see if anybody was following us. Luckily, the only thing trailing us was the autumn leave's kicking up from Terrance's speed. Looking out the back window, I noticed two flat tires on Eddie's van. *Had he been shot?* Finally, we were back at Terrance's house. Hopping out the car, we all smiled at each other, knowing we had made it out safe and everything was ok – for now. We held a weird sense of accomplishment and pride that shouldn't have been celebrated. I went to the bathroom, looked at myself in the mirror letting out a deep sigh of relief.

Later on that night, I was so happy to be in bed; I laid upright with my hands behind my head thanking God that he got me through the day. The following morning, while driving to the barbershop, I noticed bullets on the passenger side of the floor. Thankfully, I found them before my Dad did; there's no telling what he would have said. That weekend I was paranoid every time I drove my car, but I returned back to Grambling State that Sunday unharmed.

A month later, while I was leaving out of my Business Economics class, my phone rang.

"What's up Larry?"

"It's been a few weeks since you been home, boy. I know that hairline looking a mess," he said jokingly.

"Nope, I found a decent barber down here. My hairline looks like it's been blessed by God himself. Just call me Kevin Heaven," I replied.

Larry laughed so hard that he started to cough.

"I just called to tell you Eddie is still around, but he hasn't bothered Whitney since that day." I thought to myself, he was that close and still missed; I guess that was a good and bad thing. Good that he's not bothering Whitney anymore, but bad that there's always a chance Eddie might retaliate.

Lesson Learned: I'm always there for my friends and they're always there for me. We've been through a lot; partied together, laughed together, fought together and buried a few of our friends together. But you don't have to do everything together. Their battle is not always yours, especially in a situation like this. I could have easily said "no" to Larry about taking my car, but I didn't think twice about it. I put my parents and myself in danger.

That was my first year in college and, if that situation would've turned out differently, it might have been my last. The police could have caught us or Eddie could have retaliated that same weekend. In America, every 70 minutes a person under the age of 25 dies from gunfire. Gun violence not only takes the life of the victim, but also ruins the life of the shooter.[11] Far too often we neglect the other groups affected, which are the friends and, most importantly, the families of the victims. Numerous times I've seen the stress of parents burying their child and the hurt of their friends saying their last goodbyes. In the heat of the moment, when you're angered, try to remember who all will be affected by your actions. We're all somebody's son, daughter, friend, father, mother, cousin, nephew, niece, husband, wife, friend, co-worker, etc. You're not only taking a life, but also taking a life from somebody.

Everybody has a handful of friends that are impulsive and don't always make the right choice, but as a friend you have the power to lead them down the right path instead of the wrong one. Most of the time, they will listen; you just have to speak up. You have your whole life in front of you and, in situations like this, you should stop and think: "Is it really worth going to jail, getting shot, or having your parents and friends bury you?" Some people were raised in poverty-stricken neighborhoods and they sometimes bring that mentality to college or their jobs. They end up getting into arguments and fights over petty situations at their university. You have to practice separating the two because in the real world it won't be tolerated. When you step into corporate America, you must learn to leave your inner problems at the door and focus on your task at hand. Your wrong thinking will keep you from your destiny, purpose, and what God has planned for you. I changed my way of thinking and was blessed to graduate with honors from Grambling. Unfortunate situations may be your current reality, but your circumstances will change once you transform into a better you.

Chapter 14: Under The Influence

"Wait for me before you go to Criminal Justice class, Noelle," I said while on the phone rushing to leave out my apartment. Noelle was one of my closest friends from Providence, Rhode Island. Ever since freshman year at Clark University, she's looked out for me, always making me think twice before I made some off the wall decision.

"For what, Devin, didn't you study? I don't think you have to cheat on this one," she said laughing at me. We were both headed to take our Criminal Justice final exam and if I needed help from anyone, Noelle would be perfect. I wasn't confident about taking the test, I wasn't trying to be a cop or lawyer so I didn't take this class serious. But it cost too much to repeat, plus it wasn't a part of my core major classes. I was a Business Major, not Criminal Justice. My professor, Dr. Mossinger, warned me if I didn't pass this exam with a B I would fail. She was a no nonsense professor, but she truly cared. I remember she called me the week before exams and told me to get my butt out of bed and come study with the other students. Professors like that are rare and I respected her for that. The exam lasted two hours and when it was over I felt great. I didn't even need Noelle's answers.

After I finished I walked up to Dr. Mossinger desk to turn in my test.

"Do you want to know if you passed today or later on in the week, Devin?" Dr. Mossinger asked.

"Today," I replied. I wanted to know immediately because, if I didn't pass, I would need to sign up for summer school. After class Noelle and I walked to her dorm and hung out there for a while. She was beautiful. Her mother's Irish background mixed with her father's Jamaican culture created one amazing being inside and out. Her sepia skin glowed in the sun, radiating her distinct features. We played around and told people we were cousins, but of course I was from her father's side. Students on campus always said I favored the Jamaican Olympian, Usain Bolt. "Me and my friends are going to the Crime Mob party tonight. You have to come with us," she said. I was stunned! Noelle and her friends rarely came out. They were serious about their schoolwork, so you barely saw them; but they were gorgeous and knew how to have a good time. Before I left Noelle's dorm, Dr. Mossinger called me, "Devin you passed with a B-. Congrats!" I told Noelle the news and she was happier than me. "I'm so proud of you Devin. Drinks on me tonight!" It was funny to hear her say that; she wasn't 21 and neither was I, but we both had fake IDs.

This was going to be one of the biggest end-of-the year parties in Atlanta. The whole Atlanta University Center (AUC) was probably going to be there. Not only did I go to school in Atlanta, Georgia, one of the best cities in America, but campus life was a sight to see. Clark Atlanta University, Morehouse College, Georgia State University, Georgia Tech, and Spelman were all within minutes of each other. Before the party, I went home to take a nap. When I woke up, I found my roommate, Maurice, sitting at the dining room table shuffling a deck of cards with a look of distress on his face.

"What's wrong with you? Classes are over, you should be happy," I said.

"Man, I just lost $800.00 in a card game. I was going to use that money to buy a new computer so I could start selling DVDs and CDs again." Maurice was a hustler and anyway he could make a dollar he was going to do it. "I'm not going to the party tonight; you'll have to go without me," he said. If I lost

$800.00, I would be depressed too, so I didn't blame him for cancelling. Plus, Noelle and her friends were still going.

I threw on my LRG jeans and LRG black Jungle Polo while taking shots of Absolute Vodka and jetted out the door. Coasting in my black 2005 Dodge Magnum, I valet parked at Club Atrium and walked right to the front. Atrium was one of the hottest spots in Atlanta. There was an actual pool on the inside and every night girls would literally get in the pool and party. I could see Noelle and her friends standing in front of the line. Right on time. I walked confidently to the front to meet them. The six of them looked so good, with their cowgirl boots on, denim shorts, and spaghetti strap tops, but Noelle definitely stood out. I was proud to be with the finest girls, not to mention they were all Delta's. I placed my arm around Noelle and she looked at me in disgust.

"Damn, Devin did you drink the whole bottle before you came? You smell like liquor and John Paul Gaultier cologne," she said.

"Well, I smell like I'm ready for tonight then right?" I replied laughing. I paid their way in the club; I had a part time job at Walter's, a popular shoe store in downtown Atlanta, so money wasn't a problem.

The club was packed from wall to wall. I led them through the crowd. As I glanced to the right, I saw my manager, Renaldo from my V-103 radio internship, signaling for me to come in V.I.P. Thank God he was there because I didn't feel like being in the mosh pit. We started partying as soon as we got into V.I.P. The drinks were flowing endlessly and DJ Scream kept the club hype as the locals, sporting their long white t-shirts, were shaking their "Laffy Taffy," a popular dance in Atlanta.

Crime Mob finally hit the stage around 1:30 a.m. and performed their hit songs "Stilettos (Pumps)" and their club banger "Knuck If You Buck." The energy was captivating; to see the entire club dancing and putting their fist and hands together as the song banged through the speakers was amazing. The people in the pool even joined in, dancing and splashing to the beat. I attempted to follow suit with the crowd, but I couldn't because I had a drink in both hands. Noelle kept her word and bought me a drink; but once she saw how I easily gulped down the first one, she looked at me suspiciously.

"Devin, are you sure you need this drink. I know you're celebrating, but you're already drunk and you have to drive home."

"Girl if you don't give me this drink! You know this isn't the first time I've been drunk and drove myself home!"

"Ok, but I'm not buying you another one. You know these are Zombies right?"
A Zombie was a drink mixed with Bacardi 151, black rum, white rum, and mix of juices.

"Yeah, I could tell. You always buying cheap drinks." I said with a sneer.

"You're lucky I bought you anything."
Renaldo had two bottles of Grey Goose on the table, which was more than enough to last for the next hour. Honestly, if Noelle bought me another drink or not I didn't care.

The lights came on one by one and instantly my ears started ringing from being so close to the speaker. It was 3:45 a.m. and my stomach was talking to me like I hadn't fed it in days. Abruptly, Noelle shoved me against the brick wall.

"Girl what the hell is wrong with you!" I yelled at her.

"Give me your keys, Devin. Look at you stumbling everywhere; you're not about to drive like this. I'm driving your car."

"Everything alright over here?" security asked.

"Yes, sir." Noelle replied with her arm still holding me against the wall.

"You're not driving my car, not today, not tomorrow, not ever. So go get in the car with your friends and I'll meet you at Waffle House on Howell Mill Road. I'm fine."

"I'm not letting you drive like this, Devin."

"Girl didn't I just say I'm fine. Look, I can walk a straight line." I replied while sarcastically walking an imaginary line so she would leave me alone. I don't know what she was thinking; I was drunk, but I wasn't about to let her drive my Dodge Magnum. My Dad just bought me that car and I wasn't going to let anyone drive it; that car was my baby.

I tried to sober up, but when I found myself still raising my fists and dancing like I was in the club, I knew I was plastered. Driving down Northside Drive, I picked up some speed. Noelle was already at the Waffle House and I didn't want her worrying. Boom! I heard from my car as it ascended in the air from the left tire hitting the median in the middle of the street. Fighting to gain control, I realized I had suddenly dozed off but quickly woke up from the loud noise. Dodging the traffic to the right, I blew the horn fiercely at the other cars. "Didn't you see me hit the median!" I yelled to the driver. Finally gaining back control of the car, I could feel my left front tire rumbling. Hastily, my car started to rattle, causing me to pull over in the Good Year parking lot. My adrenaline was rushing and, thank God, I was safe; but, if my car was scratched, my Dad was going to ring my neck. I hopped out to look for scratches, but only found my left tire flat. Looking at the store sign, I grunted. My tire is flat and I'm in the Good Year parking lot, how ironic.

Rushing to the trunk, I pushed my junk to the side, pulling out a spare tire. I started to panic; I didn't want Noelle to think something bad happened, plus the All-Star Special with an orange juice from Waffle House was calling my name. I was ready to devour every last bite. I had all my tools for changing the tire, but I couldn't find the lug wrench. I was rummaging all through my trunk, but I found nothing. I needed help and I needed help fast. I didn't want to call Noelle because I would have to hear her mouth. Maurice didn't answer his phone either; he was probably still depressed from the card game. My last option was to dial 911. I couldn't believe it took me through so many prompts just to talk to an operator. Working up a sweat, pacing back and forth, I became frustrated, hanging up after the 2 minutes. If it were a real emergency, I would have been dead.

Just in time, a cop was riding past and quickly I started waving him down, almost chasing him to stop. When he finally noticed me, he turned around at the same median and pulled up, rolling his window down.

"Everything ok over here?

"Yes, I just need a lug wrench and jack lift to change my tire. Would you happen to have one?

"Sure." He replied yawning while stepping out his navy Atlanta Police Department car. Opening his trunk, he grabbed the wrench, but when handing me the tool, he wouldn't let go.

"Have you been drinking? You smell like cigarettes and liquor?" He asked while strongly gripping my hands and the wrench at the same time. *Damn, where was he from, the amazon? It felt like a death grip.*

"No, I just left the club, Sir. That's probably what you smell." I answered avoiding eye contact.

"Left the club? That explains why you smell like that?" He replied looking suspicious. *Left the club? Really, Devin; now he's really going to think you were drinking.*

I started worrying about all of the consequences that could happen. I was so dumb and drunk that I waved a police officer down, completely forgetting I was intoxicated. I shook my head in disbelief. The officer pulled his flash light out and pointed it directly in my face. The light was so bright, I put my hands up covering my eyes. At the same time, my phone was buzzing in my right pocket. Oh no! It's probably Noelle; I'm sure she's worried to death. I felt so bad that I couldn't answer the phone and I knew she was two seconds from looking for me. After the officer turned his flashlight off, I got to see his nametag, Officer Porter. I will address him as such; maybe he'll be lenient if I'm respectful.

"What's your name son?"

"Devin, Officer Porter."

"I'm going to ask you to do some tests, and, if you pass, you can go home; if not, well, you know what will happen from there."

"I want you to walk on the white parking space lines heel to toe."

Was God punishing me after I just sarcastically walked the line for Noelle? Lord, please hold me up while I try to do this. God knows I'm too drunk for this. Stepping one foot in front of the other, I walked straight for the first four steps then stumbled. *It's a wrap! I'm done, I'm going to jail and I'm going to be on Scared Straight, College Edition!* I could see Officer Porter shaking his head from the corner of my eye.

"One last test and you better hope you pass this."

He walked to his trunk and I could hear him unlocking what sounded like a case. As he walked back over holding a square-shaped object in his hand, I realized it was a breathalyzer test.

"Blow into this for me."

Placing my lips on the plastic tube, I blew into the machine. His eyes widened as he looked at the results.

"Your test came to a 0.12%; you're way above the legal limit. Give me your driver's license."

I reached for my wallet, handing him my license.

"Texas huh? You come to Atlanta thinking you can just drive drunk in these streets? And you're under 21. What are you doing in Atlanta anyway? "

"I go to Clark University, Officer Porter?"

"College boy out here drinking at 4:00 a.m, and you smell like you drunk the whole bottle. I'm taking you in son. I'm sorry."

While Officer Porter was placing me in the back seat of the squad car, a black Monte Carlo pulled into the parking lot. It was Maurice! I had never been so excited to see him in my life. I was praying Officer Porter would let me leave with him. To top it off, Maurice's girlfriend was with him, so she could drive my car home.

"Hey, that's my roommate, Officer," Maurice said.

"So," the officer replied.

"You said I was too drunk to drive and now I have a ride. His girlfriend can drive my car home and you can let me go," I said.

"Is everything ok here Officer?" Maurice asked.

"No, your friend here thinks its ok to drink and drive. Then he has the nerve to be under age."

"I'm sure it's just a misunderstanding officer." Maurice replied.

He quickly pointed his flashlight in Maurice's face.

"How about you? Have you been drinking, because you can join him if you like?"

"No, sir." Maurice quickly replied.

I couldn't believe I was getting arrested for a DUI on the last day of class. Luckily, I didn't have to call a tow truck; the officer let Maurice change the tire and his girlfriend drove my car home. Officer Porter pulled off slowly. My eyes connected to Maurice's while he was sitting in his car. From the look on his face, I knew he felt bad. I couldn't hear him, but I read his lips right before leaving out the parking lot, "Damn, Devin."

I gazed out the window as the cop headed towards Fulton County Jail. Turning forward, my eyes met with Officer Porter in the rear view mirror as he started to talk.

"You know, son, you college kids have to be more responsible. Every week we book multiple students from one of the universities in the city and 90% of the time it's for drugs or drinking; it never fails. You guys have opportunities other kids would die for, but you consistently risk it. Do you know how dangerous it is to be under the influence and driving? I've seen so many accidents and deaths it's scary. Do you understand?"

He's called me son one too many times. Does he think he's my father or something?

"I understand, but I was driving right around the corner to Waffle House. I was only celebrating because it was the last day of class." I replied, starring out the backseat window.

"Most accidents happen right around the corner from the victim's house."

I huffed and puffed, intentionally not answering his question.

"You don't want to hear what I have to say huh? I'm going to leave you with this. What would your parents think? Do you know how much it would hurt if they got a call saying something happened to you. The pain they would feel, the grief that would impact them?" I sat in silence. His last statement struck a chord with me. As much as I didn't want to hear what he was saying, he was right.

I looked up at the tall jail building as we pulled in the parking lot; I couldn't believe I was about to be an inmate at the Fulton County Jail. This was Rice Street. So many celebrities have walked through these doors; I just hoped I could make bond as quick as them. They took all my belongings and I was allowed one phone call, but I was torn between Noelle and my parents. When I thought about what Officer Porter said, I called Noelle. I didn't want to place that burden on my parents. I leaned against the side of the phone booth waiting for her to pick up.

"Devin, is this you?"
I looked at the phone confused how did she know?

"What? How did you know?" I quietly said.

"I talked to Maurice and he told me everything that happened. Look, we're coming to get you."

"I don't have a chance of that happening until I talk to the magistrate, so hold off on that."

"See, I told you, Devin. I told you that you should have let me drive."
I cut her off completely.

"You think I don't know that, Noelle! I'm here now, ok! I don't want to hear that. If I wanted to hear that, I would have called my Dad!"
Silence took over the phone, leaving me feeling wretched. She was just trying to help.

"I'm sorry for yelling, but I'm already going through enough. My time is up on the phone; I'll call you in a few to let you know what's going on."

The white cement walls were scratched with writing and the smell of urine consumed the air from the one toilet that was shared amongst 15 inmates. The benches surrounding the walls were full, but thank God I spotted a seat in the corner and went straight for it. Multiple conversations conveyed throughout the cell. One inmate wearing a black hoodie with yellow eyes consistently threatened the guards while another inmate claimed he had just finished singing with the legendary Atlanta rap group, Outkast. He continued to sing "Don't you think I'm so sexy, I dress so fresh so clean." The drugs consumed in his system had him feeling every bit of *Southernplayalistc.* The guards lined us up one by one to take our pictures and weight. They even gave us an HIV test. Who the hell knew you had to take an HIV test? Was I at the doctor's office or jail?

Three hours and a million conversations with Atlanta's local drug dealers, robbers, pimps, players, and ballers later, it was finally my turn to talk to the magistrate. I stood behind the wooden table as I looked up at the magistrate sitting on her throne.

"Mr. Devin Williams, arrested for a DUI; and would you look at this, you're underage. What do you have to say for yourself young man?"

Her pinecone skin, short hair, glasses, and authoritative voice made me feel comfortable, for some reason reminding me of my Aunt Cheryl, who's as stern as they come.

"I really have no excuse ma'am. It was the last day of class and I was celebrating passing my Criminal Justice class with a B-. If I didn't pass, I would have to attend summer school."

She stared at me, looking totally unamused.

"You college kids sure know how to party; always going full throttle at the end of the year. A B-; you should have got an A, Mr. Williams."

"I was trying your honor."

"You didn't try hard enough!"

She glanced at the paper in front of her then glanced back at me as if she had an epiphany.

"Wait a minute, what's your name again?"

"Devin Williams, ma'am." A smile appeared on her face. I wasn't sure if I should smile back or be afraid. I stood in front of her not knowing what to do.

"Let me tell you something, Mr. Williams. You have some good friends. For the past two hours, five of your friends have been trying to persuade me to let you go. They told me how much of a good person you are and that you're never like this. Your girlfriend even blamed herself for giving you too much to drink."

I looked at her in shock. What friends? I don't have a girlfriend. Then it hit me; she could only be talking about Noelle. Were Noelle and her friends outside of the jail vouching for me? I was smiling on the inside; once again she had come to my rescue.

"Today is your lucky day, Mr. Williams."

"Really?" I replied with a smile on my face.

"Yes. If a group of people will stand outside of my building trying to convince me to let you go for hours, there must be some truth in it; but you're not getting off that easy."

My smile went to a straight line. What was she going to do? What was my punishment?

"I hear by order Mr. Devin Williams Saturday driving classes in addition to a $1,000.00 fine, with a suspension of driving privileges in the state of Georgia for 90 days."

"Do you have any questions Mr. Williams?"

"Yes. How am I supposed to get to driving class if my license is suspended?"

"You'll have to figure that out. If you want to drink like an adult, then you will get treated like one. We have additional community services programs that can drop your 90-day suspension to 30 days if that will help you. You won't be going to summer school, but you will be attending driving class."

"Yes ma'am," I replied in a somber voice.
With a look of shock on my face from her decision she quickly replied.

"Mr. Williams, I know this may seem like a lot, but for your sake this is nothing. Your breathalyzer test was at a staggering 0.12%. You put yourself and others at risk and you're not even 21 yet. I could fine you $3,000.00, lock you up for 30 days, put you on probation, and suspend your license until you turn 21."

When she explained what could've happened, I humbly accepted her first offer. As I was leaving out of the court, Officer Porter walked me to the front of the jail. "I don't want to see you back in here again. Do you hear me?" He said while handing me a stack of papers to read and sign.

The morning sun was beaming in my face as I walked out the front doors. I assumed I was going to see all of them standing outside waiting for me like a movie, but they were nowhere to be found. I looked around and saw Maurice's Monte Carlo sitting in the parking lot. As I got closer, I could see all of their heads slouched down in the car. *What are they doing?* I walked over to see Noelle sitting in the passenger seat sleeping; the others were doing the same. I made one of the scariest faces I could make and tapped on the window.

Opening her eyes, she screamed, waking Maurice and the others up. Realizing it was me, she jumped out the car playfully hitting me. "Don't you ever scare me like that again; and next time listen when I say give me the keys, Devin!" I stopped her in the middle of her rant and hugged her tight, placing a small kiss upon her forehead. "Aww y'all so cute," everyone in the car said. "Can y'all save that for later; none of us have eaten and I'm hungry," Maurice sarcastically said. I felt bad about what happened and I couldn't be more grateful to have friends like them. "Come on y'all; were going to Waffle House and it's on me! Maurice instantly sat up in his seat and turned on the car. Looking at me in a sense of urgency, "Well come on. We need to get there before you change your mind."

Atlanta was my home for the summer and luckily my parents didn't question me about coming home. They knew I had an internship, but, thank God, they didn't know about my driving classes. Towards the end of summer, I got a call from my Dad. From his tone I could tell something was up.

"Hey son, how have you been?"

"I been good Pops, just enjoying the summer, working and going to my internship every day. How are you?"

"Oh, I'm fine. You say you're going to your internship everyday huh?"

"Yeah, it's pretty cool."

"Cool huh? So Devin let me ask you this. How have your driving classes and community service hours been?" I was stuck for words. How did he know?

"It's been good. How did you know," I replied in an undertone voice.

"Son, I know everything, especially when the Fulton County court is sending mail to my house!"
I was stooped.

"You know son, you're older now. These decisions you make are going to affect you later on in life. I'm sure you learned your lesson from this and you didn't even ask for my help; I'm actually happy about that. But you have to be more careful; there's no telling what could have happened to you that night. What would've happened if you got hurt or even died?" As soon as my Dad said that, Officer Porter's speech replayed back in my mind. This was one mistake I wasn't going to make again.

Lesson Learned: This is one of the dumbest decisions I ever made in life. The DUI stayed on my driving record for five years and doubled my insurance because I was a high risk. I believe all those prayers my grandmother said for me came through that night. I could've had an accident or served time and paid a bigger fine, but somebody had mercy on me. If you're ever intoxicated, don't try to be the big guy; let one of your friends drive, call a cab or Uber. According to the National Institute on Alcohol Abuse and Alcoholism, each year an estimated 1,825 college students between the ages of 18-24 die from alcohol-related, unintentional injuries, including motor vehicle crashes. The data also states that each year 4,860,000 students between the ages of 18-24 drive under the influence of alcohol.[12] There are numerous options to avoid driving under the influence. It's better to be safe than sorry.

I was 20 years old and I waved the cop down for help, forgetting I was intoxicated and underage. Just stupid. I was so lucky to have somebody like Noelle, who was constantly by my side; no telling what other trouble I would've gotten into if it wasn't for her. Sometimes we push people like Noelle out of our lives because they're always on our case. We may think it's annoying, but they're just trying to help. Keep them around; they have your best interest at heart. My record was expunged 5 years later, but if I never would've made that decision I could have saved thousands of dollars on my insurance. Everybody is tempted to drink in college, but wait until your 21 and be responsible. Drinking can also lead to other problems, such as injury, assault, sexual abuse, unprotected sex, academic problems, and alcohol abuse disorder. Be disciplined and know when you've had enough. If you live a lazy, undisciplined life, you will make very poor choices that you'll end up regretting.

Chapter 15: Panhellenic Commitment

"I can't take this anymore more, Brandon. You keep accusing me of doing something I'm not; calling me out of my name, snooping around in my phone, and blatantly disrespecting me. I won't keep going through this with you. I won't!" I paced back and forth in my dorm room while talking to Brandon on the phone. He must have lost his everlasting mind accusing me of cheating on him. Yes, I have been acting different. But it has nothing to do with cheating and everything to do with me pledging to become a member of Phi Eta Beta.

I was five months in and almost done with the process of becoming a part of one of the best Sororities, but Brandon, my friends, and my mother weren't making it easy. My prophytes tried to help me, but all they ever said was "Carmen, they will understand once it's all over." "Carmen you have to have patience in this new life; it will all pay off in the end." Carmen this, Carmen that! They were supportive, but nobody was giving me a good solution to ease the minds of the one's I loved. As the days went by, their patience was getting thinner and thinner.

Ever since I was a child I wanted to be a part of Phi Eta Beta, especially since my Aunt was a member. The sorority represented everything I wanted to be. They were aware of national and political issues; they gave back to the community, and promoted health awareness on campus. With my goals of one day becoming a Physical Therapist, it felt more than right to join. Phi Eta Beta's reputation on campus represented integrity, strength, and love. To be frank, we were just cooler than all of the other sororities.

Brandon continued to accuse me of cheating. After an hour of yelling back and forth, I decided to walk over to his dorm. I threw on my red Ohio State hoodie and sweat pants and swiftly brushed past the girls in my dorm. He had no idea I was coming and I didn't want him to know. I loved the element of surprise. Luckily, Ohio State's dorms weren't that far from each other. I lived in Siebert Hall and Brian stayed in Bradley Hall, both on the south side of campus. I walked to the Student Union first to get his favorite snacks.

"What are you doing, Carmen? Where are you?" he said.

"I'm in my room, Brandon, stop clocking me," I replied while grinning.

"Clocking you? It sounds like you're in a restaurant or something. See this is what I'm talking about, you keep lying!"

"Just calm down, it will all make sense soon, please."

"What do you mean calm down! I am calm!"

I grabbed a small bag of Cheetos, an orange Gatorade, and our favorite movie *Talladega Nights: The Ballad of Ricky Bobby* from the local Red Box. We quoted lines from that movie all the time, so I knew it would put a smile on his face. I didn't want to lose him in the midst of gaining something I really wanted. I was cool with Brandon's male resident advisor and I explained that I wanted to surprise him. He let me right up and I took the elevator to the third floor. Walking through the hallway I started to feel like a piece of meat. All the guys were staring at me and saying some of the most outrageous catcalling comments. "Where you going, pretty freckles?" "Long hair, don't care; you coming to my room?" Then one guy yelled from the end of the hallway "Ms. Caramel where you going?" I immediately turned around with the meanest look on my face, but the guys weren't lying. I was petite with freckles and my hair flowed down my back, but I have a name and they should use it. Brandon was a senior, a year older than me, tall, close clip haircut and played football with a smile to die for.

I could hear Brandon talking to me on the phone while I was outside of his room. "Hello? Hello? Carmen, Hello! I know she didn't just hang up on me." I giggled then knocked on his door like I was making a Hip Hop beat. He opened the door and there he was shirtless with just his basketball shorts on. He looked at his phone then looked back at me confused. "Carmen what in the hell, how did you get in here?" He pulled me in his room as he quickly looked in the hallway to make sure nobody was following me.

Brandon's room wall was filled with his hometown Baltimore Ravens paraphernalia with a few Ohio State pieces. Both of the twin beds were pushed together because his roommate relocated due to financial aid problems. I sat on his bed and pulled out the snacks and DVD that I purchased. "I'm sorry I've been acting strange lately, but there is nothing going on, I promise," I said in a soft sweet voice. He gently kissed my forehead, held me tighter and didn't ask anything else. We snuggled and laughed while watching *Talladega Nights*, but within forty-five minutes my phone started ringing uncontrollably. I was afraid to answer because I didn't want the night to end. I had just gotten my boyfriend back and didn't want to lose this moment. Brandon handed me the phone from the desk with a look of annoyance on his face. Looking at the caller ID, I saw that it was my prophyte, Sandy. I knew immediately that she wanted me to do something, and it was probably to chauffeur her and the other girls around the city. I drove them around so much I was starting to feel like I dropped out of college and was working for Uber.

I stepped in the hallway to answer the phone, causing Brandon to become even more suspicious.

"Meet me in the bookstore parking lot in 10 minutes and don't be a second late," she said in a stern voice. Rushing back into Brandon's room, I gathered my things, but not before he stopped me.

"Where you going?" he asked while blocking the doorway. "I'm sorry Brandon, but I have to go. I'm sorry," I said looking down at the ground.

"If you leave, don't come back."

"Don't be like that, I promise it's not nothing bad." Slowly he moved to the side and let me out. Swiftly I rushed across campus so I would be on time. The last time one of us was late, they had us out until the early morning.

The next morning was hell. I didn't return to my room until 4:30 a.m. from driving each prophyte around. I was chauffeuring them around to their dorms, Wal-Mart, and their boyfriends' dorms. I walked into my biochemistry class looking like death warmed over. I barely made it, but my friend Dominique always helped me through. We were both from Chicago, Illinois so we looked out for one another from time to time. If it wasn't for him, I might have failed lab last semester. While walking to my dorm to catch up on some much need sleep, I saw Brandon on the yard standing with his friends. As I walked towards him, he deliberately turned his back; that was my warning. I was too tired to explain myself and wasn't going to risk getting embarrassed.

Midway through my perfect nap, my phone started to ring. I tried to ignore the calls, but they just wouldn't stop. Looking at my phone, I had seven missed calls from my mom. She called again and before I could say hello she started yelling.

"Carmen Helen Jones!"

I knew I was in trouble once she said my whole name.

"Yes Mom," I replied while still half asleep in my bed with the sun peaking in.

"Why have you been ignoring my calls? It's 2:00 p.m. Why aren't you in class or studying?"

My Mother was a no non-sense type of person and if she was dishing out money she really wasn't having it. She wouldn't stop asking me the most ridiculous questions: "Are you pregnant?" "Do you think you're in love with Brandon? "Carmen keep your mind in those books and off them boys!" I stopped her right there.

"Mom I'm not pregnant and I'm not distracted by Brandon. You know I'm a cheerleader and we have practice every day. I'm also in the Student Government Association and to top it off I have a million assignments to finish. Your money is not going to waste." I explained every detail of my life, except that I was in the process of becoming a Beta. Before I could go on, she stopped me mid-sentence.

"Girl, do you think I'm dumb? Did you forget that I raised you? It's something else going on with you Carmen. I just know it. Whatever it is, get it together. I have to get back to work. I'll talk to you later, honey, love yah." I took the phone off of my ear and looked at it in shock. I could never get away with lying; she sniffed out lies like a canine sniffed out drugs.

Rushing down the steps of my dorm, I headed to my next class and saw the resident advisors stapling Valentine's Day decorations on the wall. I completely forgot Valentine's Day was two days away. I sent Brandon a long text message apologizing and explained that I would make it up to him on Valentine's Day. I started planning it right away and I was lucky because this year Valentine's Day fell on a Saturday, so I didn't have to worry about class the following morning. My friend Chloe rode with me to the mall. I needed her advice on what to wear; I always admired her style. Chloe was a tall, blonde cheerleader who looked like she came off the pages of Vogue. The guys on campus called us Beyoncé and Gwyneth, not only because I was black and she was white, but we had a lot in common. Her boyfriend was on the football team too, and she liked Hip Hop.

"Carmen where have you been? I haven't seen you in forever, you don't come to the kickbacks anymore and I haven't seen you at any parties. Did I do something?" she asked. I was in disbelief; everybody was questioning my whereabouts. First my boyfriend, then my mom, and now my best friend.

"I've just been so busy with class and Brandon. I'm here now though, sorry." As I parked the car, an eerie silence came over the car while Chloe looked at me as if she knew I was lying.

"What's wrong?" I asked.

"Well, you know Tim and Brandon are good friends. Brandon told him that he rarely spends time with you anymore and he didn't know if it was going to work out."
Tim was Chloe's boyfriend; he and Brandon both played on the football team together.

"That's why we're here at the mall. I'm making it up to him for Valentine's Day. I swear it's not what you think," I explained while walking into Macy's.
From the look on her face, I could tell she was still skeptical. Then she said the unthinkable.

"Carmen, if you're on line or something you can just tell me. I know you're supposed to keep it a secret; but it's ok, you're safe with me."
I couldn't bear to look her in the eyes. I've come this far without telling anybody and I didn't want to drop the ball now. I knew my secret would be safe, but I still didn't feel

comfortable telling her. As I finished paying for my dress, I turned around and looked her directly in the eyes.

"I guess," I said with a funny smirk on my face.

"I knew it!" She screamed.

She hugged me while yelling so loud that she scared a few customers. I felt content with telling her because she never brought it back up or asked questions about it. It was great to have her support, and partially have what seemed like the weight of the world lifted off my shoulders.

My roommate was gone for the weekend and Valentine's Day was finally here. I told Brandon to dress casual even though we were only going to be in my dorm room. I finished straightening my hair just in the nick of time; he knocked on my door at 8:00 p.m. on the dot. He looked so good in his black blazer, red polo, black slacks, and loafers to match. He took my hand and spun me around like a queen, admiring my red strapless dress and black high heels. He loved when I wore heels. "Baby, you are stunning and I love it," he said.

Finally taking his eyes off me, he looked around the room surprised. I had completely decorated the room to our own little Valentine's suite. I changed the light bulbs to red ones, placed chocolate Hershey Kisses on the ground, and put fake roses in a vase in the middle of the table. "This looks great, baby! I appreciate it," he said with a smile. Yes! It was working! I was on a college budget and couldn't afford to buy him expensive gifts, so I had to improvise. Plus, I was paying out of pocket to become a part of Phi Eta Beta. He also loved the steak, salad, and bake potato I prepared. After we finished eating he leaned over and picked up one of the kisses off the ground looking confused.

"Baby, why do you have Hershey Kisses on the ground?" I smiled before replying.

"This is to make up for lost time. Now that I've kissed the ground that you walked on, will you be mine, again?" He cracked a smile and started laughing so hard that I couldn't help but laugh myself.

"Who told you to say that? You didn't come up with that by yourself," he said.

"Yes I did and that's not it! The fake roses in the middle of the table represent our love that will never end. You get it? The rose is fake, so it will never die," I said jokingly as he couldn't contain from laughing.

Brandon realized that he forgot his phone in the car, so he went to get it, but while he was gone my phone rung and it was one of my prophytes. *Not again!* I know they wouldn't dare ask me to do anything tonight. For goodness sake it was Valentine's Day! I answered the phone slowly, putting it to my ear as if I was in a scary movie. "So you have time to cook for your boyfriend and make all these plans huh? I need you to meet us in front of the Buckeyes Football Stadium in the next twenty minutes!" Sandy yelled into the phone. I was baffled. How did she know I was with Brandon? Before I could ask, she hung up the phone. How was I going to get out of this? Every time I seem to get back within Brandon's good graces, they would summon me. I couldn't face telling him what I had to do. I reached for a pen and wrote him a note. "Sorry baby, an emergency came up. I'll be back soon. I Love you."

While I was driving to the stadium, Brandon was calling and texting me back to back. By the time I arrived at the stadium, I had ten missed calls and fourteen text messages from him. I couldn't believe they wanted us on Valentine's Day. I was beginning to think they were jealous, lonely, and bitter. Sandy and Tyrese were the only two prophytes there, along with the other 20 girls that were pledging with me. If one of us was summoned, then all of us had to suffer consequences. I felt bad because I didn't want the other girls to suffer because of my actions. "So, the six of you think you can be on dates having fun? How can you find time to do such? Shouldn't you be learning the history about the sorority?" she said.

All six of us had on makeup, high heels, and dresses. We looked like we were about to attend the most upscale club in Ohio. "I bet you're wondering how I know that you six were out on a date. Well, one of your prophytes told me. That's unfair to them, you all are a team; if one is on a date, all of you should be on a date. If one of you is studying, then all of you should be studying. You're only as good as your weakest link!" Tyrese yelled while we stood in front of the football stadium in the blistering cold. I couldn't believe somebody told on us. Am I supposed to apologize for having a life? Tyrese was one of the nicer prophtyes; she always had good advice and was understanding, while Sandy was the exact opposite. "Listen up girls! If you want to leave, you have to pass this history exercise," Tyrese said. I immediately started smiling because I knew I would pass.

Tyrese made the six of us sit in the two back rows of her black 2005 Ford Excursion while the other 15 stood outside in a line. Three girls sat on each row while Tyrese and Sandy set in front.

"Whoever answers these questions correctly gets to leave. You better hope your boyfriend is still there when you get back," Sandy said causing me to suck my teeth.

"Carmen is there something you want to say?" Sandy asked.

"No," I replied. I didn't want to be in any more trouble than I already was.

"Girls, I want you to recite the founders' names and the day they were born, but I want you to recite it backwards and in alphabetical order," Tyrese said. *What!* Who thinks of this stuff? I'm convinced all of them are bored. I was on the last row so I had time to think about my answers. One-by-one all of my line sisters failed, but they all gave the right answers. At least I thought they did. I still didn't understand, but a light bulb went off right before my turn. "Carmen it's your turn; you might as well give up, because you're going to be here with your sisters too," Sandy snarled. Abruptly I turned around backwards in my seat and recited each founding member's name and date of birth in alphabetical order. I could hear Tyrese laughing slightly when I did it. Finishing my answer I could hear Sandy huffing and puffing. *Was she mad because I did it right?* "Everybody has to stay except for Carmen. You can go Carmen," Sandy stated with an attitude. Rolling down the window, she let the other girls leave too. Getting out the truck, all of the girls had an attitude, but I was smiling. I knew they wanted us to be smart, but also clever. As I walked past Tyrese, she gave me the thumbs up while Sandy rolled her eyes.

I knew Brandon would be gone once I returned, but he wasn't. He was sitting on the side of the bed with the most disappointing face I had ever seen. He didn't even look this sad when he lost his championship game last year. "I can't be with you anymore; it's over," he said as I walked in the door. I tried to explain but he wouldn't listen. I reached for his hand, but he pulled back with a look of hatred on his face. "When I told you I was getting my phone, I really went to get you these flowers and gift card from H&M! But again you left me! I'm done with you! Get out my way!" He was yelling so loud I became scared. His veins were popping out of his neck as he held the flowers and card in his hand. "You can keep the flowers too; they'll be dead soon, just like you are to me!" he yelled as he threw the flowers at me. I stood in disbelief as he slammed the door storming out. With my dress still on, I laid in bed crying my eyes out. All of the kisses and roses were still spread across the floor and the candles on my desk looked just like me – melted in sorrow.

Getting out of bed, I went for a long walk and ended up crying on a bench with my head down.

"Carmen is that you?" I heard from a familiar voice. It was Tyrese.

"What's wrong? Why are you out here in the cold crying? Where's Brandon?" she asked.

"He just broke up with me. I've been keeping everything from him and he couldn't take it." I said.

Sitting down beside me, she consoled me and took a deep breathe.

"The pressures of pledging; Carmen I went through the same thing."

"Really?"

"Yeah, but not with my boyfriend; it was with my friend. She found out that I told some of my other friends, but not her and she was upset. She even cried about it."

We both giggled at the thought of somebody crying over this, but coincidently I was drying my eyes.

"If he means that much to you, then you should tell him."

"I don't understand; I thought we couldn't tell anybody."

"Well, that's the thing Carmen, you can't tell anybody; but, if he's somebody, then you can tell him. Get it? If he wasn't somebody you loved, I would say forget about it. But since you're out here at four in the morning crying your eyes out, then obviously you love him."

Hugging Tyrese goodnight, I headed straight toward Brandon's dorm. Knocking on his door softly so I wouldn't disturb his neighbors, I could see somebody looking through the peep hole.

"What do you want Carmen?" He said.

"I just want to finally explain everything, Brandon." He unlocked the door and without glancing at me got right back in his bed - so rude. As he laid down on his stomach, I smacked him on his back.

"Can you at least look at me, dang!" I said. He then rolled over, purposely closing his eyes.

"What Carmen?"

"I'm sorry for the distance and neglect you've been experiencing, but here's the truth."

"I'm on line and in the initiation process of being a Beta. There, I said it."

His eyes opened wide like he had just seen a ghost.

"What! That's awesome! It all makes sense now; you're always leaving randomly in the middle of the night and looking so tired the next morning. I mean, that's still the actions of a cheating girlfriend, but I believe you." I laughed at his reaction. We made a promise to each other that whenever I would be summoned by my prophytes, I would come to his room afterwards or he would come to mine no matter the time. That agreement took so much pressure off of me. I was grateful to have him back.

The following weeks were going smooth, but then mid-term grades were released. My grades dropped from an A average to a C average in four of my classes. I wasn't surprised, I knew they weren't going to be the best; but my mom on the other hand was. She called me the following week when my grades were sent home.

"Carmen, I knew it, I knew it! I knew something was wrong and now these grades are proving that I was right. For the last time are you pregnant? If not, what's the problem?" She said yelling in the phone. I thought about what Tyrese said and decided to tell her the truth.

"Mom, I'm pledging to be a Beta; I've been on line for the past two months. I would have told you sooner, but I wanted to do it alone." I replied as the phone became silent.

"So, you mean to tell me my baby girl has been on line all this time and hasn't told me? You know your Aunt Faye is a Beta and she started the first chapter at Ohio State. She could have called and pulled some strings for you and your grades wouldn't be how they are."

That's exactly why I didn't want to tell my mom or aunt. With my aunt being the founding member of the Phi Eta Beta's Ohio State chapter, it would've been too easy to join or they would have given me a harder time because they knew who she was. I wanted to do it on my own, without any leeway.

"Did you call your track coach from high school?" You know she's a Beta too, she said."

"Mom I know, she and Aunt Faye are the reasons I'm pledging. I just want to do everything on my own. Don't worry, I can do this and my grades are going to come up. Have I ever let you down before?"

"Well, I'm proud of you. You have everything planned out. Just make sure these grades are up by finals."
The advice Tyrese gave me was working and it helped me release so much stress. I started to see an immediate improvement in my grades.

The day was finally here. Tonight was the night the entire Ohio State University would see who the new Panhellenic Greeks were. I was nervous, excited, and anxious all in one.

Brandon told me he was stopping past before the probate because he had an away game the following day and wouldn't be able to attend. I understood and didn't complain; he's been nothing but supportive since I told him the truth. He arrived at my room with a big black sheet covering something in his hands. Uncovering the sheet, he revealed a big teddy bear wearing a shirt that said "Clever," which represented my line name. My prophytes gave me that name because I always had clever answers whenever we were being tested. He also had a plethora of other gifts, including a license plate with my sorority logo on it, a necklace, card, and various accessories of red and pink, the colors of my sorority. Suddenly, there was a knock at the door.

I opened the door and in walked my Mom, Dad, and Aunt Faye.

"Mom, what are y'all doing here?" I said.

"You didn't think we were going to miss this did you? I told your Aunt Faye you were online and she called down to see what day you were coming out, so we decided to surprise you," she explained. She just couldn't keep it to herself, but I'm glad they were here. With a look of nervousness on his face, Brandon was quiet. This was his first time meeting my parents, but luckily he was dressed nice and had just given me a ton of gifts so he was in my parent's good graces. Brandon and my Dad started talking about football and from there on I knew everything would be ok; they were football fanatics.

It was 8:01 p.m., which is the actual date of when Phi Eta Beta was founded on August 1st, 1926. It was time for the probate to begin. With all of my line sisters, we marched into the Value Center Arena wearing our matching red and pink dresses with black heels singing our sorority's song. The screams in the stadium were so loud I could hardly hear myself. There were 21 of us and I was number 10. It was my time. I stepped out of line, stomping the wooden basketball court all the way to the front of the audience.

"My name is Carmen Helen Jones! Coming all the way from the windy city! Chi-Town! And I'm the Clever 10!" I said in my loud, squeaky voice. The crowd started screaming to the top of their lungs. I could hear my mother screaming, "That's my baby, that's my baby!" and Chloe was the loudest, "Carmen! That's my best friend! Go best friend!" I watched as security came and told her to stop blowing the bullhorn. I couldn't contain my laughter as she continued to blow; nobody was stopping her.

Once the last sister went, everybody rushed the floor congratulating us. Red and pink balloons filled the arena while hugs and kisses were exchanged. I screamed "I did it! I finished!" as my parents, Aunt Faye, Chloe and my other friends surrounded me. Tyrese and Sandy came over to congratulate me. Sandy was so nice I was beginning to think she was schizophrenic. She was hugging and jumping for joy with me. My line sister, Jada, leaned over toward me "Do you see Sandy? Who knew she could be so nice," Jada said sarcastically. I later learned she was like that with all of the pledging females until they crossed over. It was her way of tough love.

My parents, Aunt Faye, Chloe, and a few of my cheerleading teammates went with me to P.F. Chang's. I decided to wear pink and red around campus the next few days, but once I hit the yard things changed. Everybody seemed to be treating me different, but in a good way. The congratulatory comments went on for days, making me feel like an overnight celebrity. Numerous students knew my name, and, to top it off, younger girls discretely asked me about joining. It was then that I realized I would be on the other side of the fence recruiting next year; but I was ready. Ready to serve the community with integrity, love, and fortitude as a member of the Phi Eta Beta Sorority.

Lesson Learned: While on your journey to becoming Greek, take every step along the way serious. Don't do it for the popularity, accolades, or because your friends are doing it. It won't benefit you because in the end you will be sacrificing certain parts of your life and wasting your time, money, and energy. I sacrificed my relationship with Brandon and it almost cost me his love. Patience is one of the main ingredients when pledging. Some of your peers won't understand and some people pledging may not cross on their first try. Sometimes the time is not yet ripe. There were 25 of us when we first started, but at the end there were only 21. Remain humble and don't change yourself; still be you.

Becoming Greek has helped me to become more persistent, balanced, and personable, allowing me to network and meet numerous people in the field that I chose to work in. All of these elements can be applied to your everyday life. Don't let the negative stories you hear about pledging deter you from joining; every campus is different. The ones who take advantage of the newcomers have lost sight of what joining a Greek organization is really about. They are stuck on having power. Listen to your conscience, remember your morals, and follow your heart. If something doesn't feel right from within, then most of the time it's not.

I love my Sorority and love the members who are active after they graduate, who continue to serve their community. Please remember that this is a lifelong pledge to support and help others who are in need. You worked hard to get those letters, so you should continue to take the oath seriously. It's not just a one-time engagement, but a lifetime partnership. If you're not consistently making somebody else's life better, then you're wasting your time. Your life will become better by making others better. Remember this one thing: after the initiation process is over, the real work begins.

Chapter 16: Two Heartbeats

"If you think we're going to keep sending you money every week without talking to you, then you are sadly mistaken. Your father and I are dishing out thousands for your education, Stacey! Thousands! Call me back or else!" *Could this situation get any worse?* My mother was threatening me over voicemail, my so-called boyfriend came straight from the pits of hell, and I hadn't been to class in days. Lying in bed, I listened to my mother's voicemail over and over. She had to be worried sick! I never acted like this; she probably thinks it has something to do with Bruce. She was right. I shook my head as I watched my favorite TV show, *Maury*. "You are not the father!" Maury yelled to the potential dad. Bruce and I would never need Maury's help; he absolutely was the father and the sole captor of my virginity.

Muscling up enough energy to close the blinds, I noticed a tinted white Lexus speeding toward my house. It was Bruce. *Oh God, what does he want?* I watched as he knocked on my door and I prayed he would leave. "I see you peeking through the blinds, Stacey. Open the door now!" he yelled. My stomach trembled as I walked downstairs; the mere sight of him made me nauseous.

"Don't track those leaves in my house, Bruce. What do you want?"

"What do you mean? I came to check on you."

"I'm fine. Can you leave now, please?"

"I'm not going anywhere. Let me upstairs. Why you acting stupid?"

"You're not staying here. What do you want?"

"Did you tell anybody?"

"Is that why you came here? No I didn't, now leave."

"Did you schedule your appointment? My friend should have the money this week."

"Not yet; I'll let you know when I do. Now leave." Little did he know I wasn't scheduling an appointment. I'm having this baby. His friend can keep that money.

I was a sophomore at St. John's University in New York and I hadn't talked to anybody since the incident. God and I weren't on good terms either. I questioned him so many times when I saw the pregnancy test. *God, how could you let this happen? How could you let him do this to me?* First I lose my virginity, now I'm pregnant. What did I do to deserve this? I even Googled "What are the chances of a pregnancy test being wrong?" But that answer did no justice. "It's possible to get a false positive, but people usually get a false negative." I got down on my knees and prayed. I'd have to tell my parents soon, so I needed all the help I could get. After praying, I decided to attend church. With my black heels on, black dress, and black church hat, I looked in the mirror wondering, am I heading to a funeral or Sunday service? I guess my look reflected how I felt - dead.

"Mom!" I yelled opening the front door. *Are my eyes deceiving me?* Are my parents and younger sister really at my house dressed for church? There she stood with her fist in the air attempting to knock on the door. Was I dreaming or did they really drive three hours from Albany, New York to Queens, New York to check on me.

"Hi, Stacey," my mother and father said simultaneously as they walked in the house.

"I was headed to church, what are y'all doing here?" I asked.

"Sit down, we want to talk to you," she sternly replied.

The mood had shifted from "we're happy to see you" to "sit down, shut up, and listen." I could feel my mother's eyes gazing into the depths of my soul. She sat with her legs crossed and fingers tapping her knees. Her demeanor said it all - she meant business.

"Did you get my voicemail?" my mom asked.

"Yes, but…"

"I don't want to hear it, Stacey! I'm sick of your excuses. I called you yesterday and today is a new day. What has had you occupied these last two weeks?"

"Nothing."

"Nothing? Have you seen Bruce? What has he done to you?"

Holy crap! How does she know? Is my house bugged? I wouldn't put it past my father. He'll do anything to make sure I'm safe and following the good book of the Lord.

"I had a dream about you last night; I could hear you screaming so loud that it woke me up. I woke your father and told him we had to come see you. So, for you to sit here and say 'nothing' is puzzling."

Did this woman just say I was screaming and needed her help? When did she become a psychic? "Did you have sex?" she asked.

God why are you doing this to me? I was dressed and ready to give you all the praise, but now things are getting worse. I'm pregnant, but my parents thought I was a virgin. I'm not getting rid of the baby and, even if I wanted to, they wouldn't let me; so I'll just tell them. Besides, I'm not a child anymore. I'm 19. What can they do?

"Yes," I uttered

"Excuse me! What did you say? Speak up please," my mom said.

"Yes," I murmured.

Leaning against the wall, my father palmed his face in his hands, letting out a huge sigh. Quickly, my mother stood up from the couch, pacing back and forth.

"After all we've taught you? After being in church from Sunday-to-Sunday, haven't you learned anything? Your father is the Youth Minister! You're a role model!" she yelled.
I looked at the ground as they continued to yell. I didn't want to hear it; the pressures of being Stacey Turner had always been too much. Abruptly a loud noise hit the wall, frightening me and my mom. Looking up, I could see my father's hand coming out the wall. He had completely lost it! Walking over towards him, my mother consoled him while taking a look at his visibly swollen hand.

Glancing at my father, I could see a small tear coming down his cheek. I couldn't believe it. He was showing emotion. All of my life, I've wondered why he reserved hugs and kisses for special occasions but never just because. Bruce was a devil, but he showed me affection that I never felt. I yearned for warmth and now it felt too late as I watched my father stand there and cry because of what happened. My Dad's emotions painted two pictures 1. That he loved me and 2. He wanted to send Bruce through the wall.

"Stacey go in your room and start packing," he said.

"Why? I have class tomorrow."

"Class? You're not going to class, you're coming home. You think you're going to be down here having sex while we're paying your tuition? You must have lost your mind. Now start packing. Tears flushed my eyes as I packed.

"I don't know why you're crying. You're the one that decided to lay down with that boy," my mom said.

Waking up the next morning, I felt lost. I couldn't believe I was home. I was starving and I could hear my parents talking from the kitchen. I decided I'd wait until they left because I didn't want to see them. I heard footsteps going up the stairs followed by their bedroom door being shut. Throwing on a big, long shirt, I headed toward the kitchen and devoured a bowl of cereal. I heard their room door open while I was eating. Just when I thought it was safe, my mother comes down the stairs in her pink robe standing in the doorway with her arms folded.

"Well good morning to you," she said.

"Good Morning."

"When you're done eating, get dressed. I'm taking you to the doctor for a checkup. Hopefully, that nasty little boy didn't give you a disease."

My palms started to sweat and I immediately started praying. *Lord please don't let them do a pregnancy test, please, Lord, please.*

Putting on my pants I caught a side glimpse of myself in the mirror. I turned to the right then turned to the left, placing my hands over my stomach. Is there really a baby in there? "Stacey cut that secular music off!" My mother yelled from the hallway. I was playing The Dream's *Love vs. Money* album and she killed my groove. I dashed for my shirt, just in case she opened the door. I couldn't bear for her to find out I was pregnant. "You know we don't allow that kind of music in here," she yelled from outside of my door. Aggressively, I waved my hands at the door like a gangbanger throwing up gang signs silently saying "shut the hell up!" For a moment I felt slight satisfaction, even though she couldn't see or hear me.

Pulling in the parking lot, my body was filled with anxiety. *What if I contracted an STD? What if the doctor decides to give me a pregnancy test?* She'll probably kill me right here. Big Bird, The Cookie Monster, Burt and Ernie, and Oscar the Grouch covered the walls of the doctor's office while I sat there looking like the biggest kid in the world. I was 19 years old still going to a children's doctor.

"Stacy Turner, Dr. Matlin will see you now," the nurse said motioning for me to come back.

"Stacey. What a surprise. How is school?" Dr. Matlin asked.

"It's going good."

"Yeah, I guess," my mother replied as Dr. Matlin stared at us confused.

"What brings you in today?"

"I wanted to get a checkup and an STD test."

"Are you sexually active?"

"She sure is," my mother replied.

"Well in that case, I'm going to give you an STD test and a pregnancy test."

My heart dropped to my knees. This is it. I'm coming home to you Lord; my mom is going to kill me right in this office.

Dr. Matlin drew my blood and sent it to the lab. Next up was the pregnancy test. She explained the STD test would come back in a week, but I would get the pregnancy results today. I wish it was the other way around. My mother and I sat silently waiting for Dr. Matlins return. *What am I going to say once the results come back?* Dr. Matlin walked in the room with a brown folder. Opening the folder she scanned the paper uttering a low "hmm."

"So, it looks like Stacey is about five weeks pregnant."

"Excuse me. What did you say?" my mom asked.

"Stacey is pregnant, Mrs. Turner."

"Are you sure?"

"The tests results are usually 99% accurate. We can take another one if you want."

"No, that's fine."

Grabbing her coat, my mother glanced at me and didn't say a word as she walked out the office.

The ride home was silent. When I attempted to part my lips, her eyes pierced through me letting me know to stay quiet. If only she knew what really happened; but I was too afraid to tell her. Bruce said if I told anybody, he would kill me and then himself.

"Where the hell you going!" she said as I walked to my room.

"I'm just going to my room," I murmured.

"Look at you, standing there pregnant from your supposedly first time having sex. How unlucky is that!" Walking up the stairs, she grabbed the back of my shirt and dragged me down the steps, slamming me against the front door. Our noses connected like two boxers at a weigh in.

"Since you want to be grown, get out and don't come back!"

"Get out of my face!" I yelled in an attempt to push her off me. Suddenly, I was struck with a mighty blow to my stomach. She hit me! I couldn't believe she hit me. She's in church every day and she just hit a pregnant teen. I crumbled to the floor in pain as my mother stepped away in shock. *What if she killed my baby?*

"Why God? Why! We've been so good to this girl! Get out, Stacey! Just get out!"

Where was I going to go? I'm 19 with no car and $50.00 to my name. I sat on the porch crying while scrolling through my phone. I needed somewhere to stay. Reaching in my purse, I grabbed my mirror. With mascara and eye shadow running down my face, I could see my mother looking at me through the window. I didn't bother turning around. At this point I didn't know who was crazier, my mom or Bruce. I looked like a true runaway as I walked to the entrance of the neighborhood.

I smiled at my neighbor as he pulled in his driveway, staring at me as if he knew something was wrong. Then I heard a yell.

"Stacey! Stacey! Come back here!"

I stopped, turned around, and then kept walking. She was a complete psycho. What did she want?

"Stacey, come back here now!" she screamed again.

"Huh?" I yelled as if I didn't understand.

"I said come back."

The following Friday, my father knocked on my door.

"Stacey, I'm coming in," he said.

"Be ready in the morning. We're going to speak with Pastor Brown."

"Pastor Brown?" I replied.

"Yes, we're going to see him. We need to figure out how we're going to move one. Be ready at 8 a.m."

What was Pastor Brown going to say besides pray? Hopefully, he would knock some sense into my parents and tell them to put me back in school.

Opening the stained doors of Mount Hope Baptist Church, I felt like a call girl who had just left the Vegas strip. I even looked in the air to see if smoke was coming from my head. I was far from evil, but being called derogatory names by my mother had taken its toll on me. This was embarrassing. My father's the Youth Minister and I'm a future youth parent. What a shame. Pastor Brown walked in, greeting us in his burgundy robe.

"I'm so glad you three could join me," he said.

"Hi, Mr. Brown" I replied in a mellow voice.

"You don't seem happy to see me, Stacey."

"Brother Turner has told me everything that's transpired and I must say it was a lot to take in."

"Tell me about it," I murmured.

"Now from what I understand, you two have taken her out of school. Correct?"

"Yes, Pastor Brown. We work hard and we didn't raise her to be in school going buck wild," my mom said as I sat visibly frustrated

"This is all very sad, but you can't keep her out of school. Now more than ever is when she'll need an education. How else is she going to provide for her child? I know you two are highly upset, as any parent would be, but that seed is your grandchild. When that child arrives, you're going to love him or her from the bottom of your heart."

Thank you Pastor Brown! Finally, somebody is on my side, willing to help me.

"And for you miss lady, you need to make sure you are focusing on God, class, those books and nothing else."

I guess I spoke too soon. My parents agreed with Pastor Brown and, before we left, he lead us in prayer that seemed to last forever. My hand started sweating because my mother's forceful grip got tighter and tighter with every word Pastor Brown said.

I was so relieved to be back in school, to be back in Queens, New York. Better yet, relieved to be away from my parents. Two months had gone by since I saw Bruce and I was going to do my best to avoid him. I was transferring to the University of Albany in the fall so I wouldn't have to worry about seeing him. Plus, my parents and I agreed it would be best if I went to a school closer once it was time for me to have the baby.

"Ms. Turner, are you ok?" Professor Walker asked.

"Yes ma'am."

"Are you sure? You don't look well and there is no sleeping in my class. Sociology majors are better than that."
I know I'm not supposed to be sleeping. What college student doesn't know that?

"I'm sorry, Professor Walker. I've had a migraine for the past week and it won't go away," I said.

"Stacey, if you've had a migraine for a week then maybe you should see a doctor."

She sounded like my mom. I told her about my migraine a few days ago and she said the same thing, but I didn't have time. I was already behind in class due to the constant morning sickness. I rubbed my stomach every day, comforting my baby, wondering if he or she felt the pain. Maybe I should go to the doctor; I hope it has nothing to do with my baby.

When I arrived at home, the same white Lexus was parked at my house. I knew right away it was Bruce. Parking my car, I attempted to rush inside. I wasn't in the mood for his antics.

"Stacey, I know you see me!" he yelled while getting out the car.

"What do you want?"

"Why you didn't tell me you were back? I missed you."

"Missed me? You didn't miss me. What do you want?"
He moved closer toward me and looked me directly in the eyes, almost scaring me.

"Did you tell your parents?"
I paused before answering, wondering if I should tell him I was keeping it. What if he hits me? If my own mother did, I'm sure he would too.

"No, but they know I'm pregnant and I'm keeping the baby."

"I knew you were going to do that! I don't care; you're a female, so you're going to have it most of the time."

He was such a jerk!

"Look, Bruce, you don't have to worry. I'm not saying anything. Can you just leave me alone? I'll contact you for my doctor's appointment in a few days and that's it."

"You know what, forget you, Stacey. I don't want to be around you anyway." He yelled, waving his fist as if he was about to hit me. I quickly stepped back, blocking my face while he gained composure and then left. That wouldn't have been his first time hitting me.

I hated hospitals and, even more, I hated being next to Bruce. With those two combined, I could tell this was about to be a visit from hell. Surprisingly, the ER wasn't packed; they were moving right along. Within 45 minutes, Bruce and I were called to the back. The primary doctor couldn't prescribe me medicine because I was pregnant, but they wanted to do an ultrasound to ensure nothing was wrong. I positioned myself on the table and waited for the doctor to come back while Bruce was sitting in the chair scrolling through his phone. If he wasn't such a jerk, it would actually be nice to have him here. The doctor moved the ultrasound camera around my stomach while we looked at the screen trying to make out what he saw.

"Hmmm" the doctor murmured while moving the camera to the right side of my stomach. He then moved it to the left and murmured "hmm" again.

"I have some great news for you; actually, it's double the news," the doctor said.

Sir, I don't have time for this, just tell me what's going on. I'm a broke college student and I'm only pregnant because of this psycho.

"Well, I don't know if you heard, but it was two heartbeats."

I knew something was wrong!

"Oh my God, is the baby going to be ok? What does that mean? Does my baby have a heart deformity or something?"
"No, of course not. I wouldn't have said it was good news," he said laughing.

"Well, what is it?"

"You're having twins. One's a boy and the other's a girl. Congrats!"
Bruce instantly dropped to his knees as if he was praying.

"Are you serious!" he yelled in the most disappointing voice.

"I can't believe this, I'm calling my mother." Bruce said, putting his phone on speaker.

"Mom, Stacey and I just found out what we're having..."

"Go ahead. What is it?"

"We're having twins, a boy and a girl."

"Twins, you're having twins? Boy, I thought you were shooting blanks!" she said.
Did she really just say that? She thought her 19 year old son was infertile. For the next 18 years this is the type of stupidity I'll have to deal with. I was starting to see where he got his ignorance from. *God please don't let my kids get his genes. Please!*

On the way home, I called my parents to give them the news. At least I knew they weren't going to say anything ignorant.

"Mom, put the phone on speaker so dad can hear me." I said while driving.

"Ok, it's on speaker."

"So, I went to the doctor for my migraine and they did an ultrasound."
I waited for a response, some sort of gasp or excitement, but the mood was calm and silent.

"Ok, go on," she replied.

"Well, the doctor saw two babies. So, um, I'm having twins."

There was complete silence. Were they lost for words?

"Hello," I said.

"We're here, baby," my mom said.

"So, what do you have to say?"

"Nothing, I kind of figured that. I could feel it in my spirit."

"All of y'all are crazy," Bruce whispered in the car as I gave him a sinister gaze. I was five seconds away from saying something about his ignorant mother, but I let it go.

Today was my last day at St. John's University and I couldn't stop the tears. I only experienced 1 and ½ years of being alone in college. Looking out the window, I watched as my mother and father carried my belongings to the car. Fall semester was over and it was time for me to head home. I cried my eyes out thinking how I never enjoyed college. I never partied or socialized. I was leaving behind a life of innocent discovery to be responsible for two lives, even though I hadn't fully discovered my own.

Before I could settle in, my parents called me to the living room. Walking down the steps, they looked disturbed. What was it now? I swear every day it was something new. There were packets from Sallie Mae, Direct Loan, Department of Education, FAFSA, and scholarship information on the table. "Your mom and I were talking and we've come to terms with the pregnancy, but you still went against our rules. Because of this, we'll no longer pay for your education. I've taken the liberty of gathering financial aid information for you, if you care to continue.

What am I supposed to do? I'm about to have twins and now I have to pay for college. The odds were stacked against me.

"Ok," I replied as I stood up and headed toward my room.

"Wait one last thing. We're going to make a confession before the church tomorrow. You should probably be prepared to talk."

"Confess? Why?"

Is he crazy? I'm not going in front of the church.

"Because you're my child and as leaders we owe them our accountability. We can't just sweep it under the rug while your belly grows; we have to address it.

I didn't respond to my father; he looked disappointed. My mother rubbed his back to console him, "everything is going to be ok," she whispered. I felt bad.

My parents, sister, and I sat on the front row. I was praying some sort of electric malfunction would happen, but the lights were shining brighter than the heaven gates. Prayer requests were usually written down, but, no, we had to go in front of the church. Jesus help me! The choir was singing my favorite song, "I'll Fly Away," by Hezekiah Walker, and I wished I could do just that. All of the deacons stood in the aisle as Pastor Brown prayed for the tithes and offering. The collection plate seemed to be moving faster than ever. I took my time passing the plate to prolong the service. "Girl, if you don't pass this collection plate. What is wrong with you?" My mother said while grabbing the plate. Pastor Brown stood at the podium with sweat dripping from his head. Pulling out a handkerchief, he patted his face and looked down at us.

"Today's confession is going to be a little different. Minister Turner and his family are going to come up. Let's give them a warm Mount Hope welcome," he said. As they clapped, I stood nervously in front of 500 people preparing to tell them the unthinkable. The bright lights shining down on me made it even worse. The true definition of being in the spotlight.

"Good Morning, church. I'm sure many of you are wondering why we're standing here. Well, we've fallen short and as the leader of the Youth Ministry, I'm asking for your prayers. See, well…." My father started to stumble over his words. I couldn't take it anymore. I looked toward the back wall and kept my eyes there. "Well, my daughter, Stacey, is with child and we're asking for your help and prayers at this time." Instantly, ripple effects of loud gasps filled the room. My father handed me the microphone, but I didn't know what to say.

"Hello, church. Yes, I've fallen short; but this isn't the end. I know it's shocking, but I'm just asking for your support and prayers. My time at St. John's University is over, but I'll be attending Albany University in the spring, so I can care for my children and attend school. Again, I'm just asking for your help and prayers." Pastor Brown came down from the stage and told the congregation to stand as he prayed for us. I could hear multiple people saying "yes Lord," "please Jesus," yes mighty father" as Pastor Brown prayed. Tears flowed down my cheeks as I headed to my seat. Multiple members rubbed my back, telling me it was going to be alright, and that was honestly the first time I felt everything was alright.

Love was in the air as my family and I sat down for breakfast. I was so happy things were back to normal; I could tell my Dad was too. While we were eating, the doorbell rang. "Mrs. Mae, It's good to see you. Come on in. We were just finishing up our breakfast," my father said. What is she doing here? She never comes over. I looked to the left and there she stood, in her usher's uniform with her long silver hair flowing down her back. I stood up to give her a hug. She was so small and sweet, everybody loved Mrs. Mae. She embraced me like a long lost friend she hadn't seen in years.

"Mrs. Mae, please sit and have some food," my mother said. Mrs. Mae sat across from me and just kept smiling. I smiled back and wondered what was up with her. Did she drink too much communion today?

"I heard your message this morning and it really moved me. It reminded me of myself," she said.

"You had a child at 19 too?" I asked.

"No sweetie, but my uncle abused me. I know it's different, but it's something I had to overcome. I feel a connection between us," she said.
My parents started to smile when she told her story. I was still lost, but appreciated her compassion.

"I don't know your plans, but God put it in my heart to babysit for you," she said.
The sound of my fork dropping on the plate echoed through the kitchen as I looked at her in shock.
"No, I'm sorry Ms. Mae, I can't. I don't have the money, and my parents have already dished out enough at St. Johns. I can't."
She laughed at my response. What was so funny?

"Sweetie, I didn't ask for money. I said God put it in my heart, so I'm willing to help you for free and that's that."
I smiled from ear to ear and gave her the biggest hug I could give somebody. Confessing my sins might have been the best thing I've done. I should do it more often if I'm going to receive these kinds of blessings.

It was time for my annual checkup. Dr. Matlin had been so good at making me feel comfortable that I was excited to go. The babies were healthy and my due date was June 25[h].

"How are you doing?" Dr. Matlin asked showing all 32 of her pearly white teeth.

"I'm great; I should be starting class in two weeks since, I'm having my children in June."

"Ok! You seem to have it all planned out. So many girls take a break from school or completely stop. It's good to see you're on top of it. I'm proud of you!"

"Thank you! I can't let this stop me. How can I? I'll have two mouths to feed."

"You're so right. Lay back for me so I can check on these two."

The lights were beaming and I could feel her touching my stomach, but it felt like she was checking for pressure points rather than the babies.

"You don't feel that?" she asked.

"No, feel what?"

"Hold on let me see something. I want you to spread your legs for me while I check your cervix."
Placing her fingers in my cervix she asked again.

"Can you feel that?"

"Yes, I can. What is that?"

"That's your son's head; he's near your cervix. You're not contracting or anything are you?"

"No, I mean, I don't think so."
I didn't know if I was contracting. Hell, I didn't even know what it felt like.

"Did you drive here?"

"Yes, ma'am."

"Well you're not driving home. You're staying here for a few nights. We're going to do an emergency surgery called a cerclage. Your cervix is weak and the cerclage will tighten the opening of your cervix to ensure that you don't prematurely have your babies."

All my plans were killed. I was put on bed rest for the next four months and took six online classes at The University of Albany instead of going to school like I intended. I was secluded away in my room every day, but thank God my father put a microwave and small refrigerator in my room so I wouldn't have to walk to the kitchen. My mother also made me dinner and breakfast every day and made sure it was in my room before she went to work.

As I was studying, I heard my door slowly open; my mother came in and sat on my bed.

"How are you feeling, baby?" she asked.

"Defeated. I just wanted to finish school, but now I'm going to be behind."

"I know, baby, I know. Don't worry, God will work it out," she said as she rubbed my back.

"I was thinking I could take summer classes and catch up, what do you think?"

"I'm not sure about that. You're due on June 25th and classes start June 26th; that's too close."

"I looked at the dates. If I get my labor induced on June 15th I can start on time."

"Induced! Stacey, you're going too far. You have to give yourself time to heal."

"No, mom I need to finish school."

"I understand, but you have to rest. I'm not a doctor so when you go for your check up ask Dr. Matlin and see what she says."

I was going to ask Dr. Matlin anyway, this is my body and I can do as I please. Besides, these babies were ready to come out a few months ago; ten days early won't hurt a thing, especially if they're impatient like me.

I went in for my last checkup and asked Dr. Matlin right away.

"I want to induce my labor so I can start school on June 26th, Dr. Matlin."

"Are you crazy, Stacey? You want to have the most natural experience when giving birth and you want to give yourself time to heal. Also, your little girl is breach and you might have to deliver her the following day."

"What do you mean she's breach, how did that happen?"

"Sometimes it happens. You need to get some rest. It's your decision to induce your labor, but I wouldn't recommend it."

I didn't change my mind and my daughter was coming the same day, breach or not. I will not be delayed!

Today was the day. It was June 15th, everything was in order and I was headed to the hospital. Bruce was also in town. I tried to disregard him from the delivery, but he's their father so I had no choice, especially since he gave me hell about not being in the delivery room. I was only allowed to have one person in the room because I was a high risk, so I choose my mom. He hadn't been around in months, so I felt he hadn't earned his rights.

Suddenly, before Dr. Matlin started the inducing procedure, Bruce showed up to the hospital raising hell.

"Why are you trying to keep me from them?" he asked walking into the room.

"Really? Of all days you want to act crazy today?" I yelled.

"Right now is not the time for that young man." my father said to Bruce.

"No! I never get my time," Bruce replied.

My father, who is 6'3 and built like an NFL player, stood up and told Bruce to leave, but he refused. They continued to argue back and forth. Luckily, security arrived in the nick of time and escorted him out; he resisted as they tackled him to the floor, causing him to curse and yell.

The head medical director came running into the delivery room with a tense look upon her face.

"What is going on?" she asked.

"That's my children's father; he's upset." I replied with tears coming down my eyes.

"I'm sorry Stacey, but we can't induce you today. You're in no shape for this. When a woman delivers her child, it should be peaceful. This young man is putting you and everybody at risk."

"Please, no. I need this done today," I replied.

"I'm sorry Stacey. Come back in two days and come back quietly. Do you understand what I'm saying?"

I knew exactly what she meant and I was going to do just that. I'm not notifying Bruce until they're almost here. I was getting these babies out in two days with or without him.

I arrived at the hospital just how the medical director said - as quiet as a mouse. I told my mom to call Bruce once I was close to pushing out the first baby. I wanted the pregnancy to be as calm as possible.

"Push, Stacey, push," my mother yelled while holding my hand.

"I'm trying, I'm trying!" I screamed out, feeling exasperated.

"Come on, one more time, Stacey. I see the head!" Dr. Matlin yelled out.

"It's a boy, it's the boy!" Dr. Matlin screamed.

"Yes!" I yelled out as I watched the nurse clean his body while his cries echoed through the room. Twenty minutes later, Dr. Matlin examined me with a look of shock on her face.

"Oh God! It looks like the little girl has turned and she's coming today too. Come on, Stacey. I need you to concentrate; you have one more to push out!" Dr. Matlin said.

"Oh my God!" I said grunting

"Push, baby, push!" my mother yelled out!

"She's here, she's here." Dr. Matlin said as she placed her on my chest. Not one cry or sound came from her; she was the tough one.

Dr. Matlin placed Amir in my right arm and Eunice in my left. Their bright eyes shined into mine, creating an inseparable connection.

"Aww look at the babies. Over here, Stacey, smile," I heard my mother say while taking a picture with her cell phone.

"Mom! I look a mess, geesh!" I yelled.

"Girl please, I looked a mess when I had you. Now smile one more time."

Suddenly, her smile became a frown as she dropped the phone by her side staring at the entrance of the doorway. I turned to the right and there was Bruce, standing in the doorway with his mouth dropped to the floor. Slowly, he walked toward me, staring at Amir and Eunice in total disbelief.

"I'm a father. I can't believe I'm a father," he murmured.

Just how I planned, the following week I started school. Standing in the mirror, I turned from side to side, trying to convince myself that my stomach had gone down. I knew I wasn't fooling anybody. It had only been nine days since the delivery and I still looked pregnant. I didn't care; me and my pouch were headed to class and I dared anybody to stop me. Plus, my extra-large t-shirt hid it well. In class, I made sure I sat in the front. I wished I could mix and mingle, but I had two babies waiting for me at home. Leaving campus, I became sad as I looked at the other students socializing, wishing I would have taken advantage of my freedom at St. Johns.

Part 2: Two Heartbeats

Seven months, seven whole months have passed and now Bruce wants to call me. Really? I have no words for him.

"What!" I yelled answering the phone while changing Amir's diaper.

"What you mean what?"

"Just what it sound like. You haven't seen them in seven months, but you're calling me when you should be changing diapers."

"Look, I'll be down there, but this weekend I want to take them to Philadelphia, Pennsylvania. I also want you to sign these custody papers."

Bruce was from Philadelphia.

"Custody? You haven't even seen them since the hospital."

"You can get Eunice and I can keep Amir. A boy needs to be with his father."

"No, Amir and Eunice need their mother and father."

I hung the phone up and continued to change Amir's diaper. There was no way in hell he was getting custody of my kids.

Who is this knocking at my door early in the morning like the police? I rolled over to look out the window and to my surprise it was the police, the Albany State police.

"Stacey! Come to the door!" my father yelled from downstairs.

Walking downstairs, I saw two cops standing there. *What and who do they want?*

"Hello officers. How may I help you?" I asked.

"Are you Stacey Turner?" they asked.

"Yes, I am."

"You've been ordered to appear in court, Ms. Turner. You've been served."

273

Are you kidding me? Bruce was serious about this custody battle.

Instantly, I ran upstairs to call Bruce.

"Really? You think you're getting custody of my babies? It will be a cold day in hell before that happens!"

"See that's your problem. Those aren't your babies, those are our babies," he said before hanging up.

Sitting at the front table of the courtroom, my parents sat behind me as we waited for the judge to announce the decision on me and Bruce's case.

"Let me get a few things straight with you two. When a child is born, nobody has custody until you establish custody with the courts. Filing for custody means that you're acknowledging that you and the other parent can't successfully co-parent. So you're giving the state permission to teach you how. Is that what you're telling the court?"

"Yes, your honor," I replied.

"Yes, your honor, but if she would've let me see my kids, we wouldn't be here."

"Young man, I didn't ask you that. Simply answer the question yes or no?" The judge said.

"Yes, your honor."

"Thank you. In the case of Amir and Eunice Turner, Stacey Turner is granted full custody. Mr. Bruce Westfield is granted visitation rights and access to the children's legal and medical records. Before you leave the courtroom Ms. Turner, you will make a visitation schedule for Mr. Westfield. Do you understand?"

"Yes, your honor."

There was nothing I could do. Alternating weekends were set-aside for him and he could take them to Philadelphia or wherever else he pleased. I was powerless.

"I'm coming to get them next week."

"Where are you going to stay?" I asked.

"I'm probably going to book a hotel and take them out somewhere; you know, do the father thing."

I didn't feel comfortable leaving him with them. He didn't know the first thing about being a father. Does he even know how to change a diaper?

"Ok, but…"

"But what? You can't say nothing, the judge granted me custody. Don't make me get the cops again because this time it will surely work in my favor."

"I wasn't going to say that, Bruce. Just tell me what day you're coming." I murmured.

I didn't feel like arguing and he was right, there was nothing I could do. I started brainstorming. Maybe somehow, some way, I could convince my father to let him stay here. The kids were sleeping, so this would be the best time to ask. I crept down the steps as if I was on a secret James Bond mission. My father was sitting on the couch laughing at reruns of Seinfeld.

"Daddyyyyyy." I said smiling while making my way to sit next to him.

"What do you want Stacey?"

"What do you mean, what do I want?"

"The only time you call me daddy is when you want something, so what do you want?" He said smiling.

Great! If he smiles throughout the conversation, there's a possibility he'll say yes.

"So, I was thinking. Since the judge granted Bruce visitation rights and he's coming in town next week…."

He sat straight up and put the TV on mute, giving me his undivided attention.

"Ok. What does that have to do with us?"

"Well, I was wondering. Can he stay here?"

"Are you crazy, Stacey? Not under my roof. I won't condone that."

"I know daddy, but he can sleep downstairs. He is their father. I was thinking about the situation. I have to deal with him for the next 18 years, so he and I should be cordial and develop a healthy relationship."

Did I really just say that? I sounded so mature. I mainly wanted to keep an eye on him because I knew he had mental issues. My father sat back on the couch and took a deep breath. "Ok Stacey, but let's make one thing clear. If I catch him upstairs, only God himself will be able to peel me off him."

It worked! It worked! I placed a huge kiss on my dad's cheek and ran upstairs.

Diving on my bed like a kid with a huge smile, I called Bruce. He always complained about not having enough money, so pitching this idea would be a piece of cake.

"So, I was thinking. Since your money is low, you should stay here instead of a hotel."

"Stay with you? Yeah, right. You know damn well your father too holy for that," he said laughing.

"I already asked him and he said it was cool, as long as you stay in the basement."

"Really?"

"Yeah, I'm shocked myself."

"Well, I guess. Tell him I said thanks."

"Tell him yourself, he'll appreciate it."

"You know I'm scared of your father," he said as I laughed at his reaction.

That was the first time we'd laughed together in a while, but I still didn't trust him. The grudge I had for him was like poison. I wanted him to feel my pain slowly, until he couldn't bear it anymore. Just like Joseph from the bible made his brothers jump through hoops to trust them again, I was doing the same to Bruce.

Throughout the next year, we grew closer and I tried to forget everything he did, but it still lingered in the back of my head. I strategically rekindled our relationship so that I could be present during his weekends with the kids. For a short time, our life together ran fairly smooth. We alternated trips to his home and mine and shared our weekends with the kids as a family.

I was 21 now, not 19. Walking in the house from the store, my mother was sitting on the couch. She patted the seat signaling for me to sit.

"So are you ready for graduation?

"Yeah, but I'm not walking."

"What! Why? I want to see you walk across the stage. Do you know how proud that'll make me?"

"I know mom, but all of my friends have graduated and I already feel left behind. I just want to get my diploma, that's it."

"No, I really want you to walk!"

"It's not your decision; you gave that up when I started paying for college. Plus, I already have a job making 40K. I'm fine"

"Well, you seem to have it all figured out, don't you?"

"I'm not trying to be rude mom, but let it go, please. I don't want to argue, this is my decision.

Time was flying. Bruce and I were on good terms and he even started talking about marriage. I became so comfortable with him that I started to fall back in love; he was finally starting to act like a man - until social media intervened. One day, I decided to post a picture of us on Facebook to show the world how happy we were. My phone notifications kept going off from people liking and leaving comments under the picture. I tagged Bruce in the picture, making his friends able to see it. I was shocked to see his friends were giving us compliments because guys rarely did that.

Late in the night, I received a text from my friend, Rachel. "Girl, who is Shanice Long? She commented *I guess so lol,* on your picture." I was confused, but I surely investigated the situation. I was looking through Shanice's page like the FBI. This wasn't the first time I'd seen her. A few months ago, Bruce was tagged in a picture with Shanice, but it mysteriously got deleted off of his page. She lived in the same state as him and was the same age as him. Looking through her pictures, I saw comments from Bruce and he even left a heart on one picture, leaving me furious. The evidence was clear, so I called him right away.

"Who is Shanice?"

"Shanice who? What are you talking about now?"

"I'm not stupid, Bruce. I already saw the comments you left on her page."

"You stalking me now? I feel like you got me under a looking glass, always trying to find something."

"I don't have you under a glass, but at the end of the day, I'm taking care of your kids and, to be honest, I don't feel appreciated."

"You know what? Get off my phone; I don't feel like hearing this today, Stacey!"

"Hello. Hello!" Did he just hang up on me?" I said to myself.

I called his phone back to back to back, but he wouldn't answer. I sat on the bed and started texting him, but before I could finish, he called.

"What do you want!" I yelled.

Two Heartbeats ❤❤

"I really don't think I could ever be happy with you," he said.

Suddenly, everything he'd done to me started replaying in my head and I made the decision that I was finally done with him. This was the last time he'd hurt me.

"Ok," I replied nonchalantly.

"What do you think?" He asked.

"I couldn't agree more." I replied before hanging up.

My phone vibrated throughout the night from him repeatedly calling me until it eventually died. He wasn't going to manipulate his way back in my life; I was completely done.

Five more minutes, five more minutes I said to myself as I looked at the clock waiting for 4 p.m. The weekend was here and I was ready to go home. A month had passed since I'd talk to Bruce. I was avoiding his calls and I was finally starting to feel happy, but since he had legal rights to see our children, I couldn't hold out much longer. Driving on I-95 I received a text from him.

"If I don't see my kids, I'm calling the cops."

"I don't care call them."

Why did I text that? Knowing I didn't want that drama showing up at my house.

"That's how you feel? You got some balls now, huh?"

"Yup, bigger than the ones you got."

"I swear I can't stand you. That's why I did what I did in college and you know exactly what I'm talking about."

After all these years, I thought the pain from that day was gone, but in an instant those feelings resurfaced. At a red light, I sat in my car and couldn't believe it. Bruce had completely sucked the energy out of me, like a vampire draining his latest victim. He was a true monster. The loud horns behind me

279

prompted me to drive, but I couldn't go far. Pulling on the side of the road I couldn't stop the tears from flowing.

I couldn't take it anymore. I called my mother crying; I had to tell her the truth, even if it killed me.

"Stacey, Stacey. Hello Stacey, what's wrong with you? Why are you crying, baby?"

I could hardly speak I was crying so much.

"Mom, mom, I was….."

"You were what, baby?"

"I was raped."

After three years my heart-stricken past was finally out.

"What! When? By who? Are you there? Say something, baby."

"It was Bruce. That's how I got pregnant; that's what really happened. That's the truth. I never meant to get pregnant. I'm so sorry." I said with tears streaming down my cheeks.

"Are you serious? Why didn't you tell us when it first happened, so we could take action?"

"I was scared. Bruce said he would kill himself and me if I told anyone. I didn't know what to do."

"It's ok. You hear me? Everything is going to be fine. Please come home; we have to tell your father."

"No, please don't tell dad, there's no telling what he'll do."

"Stacey, we have to tell him; he's your father!"

"Please, mom, please. I won't tell you anything else if you do."

"Stacey, why do you have to be like this! God! Ok I won't tell him, but please come home so we can talk."

I was terrified to go home. If I know my mom, I know she was going to tell him anyway. As I walked up the steps to my house, the front door swung open and there my dad stood with a look of sadness upon his face. He hugged me with tears coming down his eyes. "I'm so sorry, baby. I'm so sorry. Why didn't you tell us? How did this happen?" he asked as we walked to the living room couch.

"After I came back from freshmen summer break, me and Bruce reconnected and I forgave him for how he acted the year before. I never told you guys this, but we broke up because I wouldn't have sex with him." My father's eyes grew bigger.

"He was consistent about me coming to his dorm. As freshmen, we weren't allowed to have co-ed visitation; but as sophomores we were, so I agreed."

"Why would you go over there, Stacey?" my father yelled.

"Let her finish," my mother replied.

"Once we got to his room, the door was still open, but once I sat on his bed he closed it. There was nowhere else to sit and I didn't plan on staying. He sat beside me and started to tell me how much he missed me and that he didn't want to lose me again. He seemed so sincere. He took his right hand and softly grabbed my chin and started kissing me forcing his weight on me. After a few more kisses, he started to unzip my pants. I should have stopped him, but he said he wasn't going to do anything; he just wanted to make me comfortable. My pants slid off and we were still just kissing. I told him to get up and stop playing because I wasn't going any further.

"In a matter of seconds, he went from a sweet puppy to a raging pit-bull. He kept telling me to stop fighting it because he knew I wanted it, that I needed it. I tried to push him off, but he pinned his legs down on my legs and held my arms down with his arms as he started to rape me, he had tunnel vision, and nothing or nobody was stopping him. I kept trying to kick him off. When I screamed, he covered my mouth, threatening to kill me. I started praying and wishing that I was invisible. He finally stopped. I couldn't stop crying, so he covered my mouth again then looked at me "Stacey, if you tell anybody, I'm just going to say you were drunk. Plus, it'll be a disgrace to your family because your father is the Youth Minister." I looked down and could see that I was bleeding on his sheets. "I have to leave, I can't be here; I'm bleeding. I can't believe you did this to me. I was a virgin!" I yelled. He then covered my mouth and started holding me as if he was comforting me, rocking me back and forth. "After this? I already got you, it's over now," he said referring to taking my virginity. I stood up and tried to leave, but he pleaded for me to stay and even started crying. "I can't go to jail; I have to finish school. Please, Stacey, please!" After 20 minutes, he finally let me leave, but not without telling me he would kill me and himself if I ever told anybody. That's the reason I acted so different when you were calling me that month. I was so scared something was going to happen, so I never told."

My father started pacing back and forth through the living room. My mother kept repeating how sorry she was and that she wished I would have told her so they could have called the police.

"We can't call the police now?" I asked.

"No, honey we can't. There are statutes of limitations for crimes, it's been too many years; but I have a better plan," my father said. Marching up the steps, he went to his bedroom, rambled through his closet, grabbed his coat, and told us that he was heading to Philadelphia. The way he walked to his car indicated that something was in his waist. My mother and I knew what it was - a gun. My mother ran out of the house chasing after him, begging him to stop; but he pushed her out of the way and sped off.

"Don't do this, please come back," I said over the phone as I pleaded for my father to turn around. My mother grabbed the phone and demanded that he come back. She quickly dialed three numbers.

"Hello, 911; please help. I'm scared my husband is going to kill my daughter's ex-boyfriend," she said crying into the phone.

"Ma'am where is he?" the operator asked.

"I don't know, but he left in a rage. He's probably on I-295 headed towards Philadelphia."

"Philadelphia? Ok, let me understand this correctly ma'am. Your husband left your house with intentions to hurt your daughter's ex-boyfriend who lives in Philadelphia, correct?"

"Yes."

"What kind of car does your husband drive?"

"A blue 2009 Lincoln Navigator. He's 6'3, short haircut, muscular build, with a beard, and he's 56 years old."

"Ok, ma'am, can you give us his cell phone number, so we can possibly calm him down?

"917-555-4352."

"Ma'am I want you to keep calling him. We will call you back when we hear something."

My mother and I continued to call my dad, but he wouldn't answer; my call log was filled with outgoing calls to him. Two hours went past and still nothing. My mother quickly grabbed my hand and started praying. She dialed his number again, closing her eyes, hoping he would answer, but it went straight to voicemail. Why is his phone off? We sat and waited, and still nothing. Suddenly, I could hear the garage door opening and my father walked in through the kitchen door.

"Y'all called the cops?"

"We didn't want you to do anything stupid," my mom said. He stared into my eyes and suddenly collapsed on the floor, crying and screaming, "I failed as a father, I failed you!"

Walking over to him, I consoled him on the floor with tears dripping on the ground. There was only one thing I could say.

"Dad I love you. You have always given me all I need by raising me in Christ and showing me what it means to live right."

Lesson Learned: If you've had a similar experience, please remember you're not alone. One in four women have reported a rape or an attempted rape, and survived rape in college.[13] Through time, healing, and therapy, I learned why I stayed in that situation and how it affected me mentally. Every time Bruce abused me, he'd console me, letting his emotions out and cry uncontrollably. He did the same thing when he raped me. It was confusing, causing me to feel sorry for him. His manipulation catapulted me back and forth between victim and confidant. In the same way, my abuser became my comforter, allowing him to control me. I was spun into a web of emotions. He knew everything about me, so it was easy for him to manipulate me and use what I told him against me. For example, he knew my father was the Youth Minister and he constantly said if I told my parents, it would bring a disgrace to my family. For those reasons alone I never told.

Never be afraid to contact the authorities or your family to get help. After I told my parents what happened, I started seeing a therapist; it was one of the best decisions I made. During my sessions, I learned the signs of a possessive and abusive man and realized I had plenty of red flags. Bruce was very aggressive and easily angered at the slightest of things. The verbal abuse started, then the physical abuse. First it was the mild twisting of the arms. Then it escalated to slaps and punches. He also ignored my personal space. When I told him to leave my house, he wouldn't; and, when we first started dating, he insisted on being alone. If I would rather study than party, he'd make me feel guilty and say I was "uptight" and "lame"; because of that, I believed I was. If your significant other has these traits, leave him immediately.

Therapy allowed me to open up and speak about my experience. I decided I would take my situation and help women who were in my shoes. For four years I held an annual conference at my church for young people. We discussed abuse, sex, drugs, and how all of those things divert you from your purpose and God's plan for you. We also talked about confidence, something I didn't have in college, but gained over time, allowing me to leave Bruce. When you have a reasonable degree of self-confidence, you're able to walk away from any situation that you feel isn't benefiting you. If you've been in a similar situation, share your story and try to help others who are in your shoes. It will help you heal and it's a way of giving. You have to grow through what you go through.

If it wasn't for my relationship with God, I would've never graduated. I prayed every day for the strength and fortitude to take care of my children and finish school. I followed his word and was blessed with people like Mrs. Mae, who helped me out tremendously. Not to mention I was making $40k a year before I graduated and I make much more now. But one thing I do regret is not going to my graduation. My mother still brings it up and I feel bad she didn't have that moment. I refused to become a statistic, so I geared all of my energy into becoming successful. Always remember you can do whatever you put your mind to with faith and endurance. If you become pregnant, or are a victim of rape, hope is still there. The universe will move in your direction, if you don't give up and put your best foot forward. There are numerous colleges that assist students who are single mothers. There are programs, scholarships, grants, and financial aid geared specifically for you. Do your research and find what's best for you. Your degree is not out of reach. I went through hell, but was blessed with two beautiful kids, a degree, and a job because I knew somewhere down the line I would find my true self and happiness.

Acknowledgements

First, I would like to thank God and my Lord and Savior Jesus Christ. Without him none of this would be possible. I've had the idea to write this book since 2013 and to finally see it come to fruition is humbling and gratifying. It wouldn't be possible without the man above. I would like to thank my mother, Carla Thomas, who read numerous chapters, giving me her honest feedback and motivating me to finish when I had no energy to do so. Thank you to my father, Barry Brown, who always supports me and is willing to give a helping hand when needed. To my close friends and relatives who inspired this book, I would like to give you the biggest thanks of all. We all went through a mountain of problems in college, and it shaped us to be the people we are today. We Made It! To my support team, who read through my stories and dealt with my nagging and near harassment: my sister, Shawnda, Grandma Dorothy, Aunt Tamara, Aunt Karen, Aunt Tina, Aunt Nialah, Uncle Tyrone, Dennis, Anice, Joy, Monique, Wesley, Ronald, Rasaan, Sidney, Serenity, Quana, Herb, Joshua, Yannick, Lonique, Shawn, Taney, Kacey, Tiffany, and Shanice.

To Tyrese, Laurence, and John, you three are there for me all the time to listen to my problems and motivate me when needed. You three have been there since we were children and you're still here today. To my late friend Jeffery Cox, writing your story was one of the hardest one's to write. Each letter, word, sentence, and paragraph took me back to that same emotional state that I felt during that time. I dedicate this book to you. I know you're looking over me and "whispering in my ear," and I thank you for that. My own guardian angel, I miss you and love you brother. To Julian, one of my closest friends I met in college, thanks for the continuous support and bringing my vision for the book cover to life – your art is priceless. To my late grandmother, Audrey Brown, and grandfather, James Thomas, not a day goes past that you don't cross my mind. Thanks for everything you taught me and I love you. To my cousin, Neema, thanks for your understanding and putting up with my seclusion of being locked in my room in order to stay focused and finish this book.

To my alma mater, Johnson C. Smith University, thank you for some of the best experiences and four years of my life. I truly grew and matured during my time there and have no regrets from any of my choices. To Dr. Harris and Professor Wynn, thank you for everything you taught me. I didn't forget. To all my friends and peers who I isolated myself from for months, I am truly sorry; but I had to finish this book. It has been a vision of mine and the only way it was going to get published was with discipline and hard work. To Janis Carmichael and Maurice Garland, my editors. Thank you for taking the time to edit my book, your advice and expertise means a lot.

To everyone that was involved in creating my video trailer, I am truly grateful. Alexandria Deal from Delta Sigma Theta Inc. at The University of Texas at San Antonio, Aaron Handy of Models INC, and Videographer Kiona Robinson from Baylor University. You three didn't know me, but understood my vision and allowed me to use your videos. Jennifer Pessima, Danielle "Lu Lu" Johnson and Jessie Porter thanks for bringing my vision to life and shooting the scenes for me.

And lastly, my past - the younger me, thank you for living unapologetically and living life to the fullest. For stepping out on faith when only a few believed, for always making an effort to put a smile on people's faces and allowing them to safely open up their hearts to you, leaving them with a feeling of hope and love.

Notes

[1] Tyler Kingkade, "There Were More Than Two Dozen Reported Shootings At College Campuses In 2013," The Huffington Post, 13 Jan. 2014, 08 Sept. 2015 <http://www.huffingtonpost.com/2014/01/13/shootings-college-campuses-2013_n_4577404.html

[2] Chris Cillizza, "President Obama wants to politicize the Oregon shooting" The Washington Post 2 Oct. 2015, 07 Oct. 2015 http://www.washingtonpost.com/news/the-fix/wp/2015/10/02/president-obamas-impassioned-call-to-politicize-the-oregon-shooting-annotated/

[3] "STDs in Adolescents and Young Adults," Centers for Disease Control and Prevention, 17 Nov. 2011, 08 Sept. 2015 <http://www.cdc.gov/std/stats10/adol.htm>

[4] "The Cost of Gun Violence," Children's Safety Network, 08 Sept. 2015 <http://www.childrenssafetynetwork.org/publications/cost-firearm-violence>

[5] H. Elizabeth Peters, Nan Marie Astone, Steven Martin, "Millennial Childbearing and the Recession," Urban Institute, 28 April 2015, 08 Sept. 2015 <http://www.urban.org/research/publication/millennial-childbearing-and-recession>

[6] Cheryl Wetzstein, "U.S. fertility plummets to record low," The Washington Times, 28 May 2014, 08 Sep. 2015 <http://www.washingtontimes.com/news/2014/may/28/us-birthrate-plummets-to-record-low/?page=all

[7]   Michelle Diggles, "Millennials – Political Explorers," Third Way Fresh Thinking, March 2014, 08 Sept. 2015 <http://content.thirdway.org/publications/798/Third_Way_Rep ort_-_Millennials-Political_Explorers.pdf>

[8]   Andrew Flint, "The Odds of Playing in the NBA," Hoops Vibe, 02 Jan 2014, 08 Sept. 2015 <http://www.hoopsvibe.com/features/285631-the-odds-of-playin-in-the-nba>

[9]   "15 Economical Facts About Millenials," The White House, Oct. 2014, 08 Sept. 2015 <https://www.whitehouse.gov/sites/default/files/docs/m illennials_report.pdf>

[10]   Matt Fortuna, "Jameis Winston: Store employee 'hooked us up' with crab legs," ESPN, 22 April 2015, 06 Oct. 2015 <http://espn.go.com/nfl/draft2015/story/_/id/12739843 /jameis-winston-florida-state-seminoles-says-crab-legs-were-given-not-stolen>

[11]   Anne Johnson, Chelsea Parsons, GUNS: HOW GUN VIOLENCE IS DEVASTATING THE MILLENNIAL GENERATION, American Progress, Feb. 2014, 08 Sept. 2015 <https://www.americanprogress.org/wp-content/uploads/2014/02/CAP-Youth-Gun-Violence-report.pdf>

[12]   "College Drinking" National Institute on Alcohol Abuse and Alcoholism April 2015, 06 Oct. 2015 <http://pubs.niaaa.nih.gov/publications/CollegeFactSheet/Colle geFactSheet.pdf>

[13]   "How often does rape happen?" One In Four USA, 08 Sept. 2015 <http://www.oneinfourusa.org/statistics.php>

Bibliography

"15 Economical Facts About Millennials." *White House.* WhiteHouse.gov, 1 Oct. 2014. Web. 8 Sept. 2015.

Astone, Nan, Steven Martin, and H. Peters. "Millennial Childbearing and the Recession." *Millennial Childbearing and the Recession.* Urban.org, 28 Apr. 2015. Web. 8 Sept. 2015.

Cillizza, Chris. "President Obama wants to politicize the Oregon Shooting." *The Washington Post.* WashingtonPost.com, 2, Oct. 2015. Web 7 Oct. 2015.

"College Drinking" *National Institute on Alcohol Abuse and Alcoholism.* Niaa.nih.gov, April 2015. Web 6 Oct. 2015.

Diggles, Michelle. "Millennials - Political Explorers." *Content.Thirdway.* Content.Thirdway.org, 1 Mar. 2014. Web. 8 Sept. 2015.

Flint, Andrew. "The Odds of Playing in the NBA." *Hoopsvibe.* Hoopsvibe.com, 2 Jan. 2014. Web. 8 Sept. 2015.

Fortuna, Matt. "Jameis Winston: Store employee 'hooked us up' with crab legs." *ESPN.* espn.com, 22 April 2014. Web. 6 Oct. 2015.

Kingkade, Tyler. "There Were More Than Two Dozen Reported Shootings At College Campuses In 2013." *The Huffington Post.* TheHuffingtonPost.com, 13 Jan. 2014. Web. 8 Sept. 2015.

Parsons, Chelsea, and Anne Johnson. "Young Guns: How Gun Violence Is Devastating The Millennial Genreation." *American Progress*. AmericanProgress.org, 1 Feb. 2014. Web. 8 Sept. 2015.

Rampell, Catherine. "Bad News for Older Folks: Millennials Are Having Fewer Babies." *Washington Post*. WashingtonPost.com, 4 May 2014. Web. 8 Sept. 2015.

"STDs in Adolescents and Young Adults." *Centers for Disease Control and Prevention*. CDC.gov, 16 Dec. 2014. Web. 8 Sept. 2015.

"How often does rape happen?." *One In Four USA*. OneInFourUSA.com. Web. 8 Sept. 2015.

"The Cost of Gun Violence." *Children's Safety Network*. Children'sSafetyNetwork.org. Web. 8 Sept. 2015.

Wetzstein, Cheryl. "U.S. Fertility Plummets to Record Low." *Washington Times*. WashingtonTimes.com, 28 May 2014. Web. 8 Sept. 2015

Made in the USA
Middletown, DE
11 October 2020